IMPAIRED INTELLIGENCE

Pathology and Rehabilitation

IMPAIRED INTELLIGENCE
Pathology and Rehabilitation

CARL FRANKENSTEIN
Professor of Special Education

The Hebrew University
Jerusalem, Israel

GORDON AND BREACH SCIENCE PUBLISHERS
London New York Paris

Gordon and Breach, Science Publishers Ltd.
12 Bloomsbury Way
London W.C.1

Editorial office for the United States of America

Gordon and Breach, Science Publishers, Inc.
150 Fifth Avenue
New York, N.Y. 10011

Editorial office for France

Gordon & Breach
7–9 rue Emile Dubois
Paris 14^{e}

Library of Congress catalog card number 70–123488. ISBN 0 677 02810 5. Printed in the United Kingdom.

Contents

PART TWO: THE FUNCTION OF THE SCHOOL IN THE REHABILITATION OF INTELLIGENCE

Foreword

THE LIST OF monographic studies on feeblemindedness or mental retardation is most impressive in its length and in the sophistication of its titles. Although more studies are concerned with the rare cases of low-grade deficiencies than with the millions of borderline cases and of secondary retardation due to environmental causes, there seems, little remains unsaid about intellectual dysfunctions. This is true particularly in the light of the recent interest in children called 'socially or culturally deprived.'

But there exists a strange 'division of labor' between studies of genuine feeblemindedness and studies of so-called secondary, environmentally conditioned retardation. While questions of causation are more frequently asked in the first group of studies, descriptive analyses of modes of cognitive operation and patterns of learning and thinking seem to occupy much more the minds of psychologists and educators concerned with the welfare and the advancement of the underprivileged.

The reason for this difference of emphasis is easy to discover: genuine feeblemindedness results from congenital defects in the brain structure or from later traumatization of a neurological order. The connection between cognitive dysfunction and such causal factors as hereditary defects, glandular anomalities, brain-infections or injuries, metabolic disorders invites primarily students with a medical, biological, physiological orientation. Psychologists, social workers and educators are auxiliary rather than essential workers for them in their empirical studies. The aspects of social adjustment or maladjustment are of greater interest than a phenomenology of cognitive behavior and modes of operation, since they view intelligence as a uniform function. Only belief in changeability through education makes a differential analysis of cognitive behavior necessary.

This becomes evident when we look at the ever expanding literature on teaching the child that is handicapped by secondary retardation. But while in this area, studies on different patterns abound, it is the problem of causation that is then often oversimplified: Not only tend the laws of causal configuration* to be disregarded, the terms of 'social' and 'cultural' varieties of secondary retardation are often used synonymously, as it were (a fact which clearly proves the lack of differentiation in causal thinking).

It was precisely my thinking about this double deficiency that motivated the present study. I did not want to add another essay on causes of feeblemindedness or mental retardation to the many competent studies that are available. Nor did I want to write another manual for the teachers of the underprivileged children. But I did want to help them clarify their basic concepts. For this purpose I asked three questions which, I felt, were mostly neglected:

1) What are the essential characteristics of genuine feeblemindedness, and how are they being modified by the factor of personality types?

2) How do these essential characteristics differ from cognitive patterns in secondary retardation, those produced by adverse social conditions, such as extreme poverty, educational neglect and externalization and those produced by ambiguity of cultural values and norms, primarily in situations of transition?

3) How do these ideal type patterns appear in interaction, when the individual is exposed to the simultaneous impact of social *and* cultural conditions of secondary retardation, and when he may even be affected to some extent by negative brain conditions?

Our answer to the first question is meant to make a contribution to a more dynamic theory of feeblemindedness. For this purpose, Chapter 1 is being followed, in Chapter 2, by a tentative analysis of the feebleminded child's development. The author contends that the concept of 'Mental Age' is a fallacy: the younger child of normal intelligence *essentially* differs in each area of intellectual functioning from a 'correspondingly' older feebleminded individual. (Type-differences decisively influence each phase of his development.)

This analysis of feeblemindedness should be read as a phenomenological study in its own rights, and not only as a basis for understanding the manifestations of secondary retardation through comparing them with those of the former. On the other hand, it is precisely such a comparison between the varieties of 'impaired intelli-

* According to which partial factors become relevant only through their configurations with each other and with their causal antecedents and outcomes (see 24).

gence' that might help us answer the vital question of whether secondary retardation in a socially or a culturally deprived child differs from congenital feeblemindedness not only in degree and in reversibility but also in essence. It should be self-evident that, if our answer to this question is affirmative, basically different methods of teaching must be employed, if we want to 'rehabilitate' such a child's potentially normal intelligence.

But although I tend to believe (and hope to be able to show) that secondary retardation is indeed essentially different from genuine feeblemindedness, the answer is not as unambiguous as one would like it to be for the sake of educational clarity: Secondary retardation may indeed essentially differ from feeblemindedness, and may nevertheless be irreversible. I have dealt in other places [24, 26] at some length with the problems of reversibility and structurization. The latter concept means that a human quality, and particularly a negative one, may crystallize as the result of experience and development, until it becomes part of the individual's structure as if he had been born with that quality. (Thus, the concept of 'structurization' supplements the generally accepted dichotomy of 'nature and nurture' in causal thinking). The time required for this structurization differs from condition to condition, as I have tried to show in the second of the two just-mentioned studies [26]: institutional care, growing up under conditions of poverty, of plenty, in cultural transition, or in an affluent society—all may produce different processes of structurization. A brief summary of these analyses is included in Chapter 3.

But structurization is not the only factor that makes unequivocal diagnosis and distinction between primary and secondary retardation problematic in many cases. The often unavoidable (and not always discoverable) occurence of minor brain damage due to adverse social conditions also may work against reversibility. It is the function of Chapter 4 to show in which way the essential characteristics of secondary retardation are liable to become modified by such additional (organic) handicaps. Whether or not tests can be worked out to help us differentiate between reversible and irreversible cases of secondary retardation, is still an open question.

In the second part the role of teaching as an instrument of rehabilitating socially and culturally impaired intelligence will be discussed. The starting points and the basic aspects are different in each chapter: first, the function of the school as a substitute of that of the child's parents will be analyzed, with emphasis on the development and the limitations of autonomy in modern society (Chapter 5). The next chapter (6) will deal with the conditions of internalization through learning. Internalization of concepts, feelings and values is, both, a precondition and a result of autonomy. But it is the former rather than the latter concept (internalization rather than autonomy) that logically leads to an analysis of faulty (because externalized) thinking and of the teaching methods aimed at correcting it. This, then, will be the topic of the next-following chapter (7) in which the categories of thinking and the methods of rehabilitative teaching will be discussed.

These three chapters are meant to be independent papers, rather than three parts of one treatise. It was therefore considered legitimate not to eliminate every repetition of certain statements since they appear in different contexts. Thus, didactical as well as school-organizational problems are included in Chapters 6 and 7, though first in generalities and only later on in specifying details. Basic concepts are not only the subject of a theoretical introduction (Chapter 5) they are intrinsic elements in any rationale of methods (the two following chapters).

The categories of faulty thinking are accompanied by short descriptions of class-situations, in which the thinking processes of socially or culturally disadvantaged children in different age-groups are demonstrated. It should be obvious that and why such a presentation cannot and should not be too rigid. Learning, after all, is a continuous process and activity, hence cannot possibly be split into isolated acts. And yet—for the purposes of strengthening the teacher's awareness of his specific functions when dealing with children whose secondarily impaired intelligence he should try to rehabilitate, such organization around didactic procedures may be useful. Every teaching method means different things when employed in different contexts and for different purposes. It makes the teacher more productive and more effective when he has learned how to view his pupils' cognitive behavior from different angles.

In the end we shall deal with the question of how teachers can be sensitized for the particular task we have in mind here, how this can be done by inservice-training and/or in generic training courses.

Thanks are due to the editors of *Israel Annals of Psychiatry*, Jerusalem, and of *Acta Psychologica*, Amsterdam, for their permission to reprint articles that appeared in these periodicals in 1964 and 1965. These essays form the basis of Chapters 1, 2, and 3.

Thanks are also due to the Hebrew University Press for permission to use parts of an article printed in *Scripta Hierosolymitana*, Vol. XIII (Studies on Education), 1963, which have been included in Chapters 5 and 8; and to Urban & Schwarzenberg, München (1964) for permission to use parts of my book published by them in 1964 (Persönlichkeitswandel).

Jerusalem, Israel. CARL FRANKENSTEIN

PART ONE

Theory

CHAPTER ONE

On Feeblemindedness

*An Analysis of Essential Elements and Types**

1 INTRODUCTORY REMARKS

IN HIS ESSAY on feeblemindedness [36] Kurt Lewin analyses the major symptoms and implications of rigidity which he defines as: lack of differentiation and fixation to known situations, concreteness, primary (that is, non-reactive) pedantry, relative inability to re-organize a field or to re-arrange parts into a new whole, difficulties in transformation, etc. At the same time, he mentions—as seemingly contradicting signs of behavior—the feebleminded individual's divertibility, his sensitiveness to distractions and his susceptibility to outside influences. We shall try to show that these seemingly contradictory traits are in fact complementary aspects of one and the same quality—lack of structure.

There is no definition of intelligence of which abstraction does not form an essential part, whether *expressis verbis* or by implication. Even in Thorndike's so-called social and mechanical intelligences [54] some elements of abstraction can be discovered, as shown by Goldstein [29], whose analysis of abstraction is undoubtedly the most comprehensive and sophisticated one.

According to Goldstein, abstraction manifests itself as ability to grasp the essentials of a given whole and the significance, within the whole, of its parts; the latter should be capable of being isolated not only as such but also as potential parts of other wholes (in other words: should be objects not only of analysis but also of synthesis). Structurally, this ability is based on the ego's power to detach itself from the outer world of givens as well as from inner experience (to distantiate itself from the objects of its contemplation and elaboration), and to shift—willfully and consciously—from one aspect of an object or a situation to another, while holding in mind its various

---

* Reprinted, with minor alterations, from: *The Israel Annals of Psychiatry and Related Disciplines*, Vol. 2, No. 2, October 1964.

aspects. Goldstein also mentions the ability to form hierarchic concepts and to think and formulate in symbols for the purpose of accounting to oneself and to others as essential elements of abstraction. (It is the latter qualification that is valid for one of Thorndike's intelligences only, since both mechanical and social intelligence can operate without concept-formation or communication with the aid of formulated symbols.)

Definitions of intelligence may include additional elements, particularly of a non-cognitive order, such as Stoddard's 'social value', 'perseverance', 'resistance to emotional interferences', or the ability to find the solution of a problem 'economically' (that is, with a minimum of trial and error) or what he calls 'the emergence of originals' [51]. But it is obvious that, although in the absence of such, mostly non-cognitive, elements, intelligent behavior will be curtailed, they do not by themselves *constitute* intelligence. We can speak of an intelligent neurotic or an intelligent psychopath, but we would not call intelligent the behavior of a socially well adjusted, patient and persevering person who is unable to solve his problems by way of abstraction (as defined by Goldstein).

We shall now proceed to defining, and analyzing, the essential elements of *impaired* intelligence in its unambiguous form called feeblemindedness.

2 SOME ELEMENTS OF DEFINITION

The feebleminded does *not understand the essentials* separating between different wholes but is liable to identify them under the influence of chance similarities between non-essential details. He does not see the whole-vector of observable details, fails to understand their specific functions in different and changing contexts and is unable to manipulate and modify his wholes.

This explains, *inter-alia,* why he cannot recall at will facts known to him, why he has *no freely available memory* (in spite of its occasional hypertrophic manifestations—see below). Normally, memory has to be maintained constantly against the tendency inherent in each detail of our knowledge to enter into new and ever-changing whole-contexts. We propose to call this the 'protective effort of memory-as-activity'. It aims not only at defining the specific function of each knowable detail within its whole-context but also at protecting the whole against the danger of losing its whole-character.

It is, paradoxically, this protective effort that explains the limitations of our memory-span: the psychic energy required for protecting the whole-vector of the detail and the whole-character of the whole makes a memory retention of too many objects of knowledge dynamically impossible. This is the basis for the selective nature of our memory; it also explains why an unusual memory-capacity is liable to impair the creative aspects of the thinking process: Too much of the protective effort absorbs too much mental energy and leaves not enough room for the kind of receptivity which is indispensable for creative thinking.

In the feebleminded, on the other hand, who is (one could say: by definition) incapable of making this protective effort, two things are liable to happen:

a) Details are not identified as belonging to this or that whole-context and are therefore allowed to move from one context to another, as it were, without leaving recallable memory-traces; and wholes, not being recognized as such in the first instance, are frequently replaced by one of their—non-representative—details so that memory-retention, and, of course, also recall are bound to be inadequate, both quantitatively and qualitatively.

b) On the other hand, relative absence of the ability to identify details and wholes functionally and the relative or total absence of selection account for the amazing capacity of certain feebleminded persons (and particularly of the lower grades) for reproducing, as it were, mechanically recorded imprints—a phenomenon which should, of course, not be identified with memory-retention and recall. This 'tape-recorder'-type of reproduction is probably linked with certain, not yet known, cerebral peculiarities.

Inability of the ego to detach itself from a given object or situation is known as *rigidity*. It is a symptom of various pathologies: of compulsion-neurosis, of certain character-disorders, of some psychoses, of cerebral injuries, of feeblemindedness. The neurotic and psychotic varieties of rigidity are the results of the ego's defensive self-restriction in its struggle against unconscious drives and tendencies; the organic variety is the result of cerebral de-differentiation and/or of the organism's defence against disturbances of the homeostatic function. The feebleminded variety is primary, not reactive. We can either consider it an epiphenomenon of cortical deficiencies (in those cases in which such deficiencies can be proven), or an integral, irreducible element of feeblemindedness *per se*.

This, however, does not preclude the possibility of its being reinforced by frequent experiences of failure, particularly in the borderline cases of retardation in which such experiences are still traumatic and withdrawal into rigidity may be, at least in part, a useful defence.

We shall later discuss the various personality types of feeblemindedness of which apathy, submissiveness, suspiciousness and aggressiveness are the most important characteristics. We shall then see in what different forms rigidity appears under the influence of these type-conditions. Here, we wish to emphasize the common element only, absence of ego-activity. Rigidity is the perversion of staticness. In rigidity, the condition to which the individual clings is no longer a basis for change and development; it is no longer the ground from which movement and activity start and in which tendencies towards expansion and growth should be rooted in order not to degenerate into wild whole-disruptions [16]; in rigidity the 'present condition' becomes the only valid reality, to the exclusion of all possible change and development. Absence of ego-activity here means not only passiveness but also a seemingly active attempt to prevent change. This pseudo-activity of the rigid ego that is well reconcilable with passiveness in other respects and with complete lack of adequate initiative in the face of changing reality-tasks, is an expression of that basic deficiency that we have defined elsewhere as non-exchangeability of the ego's subject-object positions [24].

Genuine activity is characterized by simultaneous relatedness of each action to the subject *and* to the object of change, to the ego *and* the non-ego. It means, in other words, ego-involvement and ego-investment, on the one hand, and ego-transcendence, on the other. In rigidity, genuine ego-involvement is replaced by external ego-emphasis, which tends to grow in intensity proportionally to its objective inadequacy; and ego-transcendence through reality-related actions is replaced by exaggerated dependence on the non-ego, on environmental determinants. In this sense, rigidity excludes what we have called the exchangeability of subject-object positions, the latter concept meaning that the ego is able to experience itself as responsible for determination and change (as subject) at the very moment that it feels itself determined (as object).

Here is the place to come back to the problem we have mentioned at the beginning, that of the seeming contradiction between automatic continuation of processes, this typical sign of feebleminded rigidity, and distractibility or divertibility (cf. K. Lewin's treatise on feeblemindedness).

Distractibility means—in this case—almost automatic reaction to changing stimuli. It indicates the absence of ego-selection and ego-direction, probably due to some basic disturbance in the relationships between what Rothschild [46] calls the *Körperpol* (the representative in the central nervous system of the body) and the *Weltpol* (the representative of the environment). In fact, we should not speak here of 'reaction': what goes on is *not* the result of a polar relationship between a reacting ego and a stimulating non-ego, but resembles more a purely mechanical result of physical pressure-processes.

This is, of course, an extreme formulation only. In reality, we will probably find not one feebleminded individual (with the exception of the lowest grades of intellectual functioning) who is completely devoid of ego-regulation and of stimulus-selection. But for the purpose of a phenomenological analysis of distractibility we need such a definition *ab extremo*.

Automatic, quasi-mechanical 'reaction', that is, distractibility, is a kind of *Erzatz* for truly polar relationships: in their absence, non-selective, automatic responses to changing stimuli provide the feebleminded with an illusion of contact with the non-ego, while in actual fact he has no ego that could be in contact with the non-ego ('contact' meaning polar, dialogic, relationships and exchangeability of the subject-object positions); he has a pseudo-ego only, mirroring, as it were, the ever changing environment.

We should beware of interpreting teleologically this substitute character of automatic reactions and the illusion of contact provided by it. The feebleminded, in contrast to the intellectually normal individual—both the emotionally healthy and the emotionally disturbed one—is neither in need of, nor capable of using, defences, since he is not aware, consciously or preconsciously, of dangers threatening him from the internal non-ego.

The second, seemingly contradictory characteristic of feeblemindedness is the tendency of movements and actions, once set in motion, to continue automatically, without relatedness to the ego or to changing conditions (often in a way reminiscent of catatonic perseverations). In the second chapter, in which the feebleminded will be compared with the chronologically younger child and the fallacy of the concept of mental age will be shown, an attempt will also be mode to define the essential difference between the feebleminded and the younger child in regard to their respective reaction to this repetition-pattern. Here, it may suffice to point out that the degree of ego-participation in these patterns is much lower in the feebleminded than in the young child.

Just as the term 'reaction' is inadequate for describing the feebleminded pattern of automatic response to ever-changing external stimuli, so the term 'repetition' seems to be inadequate for circumscribing the automatism of feebleminded continuation processes. Both, reaction and repetition, are terms that presuppose the existence of an organizing principle—unless we add the word 'automatic' to denote their pathological character. And just as we have warned against the use of teleological concepts in an interpretation of automatic reactions in the feebleminded, so we must warn now against trying to make feebleminded perseverations intelligible as a means to satisfy the individual by way of artificially limiting and restricting the area of the unknown and the new, and to provide him with the illusion of thus being able to master his reality. True enough, the feebleminded may himself believe that repetition proves mastery; but he does not *seek* this feeling of mastery. Repetition-processes go on as long as there is no counterforce to stop or to replace them. And to the extent that the feebleminded derives satisfaction from repetitions, it is more in the order of a physiological than of a psychological experience.*

Here, however, we see the link between the two seemingly contradictory manifestations of feebleminded behavior, and we understand why both can be subsumed under the general term of rigidity. Rigidity means, in this context, 'inability to adapt attitudes and reactions to different and changing reality-conditions and fixatedness to a certain unchangeable pattern of behavior' [21, p. 46]. It is, accordingly, the weakness or absence of ego-regulation and integration that

---

* In a previous publication [18] the author has summarized this teleological interpretation of perseverative tendencies in the feebleminded as follows:

'. . . satisfaction is liable to be derived from the very fact of repetition by which the area of the unknown is artificially limited (with repetition the danger grows smaller that something new, unknown and therefore threatening may happen); . . . the illusion of ego-strength is liable to be produced as the result of the fact that the individual remains within the narrow boundaries of what is known and therefore manageable.'

This interpretation is correct, at least in part, as long as we see in it an attempt to explain repetition in the behaviour of the feebleminded as *resulting* from lack of structural differentiation and *causing* satisfaction (through the illusion of knownness and mastery as well as through other factors mentioned later). It is inadequate, when we see in it an attempt to ascribe to the feebleminded a conscious or unconscious *intention*—a kind of defence mechanism. For, this would presuppose some sort of anxiety, of fear of ego-loss, hence a degree of structurality and of differentiation which is irreconcilable with the essential lack of structure in feeblemindedness.

produces rigidity in this case.* Both, unrestricted response to changing external influences and the perseveration-like repetition of one and the same movement or action indicate that absence of controls from within that we have called lack of ego-regulation and lack of integrative ego-functions.

But both also indicate fixation to an unalterable pattern, that of dependence on external, chance-determined, *stimulations.* We find in one and the same feebleminded individual distractibility at one time and perseveration at another. The change is probably due to (physiologically caused?) temporary changes in the prevalence of one of the two basic life-tendencies: When the tendency towards staticness prevails, perseveration, when that towards expansion prevails, distractibility will be in evidence. To the extent that one of the two tendencies structurally predominates in a certain feebleminded individual we shall find a preference for distractibility or for perseveration (we shall see later that this structural preference constitutes one of the characteristics of the apathetic, the submissive, the suspicious and the aggressive types).

On the other hand, we now understand the difference between feebleminded rigidity and externalized 'fixation to the known'. In children of normal intelligence, the latter pattern can be interpreted as the result of conditioning and avoidance; it emerges at the end of a long process of growing-up under the influence of externalizing factors, such as want and insecurity; feebleminded rigidity, on the other hand, is a structural given and not the result of a process of development. Moreover, to the extent that there is an area of the known in the life of the feebleminded, it is not only much more restricted than that of man living under conditions of externalization, but also loses its knownness-character much easier than the 'moratory' area [20, 26] of the immediate neighborhood in the life of poverty and neglect.

Lack of structure is, as we have said (p. 3), the essential characteristic of feeblemindedness. 'When we speak of a structured ego, we mean to say that each of its functions, each of its reaction-patterns owes its emergence to the participation of all others, with the ego serving as agent of co-ordination and integration.' On the other hand, 'structurality presupposes differentiation' [24].

* In the neurotic variety of rigidity, ego-regulation is eliminated secondarily, reflecting, as it were, the functional autonomy [2] of those defence mechanisms, for whose mobilization the ego was responsible when its regulating function was still strong enough.

It is lack of structure in this sense that renders possible a clear distinction between the behavior and the thinking-processes in the feebleminded, on the one hand, and in the intellectually normal but chronologically younger child, on the other. Lack of structure manifests itself in all function-areas as well as in each stage of development.

We have already pointed out that the non-selective, automatic character of reactions, and of mental processes in general, is due to the absence of ego-direction and of polar relationships between the ego and the non-ego in its different connotations. Apperception, memory, concept-formation, imagination, application are the major cognitive processes in which this lack of structure of the feebleminded can be recognized.

Let us consider, for instance, the inability of the feebleminded to recognize details within a given whole as belonging to this whole, as fulfilling their specific function in the determination of its meaning; we have said above that, as a result, the details are not freely available for re-synthesis, and the wholes are liable to appear, again and again, as new and unfamiliar. In contrast to the theory of feeblemindedness, according to which defective apperception is *based* on memory deficiencies, we maintain that the former *produces* memory deficiencies; lack of apperceptive organization and the resulting need for repeating the apperceptive effort time and again constitute too heavy a burden on the memory, which, consequently, is liable to shrink.

Apperception implies some form of *abstraction* (just as complexity —in the definition of intelligence as suggested by Stoddard [51]— implies abstraction). It is the element of meaningfulness, that is, of reaching out *behind* the perceived phenomenon, that constitutes apperception. We can speak of the tridimensionality of apperception, as against the bidimensionality of perception; the former is indicative of a similar polarity between the ego and the object of apperception, a similar self-distantiation and willfulness of attention-shifting and a similar awareness of essentials as are required for abstraction. This is why apperceptivity is a condition *sine qua non* of concept-formation (the essential difference between the two lying, of course, in the degree of ego-initiative required).

The feebleminded differ among themselves in the extent to which their apperceptivity still functions more or less normally, at least in certain reality-areas, although they may be equally weak in abstractive capacities. It would seem that this difference should not be regarded as indicative of different *levels* of intelligence, as commonly measured in terms of IQ, but rather of type-conditions to which we shall refer soon in some detail. But even when apperceptivity is still relatively intact, the ability for *willful* self-distantiation from the objects of perception is defective in all feebleminded.

It is insufficient to interpret this excessive clinging of the feebleminded to his objects as a symptom of structural rigidity only, without considering the impact it is bound to have on the development of his intellectual functions. It is a generally accepted fact that the intellectual capacities of the feebleminded child tend to decline, unless he is exposed to consistent educational stimulation. This is due not so much to lack of distance, as such, from the objects, as it is due to lack of willfulness in the *act* of self-distantiation, not so much to rigidity *per se*, as to lack of ego-intentionality and activity. (And although the latter is, of course, also a *symptom* of rigidity, it is at the same time an independent variable, which, when dealt with adequately in the educational process, may even contribute, though to some limited extent only, to loosening the structural rigidity.)

The point made here is that rigidity may have its cerebral corollaries in the feebleminded, thus being a constitutional determinant of behavior and functioning; but it is the ego's organizational weakness which, though at least in part being a *symptom* of rigidity, also *determines* its degree in each individual case: Organizational weakness affects apperceptive abilities; as a result, the understanding of differences remains inadequate, and rigidity increases; rigidity manifests itself *inter alia* in defective differentiation, and, as a result, apperceptive abilities remain undeveloped. This inherent causal ambiguity is evident in the area of apperception more than in the area of concept-formation. The latter requires so much more dynamic strength and mental energy than the feebleminded can raise under any circumstances that inability to operate conceptually is but a symptom of rigidity and no longer influences the level of functioning.

The distinction between the feebleminded individual's defectiveness in the areas of apperception and concept-formation respectively is far from being an academic issue; it is of importance for the educator when he plans his rehabilitative strategies: it is through apperception, not through concept-formation that the feebleminded is capable of acquiring, to some extent at least, mental mobility, awareness of meaning in different contexts and thus polar relationships.

Abstraction cannot be unstructured without losing its essence. We define structurality (a) as the dynamic inter-relatedness of differentiated contexts and functions, (b) with the ego acting as integrator.

Relational mobility, recognition of essentials and conceptual organization—to mention only these three elements of abstraction—require both components of structurality. We know, of course, of what might be called pseudo-abstraction, for instance in neurosis, in psychotic alienation or in externalized orientation towards the haveable. But in *neurotic* distortion the details of a given whole tend to relate to the ego more than to each other, and the ego, though operating as a center of selection and integration, does so in defence of its own positions rather than for the purpose of reality-organization and communication. This is still more in evidence when we consider *psychotic* attempts at systematization and what psychoanalysts call 'reality-restitution in schizophrenia' [13]. In *externalization* we find pseudo-abstraction in the reduction of all objects and events to the common denominator of want and of the haveable [20, 26].

It therefore is safe to say that the feebleminded can never learn abstraction: to the extent that his field of reality-contents and -functions can be organized, at least partly, through rehabilitational efforts, responsibility for the maintenance of this organization cannot be entrusted to the ego; to the extent that the feebleminded is trained into some sort of responsibility for the conduct of his affairs, this is not necessarily achieved through organizing his field of reality-contents and -functions, but rather by way of actional and reactional drill. (There are, of course, not a few cases in which a different educational attitude is justified and indicated; but these are, as a rule, cases in which environmental impairment of intelligence has not yet produced irreversible feeblemindedness.)

Another functional area in which lack of structure can be recognized as an essential characteristic of feeblemindedness, is that of *imagination,* in the twofold sense of the word: imagination as active orientation towards meaning behind appearance, towards discovering the dimension of the future and the possible, and imagination as receptivity, as response to processes emanating from the unconscious. In the feebleminded, the dimension of the future and the possible is practically non-existent, because of the extreme limitation of his time-consciousness. For him, the future is but a repetition of the present, the possible but a repetition of the real. Even when he imitates one of his frequently 'occurring' and changing hero-images—his brother or a cinema star, his teacher or a street-vendor, his neighbor or a passer-by—he does so again by way of automatic reaction rather than by way of imagination and rôle-playing. He is not only unaware of the discrepancies between his changing hero-images (in this respect there is little difference between—at least young—persons of different intelligence), but he is also unaware of the difference between himself (his real self) and the objects of his imitation. In other words: he does not identify himself, but only reacts to an external stimulus.

Imagination does not fulfill in his life the function it fulfills in the life of every normal child: to familiarize him with the unknown and to strengthen his courage, his readiness to face the unknown without too much fear. The feebleminded never learns how to face the unknown, and certainly not by way of imagining the future and the possible. He does not even experience the need to use adequate mental tools for dealing with the unknown, because he does not know that there is anything unknown. This unawareness, however, is a serious handicap: not knowing the dimension of the unknown means, among other things, not feeling threatened, and not feeling threatened means: being deprived of an important incentive for mobilizing imagination as a weapon in this struggle with the unknown.

The second meaning of imagination is receptivity in regard to the unconscious. This receptivity requires not only openness of the ego towards the inner non-ego but also, in order to make such openness meaningful and constructive, readiness of the ego to enter into polar relationships and ability to make adequate use of the received contents for its coordinational and organizational purposes. In psychoses we can see the effect of openness without the latter ability. In the feebleminded neither one of the two conditions is present [19, 24].

As a result, his imagination is bound to remain weak in all stages of his development: to the extent that some material capable of eliciting imaginative reactions in a normal child comes up from the unconscious, the feebleminded is liable to react to it as if it were part of his, in any case incoherent, reality. Ordinarily, however, no such material will reach his consciousness, the channels of communication between his ego and the inner non-ego being blocked or interrupted (which again can be interpreted as a symptom of lack of structure).

Here we should go into a detailed discussion of how lack of structure manifests itself in the *emotions and the impulses* of the feebleminded. This discussion, however, must be postponed, since it requires an analysis of structurality in emotion, drives, impulses and affects, irrespective of the level of intelligence. It may suffice here to point out that in this area again it is the absence of truly polar relationships between the emotions and, still more so, between the impulses, and a reacting ego that characterizes the feebleminded: his unstructured emotions and his unintegrated impulses are part of his consciousness rather than of an (internal) non-ego.

In an analysis of the cognitive aspects of feeblemindedness with which we are concerned at present, emotions, affects, drives and impulses become relevant for two reasons: they distort perception and apperception, memory-retention and recall, comprehension and phantasy, and they determine the ways in which the individual applies his learning, partial and unstable as it may be, to relationship and action.

The distorting effect is not only less decisive in feeblemindedness than in neurosis, it also has a different meaning in both behavioral entities: While it is the result of pre-conscious and unconscious intentionality in the neurotic, it is purely associative and automatic in feeblemindedness. We therefore can almost never give an unambiguous answer to the question of what *did* cause certain distortions in the thinking of the mentally retarded, faulty associations or interference of uncontrollable impulses and unstructured emotions. It seems that here again a type-factor is at work, so that we may speak of an 'association-type' and of an 'emotion-type' of thought-distortion.

More important is the other question: how do impulses and emotions in the feebleminded determine the application of learning to doing? (We wish to emphasize that we are concerned here with the cognitive aspect of application.)

Application normally implies some form of experimental procedures both before and during the act of translating into practice what has been learned. The younger the child, the more limited in duration and specificness will be this experimental stage, so limited sometimes that the observer will have difficulty in discovering it at all. And yet, it is there and can be identified. It implies an, at least half-conscious, comparison of the two areas, that of the learned contents with that of the expected and intended action. The criteria of comparison, it is true, may have been formed through *previous* learning and may only be elicited through the present one, the *applicandum*; they may be adequate or inadequate; but what counts most in the intellectual development of the child is the activity of comparing, albeit for a fleeting moment only, an actual experience (that of the newly learned content) with a hypothetical one (that of the anticipated result of application). Application is thus the most important instrument of enlarging time-consciousness.

Now, it is self-evident why the feebleminded is, one could almost say by definition, unable to apply his learning to the universe of his actions. This has been stressed—in similar or different terms—by many students of feeblemindedness. But what we are apt to overlook is the fact that inability to perform acts of comparison that are the prerequisites of application *makes room* for the illegitimate and obnoxious intervention of uncontrolled impulses and emotions, rather than *results* from such intervention.

This is of importance for the understanding of thought-processes in general and not only of feeblemindedness. We would venture to suggest the following law: *the more normal* the child's native intelligence, the more important becomes illegitimate interference of impulses and emotions with the thought-processes as a cause of intellectual failure; the *lower* the child's native intelligence, the more important becomes the inability to compare actual with hypothetical (anticipated) situations as a cause of intellectual failure; the latter may then be re-inforced only by (secondary) interference of emotions and impulses with the cognitive processes.

3 TYPOLOGY OF THE FEEBLEMINDED

Without entering into a discussion, whether—and if so, what—environmental, that is, experiental, causes may be instrumental to the emergence of type-differences in the feebleminded, we maintain that there are known at least four distinct hebavior patterns: the primarily aggressive, the primarily suspicious, the primarily submissive and the primarily apathetic types.

These, however, are not only patterns of interpersonal relationships but also typical cognitive attitudes. In the following table we try to compare some of the constituent elements of the four types.

From this comparative table we see that extraversion is here regarded as essentially connected not only with an ego experiencing itself as subject, but also with a strong tendency to imitate rather than to persevere, and with relatively lesser impairment of apperceptive abilities, than introversion. The two introvert types are in all respects so far mentioned the exact opposite of the former.

This is not difficult to understand when we remember the definition of the two types by Jung [31]: Extraversion, he says, means that the ego relates its functions and actions primarily to the universe of objects, whereas introversion manifests itself in a prevalence of libido concentration on the ego as the object of thinking and feeling. Extra-

TYPE PATTERNS

Criteria of Comparison	Aggressive	Suspicious	Submissive	Apathetic
Attitudinal type	Extravert	Introvert	Extravert	Introvert
Prevailing life-tendency	Expansion	Expansion	Staticness	Staticness
Ego modality	Subject	Object	Subject	Object
Non-ego modality	Object (hostile)	Subject (hostile)	Subject (superior)	Object (superior)
Affectivity	Strong	Strong	Weak	Weak
Quality of apperceptiveness	Relatively intact	Relatively weak	Relatively intact	Relatively weak
Thought-processes distorted mainly by	Impulses	Impulses	Associations	Associations
Activities determined by	Imitation	Perseveration	Imitation	Perseveration

vert relatedness to the universe of *objects*, however, requires a strong awareness of, and emphasis on the ego's *subject*-modality, since without such awareness and emphasis object-relatedness becomes diffuse and unstructured; introvert libido concentration on the ego means that the ego must experience not only itself as the object of thinking and feeling but also the universe of objects as separate and independent.

If so, we understand why the extravert's apperceptive abilities are less exposed to the danger of impairment even in an intellectually retarded individual: it is probably the combination of his close connectedness with objects and the relatively high degree of his initiative that protects, to some extent at least, his apperceptivity (not, of course, his ability to conceptualize and to think in abstract terms). And it is the introvert's tendency to withdraw from direct contact with objects that accounts for the relatively greater risk of his apperceptive abilities being impaired by intellectual handicaps.

Similarly, extravert object-relatedness accounts for the feebleminded individual's tendency to seek 'solutions' of his tasks through imitation, while the introvert's tendency to withdraw from reality accounts for his preference of perseveration.*

Most typologies suffer from what might be called the shortcomings of linearity, that is, of lack of depth. Not even Jung's distinction

* No need to add that all these—and other—dichotomies are to be understood as extreme points only on a scale of gradual transition. This reservation, however, holds good for every typological distinction.

between attitudinal and functional types, though undoubtedly an important step towards differentiation, has added another *dimension* to linear typology. We speak of multi-dimensional typology when each pattern can be shown to have some characteristics in common with another type, in other words: when each pattern is contrasted by *different* other patterns according to different criteria of analysis.

Thus the aggressive and the submissive types of feeblemindedness have in common extraversion, the tendency of the ego to experience itself predominantly as a subject, lesser impairment of apperceptivity and preference of imitation as an instrument of problem-solving (while the suspicious and the apathetic types are in all these respects their opposites). On the other hand, the aggressive and the suspicious types have in common a prevalence of the life-tendency towards expansion, relatively strong affectivity, a tendency to experience the environment as hostile and to have thought-processes distorted by impulses rather than by associations. The submissive and the apathetic types, on the other hand, are characterized by a prevalence of the life-tendency towards staticness over that towards expansion, a relatively weak affectivity, a tendency to experience the environment as superior rather than as hostile and to have thought-processes distorted by faulty associations rather than by impulses.

Thus, each of our four types of feeblemindedness differs from each of the others when seen under certain aspects, while resembling them when seen under other aspects. This becomes particularly evident when we analyze the meaning of attitudinal types versus typical prevalence of one of the two basic life tendencies over the other.

Here is the place to add a few remarks concerning the pathology of relationships between the two life-tendencies in general and in the case of feeblemindedness in particular.

In other studies [16, 20, 24] the present author has suggested a definition of 'normality' as the state in which the two basic life-tendencies operate in mutual relatedness: only to the extent that each change and growth, that is, each expansion of a present state, each ego-transcendence and -enlargement is directed and related to a phase of systematization and staticness, and only to the extent that systematization and staticness are not aims in themselves but a basis only for further expansion—can we speak of normal development. All developmental and behavioral deviations, whatever their constitutional and experiential causes may be, can be interpreted as the results of a disturbance in the normative balance and mutual relatedness of these two life-tendencies.

The specific form of this disturbance, however, differs from pathology to pathology.

The ideal type of externalization, for instance, which we have analyzed elsewhere [26] as the attempt of a structurally weak ego to strengthen and complete itself as it were, from without, by way of 'having', could be interpreted as the result of the life-tendency towards expansion operating in isolation from that towards staticness (systematization). Living in a world of chance-occurrences, this central characteristic of externalization is symptomatic of such an isolation of the life-tendency towards expansion.

Contrarily, the rigidity of the feebleminded indicates a relative isolation of the tendency towards staticness from that towards expansion. The feebleminded ego does not know of 'expansion through having'. The haveable does not appear in his consciousness as a possible source of (seeming) self-enlargement and self-completion but remains absolute otherness, eternally separated and outside.

This is the form of externalization characteristic of the feebleminded; automatic reactivity, inadequate repetition of a reaction, an action, an attitude, as well as imitation without assimilation are the ways that lead him towards the illusion of contact with the non-ego (which in some way is characteristic of every type of feeblemindedness). This illusion, however, prevents not only genuine ego-expansion but also genuine systematization. Their places are taken by the pseudo-expansion of consciousness through accepting the non-ego as the absolute outside and by the pseudo-staticness of rigid fixatedness to a given condition.

But how is the present claim that feeblemindedness as such, irrespectively of type-differences, is characterized by an isolation of the life-tendency towards staticness from that towards expansion reconcilable with our former claim that the aggressive and the suspicious types are characterized by a relative prevalence of the life-tendency towards expansion, in contrast to the submissive and the apathetic types in which the opposite life tendency prevails?

The answer is that the *direction* in which relative isolation of one life-tendency from the other takes place determines, though only in configuration with other factors and not by itself, the kind of pathology that may develop, but does *not* determine the final *emphasis* on one of the two tendencies. When we apply this thesis to the types of feeblemindedness we find the following:

a) In each of the four types it is the inability to experience a given condition as the basis from which a development or a change could start that characterizes feeblemindedness, rather than the inability to see change as a challenge for systematization (in other words: a relative isolation of staticness from expansion rather than of expansion from staticness).

b) On the other hand, aggressiveness and suspiciousness are essentially linked with an excessive though isolated and unstructured tendency constantly to expand the frontiers of the ego (pseudo-expansion); submissiveness and apathy are characterized by an equally excessive and again isolated and unstructured tendency to remain within the limits of a given condition (pseudo-staticness).

We now come back to what we have said above (pp. 17 ff.) on the common characteristics of the aggressive and the suspicious types, on the one hand, and of the submissive and the apathetic types, on the other hand.

In addition to pseudo-expansion (through aggressiveness) it is strong affectivity, experiencing the non-ego as hostile and impulsive distortion of thought-processes that characterize the two first-mentioned types; the two last-mentioned are characterized by pseudo-staticness, weak affectivity, experiencing the non-ego as superior rather than as hostile, and associative distortion of thought-processes.

Whereas the connection between the affective elements of these configurations is self-evident, it is the cognitive element that requires commenting: When the thought-processes are distorted by faulty associations, the results are as inadequate as they are liable to be under the influence of affects and impulses. But in the first case, the automatic, almost mechanic, nature of the distortion-process (symptom of the here prevailing pseudo-staticness) accounts for the *quantitative* inadequacy of performance; the uncontrollable character of autonomously interfering affects and impulses explains, in the second case, the *qualitative* inadequacy of feebleminded problem-solutions. Although in both cases the measurable results will be equally low, we often find ourselves intrigued by the queerness of answers and solutions offered by the aggressive and the suspicious types, in fact, so much so that diagnostic ambiguities are sometimes unavoidable.

On yet another level of comparison we find, strange as it may seem, a common element even between the aggressive and the apathetic types on the one hand, and between the suspicious and the submissive, on the other. Both the aggressive and the apathetic feebleminded see their environment, the physical and human non-ego, as object only, though the first as the hostile object of his destructive tendencies and the second as devoid of all intentionality, as 'just being there' and necessitating passiveness and resignation. Contrarily, both the suspicious and the submissive types see the non-ego as subject only, though the first as the bearer of hostile intentions and the second as the superior and trustworthy subject of determination.

In the context of our present discussion, that of typological factors in an analysis of feeblemindedness, we should consider in particular the strange similarity between the aggressive and the apathetic feebleminded, who are otherwise radically contrary types—the first being extravert, expansive, affectively strong, impulsive and imitative, the second being introvert, static, affectively weak, associative and persevering.

It is obvious that the similarity (the object-character of the environmental non-ego) has an altogether different meaning in each of the two cases: the ego of the aggressive feebleminded acts as a subject vis-à-vis the non-ego object, in the apathetic feebleminded the ego is experiencing itself as an object of the non-ego while at the same time experiencing the *latter* as an object; all is governed by uncontrollable forces operating from without and from within.

Here lies the importance of our last comparison—in spite of its seeming absurdity: it shows us the ambiguity of dichotomies like 'subject-object' in the interpretation of behavioral types. Before using such categories, we should ask: 'object of whom' and 'subject for what?' Unless we have made clear that we speak in each case of the same kind of 'objectiveness' (object of the ego or object of inner or outer forces of determination and of the same kind of 'subjectness' (subject as a center of change or as a symbol of identity), the dichotomy is liable to lose its meaning.

That the issue is not an academic one, can be understood when we think of the psycho-analytic thesis of apathy as the end-result of deeply repressed aggressiveness. There are undoubtedly cases in which apathy can indeed be explained in this way (and can be eliminated or changed by bringing the hidden aggressiveness to the surface); but it would be a serious mistake to generalize this type of etiology, by excluding from the analysis non-genetic, structural cases of apathy or by overlooking the ambiguity of the concepts of subject and object. In psychoanalysis the concept of object means—as a rule—object of the reacting, the recognizing, the sublimating, the distorting ego; the object in its independent *So-sein* is of as little interest to psychoanalysis as the Kantian *'thing by itself'* or—to give an example from a more relevant field, that of personality theory—as constitutional and structural givens and tendencies.

Hence, the apathetic feebleminded is not included in the psychoanalytic discussion of apathy being the result of repressed aggressiveness (just as constitutional apathy as such and feeblemindedness as such are not included in the psychodynamic interpretation of man).

Our analysis of rigidity and lack of structure as central characteristics of feeblemindedness in general applies to each of the four types differentially. Thus, lack of ego-intentionality, though lacking in all, will be more evident in the apathetic than in the submissive type with his strong tendency to cling to his hero-figures, more in the diffusely aggressive than in the suspicious type with his seeming directedness against his persecutors. In all four, it is true, the memory is weak and not freely available: the defect may be accounted for by lack of vitality and lack of ego-involvement in the apathetic, and by energy-diffusion in the aggressive type; in the two other types we find some sort of selective memory islands, though of course, with a different value emphasis in each. The 'tape-recording' memory seems to be confined to the submissive and, perhaps, the apathetic types, that is, to the types with a predominance of the life-tendency towards staticness over that towards expansion. Reversely, it is this predominance of staticness that accounts for the particular weakness of imagination in these two patterns, in contrast to the aggressive and the suspicious patterns with their often bewildering phantasies.

Distractibility and perseveration-like tendencies to repeat a chance-caused action—both symptomatic of feebleminded rigidity—have a different meaning in each of the four types: Distractibility is more pronounced in the aggressive and in the suspicious types, where it is affect-conditioned. It does, however, not relate to the type-specific basic attitudes of aggressiveness or suspiciousness (in which the feebleminded shows great consistency); it rather means almost complete inability to concentrate on any ego-trenscending task that implies learning, judging, adjustment. The unavoidable failure resulting from this inability reinforces (secondarily) the basic aggressiveness or suspiciousness of the feebleminded; this secondary reinforcement again operates as a factor of distraction, leading to an almost automatic escape from the task into feelings and expressions of hatred.

The submissive and the apathetic are, as we have said, less distractible than the affective types. In the former, distractibility indicates general weakness of intellectual functioning rather than the intervention of affective counterforces. Submissiveness may even help the feebleminded to mobilize mental energies required for concentration (though, of course, to a limited extent only). And apathy decreases man's readiness in general to react to, and to be attracted by, external factors of motivation. To the extent that the apathetic type *is* being distracted from his task, it is not so much an attractive counterforce that accounts for it, but his low tension-level.

The differences between the forms in which perseveration-like tendencies to repeat a certain action appear in each of the four types are best described as differences in the effect such repetition may have on the individual. The aggressive feebleminded is liable to derive quasi-sadistic satisfaction from his repetitious acts of destruction, while in the apathetic type repetitions often occur rhythmically, reminiscent of masturbatory acts. In the submissive type they are likely to be associated with a wish to please a 'hero-figure', to be recognized, accepted and loved, though the figure may have ceased in the meantime to be present and real (repetition as a kind of intercourse with phantasied realities). Perseveration in the suspicious feebleminded will be discussed in another context.

Are these—and perhaps other—type differences based on congenitally given dispositions or are they formed in reaction to earliest childhood experience only? Intellectual retardation weakens the causal rôle of reaction and experiences in the genesis of attitudes and patterns. It would therefore seem more likely that whatever type differences *do* exist as determinants in the development of the feebleminded child are there from the start and act as structural determinants. Rigidity being one of the essential elements in feeblemindedness, it is obvious that and why structural determinants are more powerful causally than reactions to earliest forms of environmental stimulation or non-stimulation.

CHAPTER TWO

*The Development of the Feebleminded**

1 INTRODUCTION

DESPITE THE criticism voiced against the concept of 'mental age' in the psychological literature of the last two decades—of which D. Wechsler [57] is one of the best-known exponents—the feebleminded continues to be regarded as resembling a younger child in behavior and thinking. It is generally maintained that the development of thinking leads towards greater specificness, clarity, differentiatedness, rationality and objectivity and is integrally connected with a gradual enlargement of the time-consciousness. The feebleminded, it is claimed, resembles the young child of his 'mental age': he tends to overlook differences, to generalize by using false analogies, he allows his feelings and emotions to interfere with his judgments and his thinking, is unable to detach himself from a situation in which he finds himself by chance, and has a limited time-span only.

In another place [24], the present author has suggested the concept of 'paternal principle of differentiation', meaning a structural factor of determination, that regulates processes of differentiation and internalization in the child's development, independently of his experience with the individual father, though being stimulated, tinged and secondarily re-inforced or weakened by such experiences. In this respect the paternal principle of differentiation is comparable to what Jung calls the archetypes with their structural rôle as categories and constituents of experience, on the one hand, and their dependence on being brought into play by environmental factors, on the other hand; the latter explain the different meaning of constitutionally similar or even identical endowments and handicaps in each individual case.

It is this paternal principle of differentiation that is defective in the feebleminded. Its structural normality is characteristic of the normal child; in each of his age-conditioned symptoms of intellectual immaturity, in his *lack* of specificness, of clarity, of differentiatedness,

* Reprinted, with minor alterations, from: *Acta Psychologica* 24 (1965), pp. 167-204.

of rationality and of objectivity, he shows a vector towards the opposite.

We can best illustrate this basic difference by comparing the feebleminded child's stages of development with those of normal development. Although we shall endeavor to look for type-differentials in every stage, completeness in this respect will be impossible, since the causal importance of each of these differentials differs from phase to phase.

But before entering into such an analysis a short definition of the population to which it refers would seem to be necessary.

What we shall have to say about the development of the feebleminded child, does *not* refer to the lowest grades of idiots and imbeciles with their frequent etiology of germ-injury, fetal, para- or postnatal traumatization affecting the brain and/or the endocrine system. Neither do we intend to include cases of infantile autism or early childhood psychosis with their specific forms of intellectual dysfunction, or, for that matter, later deterioration of intelligence under the impact of psychotic alienation, or the neurotically inhibited child of potentially normal intelligence who, if not treated adequately and in time, may deteriorate until irreparable damage has been done to his mental abilities.

All these cases would require a thorough analysis of physiological factors influencing growth and development, or a discussion of neurotic or pyschotic reality distortions in the development of the intellectually normal child and the effect such distortion may have on intellectual functioning. It would therefore not be possible to isolate the factor of feeblemindedness as a determinant of development. This, however, is the purpose of the following analysis.

In other places we have dealt with these and other questions of etiology [15, 24], including the eternal controversy of nature and nurture in regard to those cases of feeblemindedness that we have in mind here, children whose IQ's, could we establish them more or less reliably, would range between 50 or 60 and 70 or 80. These are the children who may have been born with a relatively low potential, or who may have lost some of their abilities. Such loss may have been the result of early institutionalization or of the externalizing conditions of extreme poverty and educational neglect or of the later impact of cultural ambiguity and tension. The loss of potentials may be irreversible or—at least in part—reversible. It is within this range of measurable intelligence that we find the majority of feebleminded children. We claim that, in order adequately to interpret their impairment, the concepts of constitution and environment, endogenous and exogenous pathologies, nature and nurture, must be supplemented by those of structurization and reversibility. These concepts will be found to be of particular importance for an interpretation of what we propose to call 'secondary retardation' (see ch. III); but they are relevant also in a developmental analysis of true feeblemindedness, that is, of those cases in which mental dysfunctioning is present as a determining factor from birth on.

2 THE FIRST PHASE

The infant's development is determined by the experiences of need and need-satisfaction, of tension and staticness alternating in rhythmical sequence. The ability to become aware of this sequence is rooted not only in the nature of the primary mother-child relationships but also, and no less, in such constitutional factors as thresholds of perception and frustration-bearance or in the level of intelligence.

A congenitally low level of intelligence, one of whose most significant symptoms, at the beginning of life, is a weak memory, explains why such an infant fails to learn that neither the protecting presence nor the frustrating absence of the mother are final. In other words: where the memory does not fulfil its basic function, that of bridging between contradictory states, these states remain unrelated to each other, and the experience of nearness is delayed, if it emerges at all.

Normally, it is this experience that both presupposes and furthers differentiation between the ego and the objects of its relationship. Low intelligence, contrarily, *inhibits* the process of separation between the ego and the non-ego, a process that normally starts already in the first months of life and prepares polar relationships at a later stage. This explains why the first symptoms of intentionality [30] that appear at the age of 2-3 months, in connection with the 'smiling response' [50], are lacking in the reactions of many feebleminded infants. In this case we tend to speak of the first manifestations of constitutional, type-conditioned, apathy). Sometimes these reactions do appear, but indiscriminately (in the 'submissive' type) or as early patterns of aggressiveness. (See the third paragraph of the first chapter.)

Although congenitally given predispositions undoubtedly play a decisive rôle in the 'choice' of the individual child's reaction-patterns, environmental, and particularly maternal, attitudes and reactions are of equal importance in its causal equation. It is a well-known fact that many mothers of feebleminded children are educationally inadequate, due either to their own feeblemindedness or to their being disappointed, their guilt-feelings, their unconscious projections. The common element in the various forms of educational inadequacy during the early period of the child's life is lack of spontaneous acceptance, but its expressions differ according to its causes in the mother's personality.* According to the law of causal configuration [15, 24] it is the *cause* of a factor (and particularly if this factor is a human attitude) rather than the factor itself that determines its effects. It is therefore highly probable that the mother's conscious or unconscious motives for relating to her feebleminded child inadequately participate not to a small extent in the formation of the child's reaction-type.

But when signs of a more differentiated intentionality *do* appear, with a delay of several months, it no longer can fulfil its structural function, which it fulfils in the life of a normal child at the age of 2-3 months, namely to establish contact with the environment as a source of protection. Meanwhile, a vital event may have taken place: the first tooth may have appeared, and with it the experience of intensive pain and frustration and—almost inevitably—aggressive reactions to pain from within and to lack of relief from without. The meaning of such pain and aggressiveness, however, is fundamentally different in a normal child in which it is *preceded* by a period of 'intentionality-practice' and in the feebleminded in which the latter *coincides* with the emergence of aggressive reaction to pain. Normally, this aggressive reaction forms the basis on which moral feelings and judgments develop, in other words, the preceding experience of intentionality makes new conflict and internalization-processes imperative. No such conflict and internalization take place in the feebleminded, whose reaction to intensive pain is determined by his type-condition.

The *apathetic* feebleminded is almost unaware of the fact that suffering can be used as a means of establishing contact with the adult protector. This unawareness often gives the impression, as if he suffered less, as if his sensitivity to pain were relatively weak. And

* As far as is known to me, no differential studies are available as to the correlation between maternal reactions to their child's feeblemindedness and the child's (congenitally given and/or early emerging) reaction-pattern. It is self-evident that such a study would have to refer also to later stages of the child's development, when the fact that the child is retarded can no longer be overlooked or denied.

indeed: low sensitivity may result from constitutional apathy (of contact-needs) while on the other hand, it increases apathy at least secondarily. Apathy, in any case, weakens all forms of intentionality, to the obvious detriment of problem-solving abilities.

The *submissive* type is, at least as regards his 'contact-needs', the opposite of the first. Accordingly, intensive pain increases his dependence on, his longing for, relief from without, while he is, it seems, somehow immune against the ill-effects of environmental neglect. In his case, it is the low tension-level that impedes all mental activity; at the same time his strong contact-need produces a kind of pseudo-intentionality (non-selective and imitative intake of environmental manifestations).

In the *aggressive* and the *suspicious* types, on the other hand, pain serves as a factor confirming and re-inforcing the type-conditioned reaction-pattern. Most mental energy is thereby diverted into affective channels so that little remains available for acts of cognition.

We suggest the hypothesis that it is in this phase of the feebleminded child's development that intellectual retardation becomes recognizable as such for the first time.

In the first months the feebleminded child fails to learn how to foresee the regularity in the sequence of need and need-satisfaction. Now, he fails to learn how to differentiate between positive and negative experiences. Normally, this is the age when anxiety appears, that is, fear of losing the vitally important contact with the protecting (loving) environment. It is precisely because normally the child has by now come to experience the mother as 'the near one whose regular return can be expected', has learned trust and security, that the intensive pain caused by the erupting teeth arouses anxiety; the negative experience puts to a severe test the still precarious ego-position of trust and nearness. Differentiation between positive and negative aspects is therefore the way in which the child normally overcomes, always anew, his basic anxiety: separating between good and bad allows for preserving faith in the good mother although she may be unable to relieve the bad pain or even to eliminate the child's own badness (to use Melanie Klein's argument [34], though in a different context).

The feebleminded child, on the other hand, whatever his type-condition may be, does not learn in this phase how to differentiate between good and bad, because he did not before experience anxiety. He does not experience anxiety because he has no ego to be lost. Need-satisfaction and the subsequent experience of rest and staticness which normally lead to ego-formation, remain in his case associated with the non-ego as the external source and representative of both need and need satisfaction. This is only another way of saying that for the feebleminded there exists no genuine staticness. Neither satisfaction nor frustration are experienced as mine, that is, as ego-related. Instead of producing anxiety they elicit the pre-established type-response only.

It will by now be evident that already in this first year of life it would be incorrect to compare and identify the feebleminded child of, say, 8-12 months with a normal child of a correspondingly lower chronological age. The feebleminded in the second half of the first year will *never* display the kind of intentionality which the normal child displays already at the age of three months. Neither will he at any later stage of his development be able to experience that kind of anxiety that the normal child begins to experience at the middle of his first year. To the extent that he does—later—learn to differentiate, the boundaries of his objects of differentiation will never be as clearly defined or felt as they are in the normal child. In other words: although the feebleminded may, at a later age, attain what the normal child attains earlier, the way by which he does reach a certain goal and the manner in which his achievements are being expressed in his behavior, his judgment, his thinking will always essentially differ from those of the younger normal child.

Even in the areas of such elementary activities as perceiving and observing the environment, muscle-control and moving towards an object of need or withdrawing from an object of frustration, a feebleminded infant shows qualitative and not only quantitative differences when compared with a normal child of lower age (though it is often impossible clearly to diagnose the defect in these earliest stages of development). Though he does learn how to *observe* his environment, his attention will be caught much too easily by details, so that he will be unable to perceive the whole of which these details are parts or indicators. The resulting inadequacy of *object-manipulation* not only persists longer than in a normal infant, it is a permanent characteristic of his general behavior, owing to a variety of factors: it results not only from inadequate observation but also from defective *movement-coordination*. Co-ordination of muscle-activities apparently requires some sort of intelligence,* which

* Though it may, of course, be impaired by purely somatic factors as well, for instance, by cerebral injuries not affecting intelligence, by certain sensory deficiencies, etc.

thus has an indirect bearing on such physiological functions as muscle-control or even on breathing.* This generally devitalizing effect of defective co-ordination, in turn, decreases the child's readiness to seek and establish meaningful *contacts* with his human environment, thus weakening still further his already structurally weak relational ability. (This holds good also for the submissive feebleminded who is no less unable to establish contacts than the other types, although he seems constantly to seek it.)

In addition to observation, object manipulation, movement-coordination, approaching objects of need and avoiding objects of frustration—the child learns in the first year of life how to *relive* past events in phantasy and imagination. Here again, the feebleminded child's structurally weak memory and his failure to distantiate himself from any given task and object of observation and manipulation explain his inability to relive past situations and thus gradually to enlarge his time-consciousness—this precondition of thinking.

It is self-evident that under such conditions the feebleminded child does not reach, at the end of his first year of life, that basic trust in which Erikson [11] rightly sees the essence of this stage of development. On the other hand, it would be wrong to conclude that he has, by this time, acquired *mis*trust, as may be the case when maternal inadequacy has determined a normal child's development. It would be more correct to say that the first phase has not yet come to an end, and that to the extent that the infant does show mistrust, such an attitude is type-conditioned rather than the result of reaction to the mother's inadequacy.

On the other hand, it would be as erroneous to expect the feebleminded child to acquire basic trust later, as it would be erroneous to expect a person with an IQ of 50 to reach a normal level of intellectual functioning in twice the time. 'Reaching the end of a developmental phase' does *not* mean: reaching the same *level* of functioning, irrespectively of the constitutionally given dispositions, but means: reaching the *individual optimum* of functioning. This optimum, we claim, is reached by the feebleminded later than by the normal child, that is, after the end of the first year, but it is not

---

* It has been suggested that the relative frequency of inflammations and infections in feebleminded children results, at least in part, from insufficient oxygen supply to the mucuous membranes, due, in turn, to shallow and uncoordinated breathing (beyond the earliest age, for which it is normal).

identical with the experience of 'nearness'* which normally gives the child the 'courage to be' [55] and to grow. The optimum that the feebleminded child will be able to reach (at a later age than the normal child, of course), is readiness to accept guidance from without, with the exception, we must add, of those cases in which strong type-conditioned aggressiveness excludes even this achievement.

But, in addition to type-conditions, there operates yet another, environmental and experiential, factor against the attainment of the functional optimum: the interference of education for cleanliness or, in psychoanalytic terms, the beginning of the anal phase of development *before* the oral phase has come to an end.

3 THE SECOND PHASE

This is one of the paradoxes inherent in the development of the feebleminded, that a new phase begins, and its specific tasks make themselves felt before the preceding phase has come to an end functionally. Normally, the phase-specific achievements of the second phase are relative autonomy, mutuality and ambivalence; they presuppose those of the first phase—the experience of nearness and basic trust (though the latter will become more firmly rooted in the growing child's structure, the more he succeeds in his second-phase tasks: true ambivalence, for instance, not only presupposes but also reinforces nearness, provided the environment helps the child solve his ambivalence-conflicts).

In the feebleminded, on the other hand, not even his limited first-phase optimum, (readiness to accept guidance from without) has been reached when the environment starts with its culture-conditioned demands for cleanliness and bowel-control, for which, incidentally, a feeble-minded child may be prepared physiologically not less than a normal child. Physiologically but not mentally: not only has he failed to learn that contact with 'his' adults makes response to their demands and conforming with their expectations worthwhile—he has not yet come fully to understand their *meaning*. In other words: need-satisfaction is for him still an exclusive function of the non-ego; it happens either as an outcome of adult-intervention or of body-

* All the concepts used in the present study to describe the essentials of each phase in normal development have been elaborated by the author in his books *Die Äusserlichkeit des Lebensstils* [20] and *The Roots of the Ego—a phenomenology of dynamics and of structure* [24].

processes, both of which he does not know to be controllable by his ego.

Autonomy in the normally developing child is not only an expression of sensory and muscular maturation (which enables the child to move and to act at will), it is also the outcome of reality-expansion and of change-awareness: the wider the reality-area in which the child moves, the more grows his obligation to make choices; and awareness of differences, particularly between the child himself and younger ones, is, as Ch. Bühler has emphasized [4] a function of growth and leads to a gradual recognition of change as a life-inherent process with which the child finds himself confronted as an increasingly independent ego.

Mutuality, this other characteristic of the second phase of development, results not only, as Erikson suggests [11], from the area of bowel-training (the child 'giving' faeces and 'taking' the adult's praise); it is primarily rooted in the growing autonomy and awareness of independence; mutuality is capable of alleviating the anxiety aroused by that awareness.

Ambivalence, the third characteristic, can be interpreted as another defence against the anxiety of independence or, better, as a kind of compromise: it means—primarily—negating the growingly independent ego by positing the other, the non-ego, while at the same time negating the non-ego in order to maintain the all too precarious ego-positions. As such it is a condition of normal growth, while attitudes of 'either-or' indicate a pathology of one kind or another. Ambivalence guarantees rationality, insofar as it allows for experimenting with partial ego-positions (badness does not exclude goodness, nor must one be always good).

In the feebleminded all these characteristics of the second phase are absent, and will remain absent in later phases as well: Although the process of sensory and muscular maturation may be normal, his reality-area does *not* expand meaningfully: His encounters with changing objects do not produce a need or a desire to make choices but only elicit quasi-automatic reactions. He is, and remains, unable to compare himself with younger children, since they may be superior to him. (The later friendships of feebleminded with much younger normal children only comes to confirm our thesis regarding the feebleminded child's inability realistically to compare his own position with that of others.) Obviously he will *not* become aware of change as of a life-inherent process, which forces the normal child into independence, but will, on the contrary, experience every change as something accidentally new and unknown, which only increases his helpless dependence. His bowel-training will be slower not only because the environment may be educationally incompetent but also because he does not feel a strong desire to establish mutuality-contacts with his adult environment, since there is no urgent need for alleviating anxiety (normally aroused by growing independence and ego-formation).

The second phase in the development of the feebleminded child, which not only starts later but also lasts longer than in the development of the normally intelligent child, is the period during which *heteronomy* firmly establishes itself in the child's behavior as an all-determining reaction-pattern. The danger of anal fixation, on the other hand, inherent in the normal child's experience with inadequate toilet-training, is considerably less real in the feebleminded child's development; he lacks that intentionality that normally makes for the emergence of resentment, reactive aggressiveness, fear and fixation to the phase and area of traumatization. Here again, it is much more the congenitally given type-condition (of apathy, submissiveness, aggressiveness, suspiciousness) than reaction to the quality of educational experience that determines the child's responses to toilet-training demands.

This relative immunity against environmental injuries accounts for the strange fact that the second period of development (which, in the feebleminded, often extends well into the fifth year) is not characterized by vulnerability and insecurity or by (reactive) aggressiveness; there is no ego to be defended, no inner tension to be alleviated, eliminated or projected, no unknown territory to be conquered, no expansion to be consolidated and structurized. All is process or happenings, nothing is intentional. (Whatever type-conditioned aggressiveness does appear in the behavior of the feebleminded in the second stage of his development, strongly resembles those forms of rage-eruptions that Cannon has described as 'sham-rage' in decorticated animals [7]; it has in any case no intentionality.)

Here should be added a few remarks about the early language development of the feebleminded child. Not only is his speech often badly articulated and sometimes resembles autistic monologuing; he does not, as a rule, use it for purposes of communication, when the normal child's speech has long entered into this functional phase. But the feebleminded also excels in lack of conceptual and verbal differentiation. Now, while such undifferentiatedness of speech is common to many other types of handicapped children as well (and particularly to the child who grows up under the externalizing conditions of extreme poverty and educational neglect), it is part of a specific blend in the feebleminded: it is not only poor, it is also fragmentary, not only simple but also blurred (in some respects resembling the speech of the autistic or the schizophrenic child).

What we have said here proves again the fallacy of the concept of mental age, retrospectively, as well as prospectively: the heteronomous dependence on external stimulation, the automatism of reactions, the absence of intentionality and of differentiation, which can be clearly recognized in this second phase of the feebleminded child's development, are certainly not to be interpreted as a belated attainment of the first phase goals. Autonomy is the offspring of nearness, heteronomy—of its absence in the preceding phase; mutuality emerges on the basis of trust, automatism of reactions and absence of intentionality are symptoms of that very lack of differentiation between ego and non-ego and of that very lack of polarity that characterize the feebleminded child's first phase of development. At the same time, it should be obvious that autonomy, mutuality and ambivalence will never be achieved at a later stage either. *Thus, it is safe to say that the older feebleminded does* not *resemble a younger child of normal intelligence but is a human entity with its own phases and laws of development.*

When discussing the fourth phase, we shall see that even in his learning and thinking the feebleminded does not resemble the younger normal child. (The fact that he knows the answers to certain intelligence test questions intended for younger children proves the inadequacy of the testing method rather than justifies the mental-age concept.)

A child growing up under conditions of poverty and neglect differs from the institutionalized child; the former does not know ambivalence, the place of which is taken by feelings of Either-Or, in the latter it is replaced by a feeling of Neither-Nor, an emotional vacuum. The institutionalized child learns how to play at being an ego, a tendency which, though obviously incompatible with autonomy, is not a manifestation of heteronomy. The child's behavior is more like a series of conditioned reflexes than of reactions. The institutionalized child's relative weakness of aggressive tendencies is due to the fact that he has almost no ego to defend or to protect by eliminating possible threats from without; and finally, his intellectual 'anemia' and his lack of incentive for leaving a given situation should be mentioned.

The feebleminded, in this second phase of development, differs from the institution child in that he does *not* live in a vacuum but in a world too full of stimuli to allow for adequate orientation; he is mentally ineffective rather than 'anemic'. Submissiveness is *not* identical with the emotional and relational shallowness of an institutionalized child; the feebleminded varieties of aggressiveness or suspiciousness have no equivalents in his behavior. Only the apathetic type has much in common with certain institutionalized children, so much so indeed that one would feel tempted to ask, whether this apathy is not, at least in part, an outcome of type-conditions, independent of institutionalization.

4 THE THIRD PHASE

This is a phase of whole-dissolution and of synthesis—in the areas of interpersonal relationships as well as of feeling, thinking and moral judgment. Normally, it is this phase in which maternal 'universality' comes to an end, in which sex-differences are discovered, and ambivalence centers around the child's relationships with his mother and father. It is the phase in which the structurally different needs of the boy and the girl find their sex-specific expression in so-called oedipal solutions. Guilt and anxiety over separating (in phantasy and in behavior) the parental unit leads to inner tensions, to tension-relief through masturbation and, thus, to increased tension; it also leads to apply the newly acquired technique of separating wholes, that is, of differentiation, to other, less personal problem-areas, those of thinking and judging. It is the phase in which internalization of parental images as well as of learning leads back to relative staticness, this precondition of intellectual and social learning in the next-following phase.

It is evident why relative autonomy, mutuality and ambivalence must precede differentiation and re-synthesis: without a strong desire for ego-independence, without readiness to face the non-ego in give-and-take relationships, without awareness of the co-existence of self-contradictory facts and forces, there would be no incentive for the child either to dissolve wholes into their constituent elements or to overcome the tension thus produced, by means of internalization and re-synthesis. In brief: this is the period in which the paternal principle of differentiation and internalization replaces, and changes the meaning of, maternal unity and whole-connection.

In the feebleminded, heteronomous dependence on the environment, absence of intentionality and of inner tension produce, at the end of the second phase of development, that is, in his case, at the age of four to five, a conception of reality in which opposites are excluding each other and contradictions are there to stay, not to be unified. In other words: the third phase of development is, for the feebleminded child, a phase in which he increasingly discovers that differences are absolute, and no partial similarities serve as bridges of synthesis. This lack of relativization—a symptom of feebleminded rigidity—necessarily leads to further reality-distortions. Thus, the vicious circle of lack of differentiation, reality-distortion and growing inability to recognize partial differences and similarities is being closed.

When we consider his relationships with the parents, the same lack of relativization manifests itself in the emergence of Either-Or feelings (affects) instead of ambivalences. The feebleminded child does *not* discover 'the parents as a couple'—to use Ophuijsen's term [40]—but continues to see them as convenient need-satisfiers, convenient because they are more frequently available than strangers. His erotic desires, to the extent that they do appear in this third phase of development (which may extend into the ninth year), are not specifically or even exclusively related to the mother or the father; on the contrary: since non-family educators often give the feebleminded child more loving care than the parents, they are likely to become more intensely desired objects of erotic needs than the former.

These developmental characteristics make comprehensible a particular inconsistency in the life of the feebleminded child at the age between 4-5 and 9; unlike the intellectually normal child, he is not yet ready for the school-learning processes, not even in a special class or school; at the age of six, the school-entrance age, he is in the middle of his phase of development during which, as we have maintained, his world increasingly becomes one of unbridgeable opposites, in other words, during which he learns differentiation in a typically feebleminded way. The school, however, as a rule emphasizes, in the first years at least, the *absolute* character of differences in order to strengthen the child's ability to accept the universe of learnable and knowable facts as *objecta*. Not only is such absolutism not dangerous, it is exactly what the normal child needs in the first years after the 'passing of the oedipal conflict' in order to become sufficiently de-emotionalized for the school-learning processes.

In the feebleminded child, on the other hand, this 'absolutism' is counter-indicated: he does not need a period of calm, of de-emotionalization, since he has *not* gone through a period of storm, of emotional involvement and tensions, he needs experience with relativization; better, he would need it as a counterweight against his phase-conditioned tendency to conceive of reality as of a universe of rigidly defined dichotomies, if he were not mentally incapable for such learning experience. As a result of his limitations, however, (pre-mature) schooling is bound to *support* his phase-conditioned tendency, and this means: to make him increasingly heteronomous and undifferentiated, although accruing knowledge and skills may —at the beginning at least—give the opposite impression.

In other words: For the normal child, the third period of his development is one of conflict, tension, crisis, dynamic differentiation, anxiety and internalization; it, thus, prepares him for objective learning of facts and skills as a way out of unbearable tensions. For the feebleminded, the third phase is one of external differentiation and dichotomization *without* synthesis. The normal child becomes less and less egocentric in language, thought and moral judgment and increasingly capable of intentional communication (although this process extends, of course, as Piaget has shown [42, 43], into the school-age). The feebleminded child cannot be diagnosed as egocentric, since intentionality is not sufficiently developed in him to move his weak ego into the center of his consciousness, he becomes increasingly non-ego oriented. Although this orientation, too, will always bear the character of passive dependence rather than of active intending, it fulfils a vital function in the development of the feebleminded child, insofar as it helps him establish and recognize an area of the learnable.

The educational conclusions to be drawn from this analysis seem obvious: the institutes of formal education with which the feebleminded child comes into contact during this and the following phases of his development—the Kindergarten and the special school—must try to supplement knowledge and skills by exercises in social relationships, must try to enlarge the area of the learnable in a humanly and socially meaningful direction. It is the only way in which this child can be made to experience tensions that may, in due course of time, become meaningful for his learning as well.

Learning means, of course, something different for each of the four types mentioned above. All, it is true, have lack of intellectual initiative and differentiation, poor language and poor conceptualization in common. But the discovery of opposites and the primitive dichotomization of reality that characterize here the third phase of development, have type-specific effects on the behaviour as well as on the learning and thinking processes. Thus, the *apathetic* is liable to see differences only instead of opposites, and as a result, his world becomes increasingly unstructured and primitive, his behavior increasingly ineffective, and his intellectual capacity is liable to sink below its originally given level. *Submissiveness,* on the other hand, is liable to limit understanding of differences rather than that of opposites: readiness to accept the other by way of imitation or blind obedience presupposes, in the feebleminded at least, its recognition as being 'there', 'opposite', though at the same time as being not essentially different. *Aggressiveness* and *suspiciousness* both have a distorting effect on the processes of dichotomization that take place in this third phase of development: objects of relationship and learning are being experienced in the first case as resisting, in the second as hostile; in both cases, the child's ability to accept and assimilate contents of learning therefore depends entirely on the extent to which the educational environment succeeds in weakening the affective factors interfering with the learning process. It again means that the functions of the institutes of formal education are essentially different from those they fulfil in the education of the intellectually normal child (see fourth phase!).

There is still another question that should be asked in a discussion of these early phases in the feebleminded child's development: is what psychoanalysis calls pregenital sexuality equally present in every child, irrespectively of type or intelligence? Psychoanalysis admits the existence of constitutionally different degrees of erogeneity in the various erogenous zones; these differences are sometimes made responsible—at least partly—for the 'choice' of pathology in the individual case [13]; but erogeneity as such (of this or that zone) is considered a fact of universal validity, more: a constituent element of human structure.

On the other hand, the feebleminded child is not included in the case-material on which psychoanalytic theories of development are based. It would therefore seem to be no more than an empirically unproven hypothesis to say that the libidinal strivings of the feebleminded are the same—in quality and intensity—as those of a normal child. More: the hypothesis seems unwarranted, since the concept of pregenital sexuality includes elements of specific relationships in and through which the biological and the psychological aspects of libido becomes interlinked. Relational abilities, however, are a function of both, the nature of primary child-mother experiences and such constitutional factors as thresholds, reaction-patterns, type and intelligence. Psychoanalytic theories of infantile sexuality, starting with Freud's famous essay [27], have constantly and consistently indulged in untenable abstraction from structural variables.

Such abstractions are methodologically doubtful already in regard to the intellectually normal child, in whom type-conditions determine to no small extent the intensity of libidinal needs and the ways in which the individual tries to satisfy these needs, either directly or indirectly. They are entirely unjustified in regard to the intellectually subnormal child with his essentially different mentality and his specific type-conditioned reaction-patterns. Even if no physiological differences exist, which could account for differences in the intensity and in the time of emergence of certain libidinal tendencies, there can be no doubt that the *reactions* of the feebleminded child to sexual urges are essentially different from the ways in which the normal child solves the inner conflicts aroused by them.

In other words: whatever the common physiological elements of infantile sexuality in all children may be, its psychological meaning, hence its importance as a factor of developmental determination, depends on the degree of structural differentiatedness, as it manifests itself, *inter alia*, in the individual's capacity to experience anxiety and guilt.* This capacity is definitely less developed in the feebleminded child. We therefore maintain that he does *not* pass through a period of oedipal conflicts, either at the age at which a normal child experiences them or later.

How, then, do we explain the transition of the feebleminded child from the third to the fourth stage of his development, which may take place as late as at the age of 8-9?

5 THE FOURTH PHASE

By that time, the normal child is in the middle of a process of ego-consolidation through learning. During the period here under discussion, learning has three aspects and three functions: reception and assimilation of knowledge helps establish more firmly the boundary-lines dividing between the ego and the non-ego, thus making differentiation more reliable, more objective: experimenting

* Cf. in this context R. May's analysis of anxiety [38].

with new and changing situations by way of manipulating them, preferably in the 'society of equals' (Piaget) makes the child increasingly independent in his judgments and in his thinking; the acquisition of skills and the gradual enlargement of the time-span strengthen the child's sense of security and his courage and thus further still more his learning capacity.

In a sense, these three aspects and functions reflect the essential achievements of the three preceding phases, better: their emergence depends on three conditions which could be called a 'new edition' of the essentials of those first phases: there must be trust in the guidance offered by reliable adults, though now preferably by adults *not* belonging to the affect-charged family area; there must be mutuality, though now applied to objective (and primarily cognitive) tasks rather than to emotionally charged relationships, a kind of 'translation' from the personal into the cognitive; there must be differentiation, though now without guilt and anxiety over mental acts involving separation of wholes. School-readiness, that is, readiness to learn in a non-personal setting, is a kind of reaction against prior over-involvement in guilt and anxiety.

This is true although, in the first years of his school-career, the child still needs opportunities for communicating his experience with objective contents of learning to his parents.* In these first years, objective, impersonal learning protects against regression to the preceding phases of 'emotional learning'. It is in the second half of the elementary school only that differentiation and polarization, conceptualization and abstraction no longer evoke anxiety, because they no longer are simply instruments of separation and analysis but serve as instruments of synthesis as well in the learning processes. While the first half of the learning-phase recapitulates, as it were, the *beginning* of the preceding phase (differentiation), the second half is an 'elaboration' of its *end*-achievement (synthesis). However, neither the first nor the second are identical with their past equivalents, since both are now much more content- than function-related, and what was there by implication only, now becomes explicit.

Separation between phantasies and reality, between reality within and reality without (separation that uses growing rationality) is the most important achievement of the learning phase. For, as long as the two continue to be contaminated, genuine internalization of

* One of the most dangerous shortcomings of the school in our time is that it does not do enough to make the child's learning-experience meaningful for his parents. [22].

learning cannot be achieved; the ego-autonomy required for internalization presupposes clear demarcation lines not only between the ego and the non-ego but also between the internal and the external non-ego. As long as phantasies replace or distort reality, the contents of learning are liable to remain autonomous parts of an unassimilated non-ego, as it were, instead of turning into integral parts of the ego (as concepts, values, patterns).*

In the feebleminded, the actual learning-phase starts at the age of 8 to 9 only, although he may have been placed in a special class or school at an earlier age. At that time he has 'achieved' heteronomy, that is, readiness to learn by way of responding to methods of drill and conditioning, methods which not only do not require mutuality or trust but, on the contrary, achieve their limited results only when there is *no* ego-consciousness, when there is *no* polar relationship between the learner and the object of his social or intellectual learning.

In the first chapter we have pointed out that one of the central symptoms of feeblemindedness (in all its forms) is: inability to apperceive and to comprehend the essentials of a given whole and of each of its constituent parts. What we have called the tendency of the feebleminded to dichotomize reality, that is, to see absolute contrasts instead of a variety of shades, to see details as separate but not as a challenge to active separation—is his (externalized) form of differentiation.

Teaching a child thus limited by lack of inner structure requires, paradoxically, simplifying the bewildering multitude of unconnected and unconnectable facts in his already undifferentiated universe ('simplification' meaning, in this context: cutting-out a large number of facts instead of organizing them). This, however, is bound to further the emergence of stereotypes instead of concepts, of conventional attitudes instead of values, of perseverations instead of relationships. It is the unavoidable result of conditioning an individual whose integrational abilities are so weak that there is no ego-reaction to the learning-processes.

This holds good, as already mentioned, for the child's behavior as well as for his school-learning. Repetition takes the place of discovery or mastery as primary source of satisfaction. As a result, there is not only practically no adaptability in the child's conduct, but even no perception of the need for such adaptation to different

* See, however, what we shall have to say later (pp. 133 ff) on developing active imagination as a means to rehabilitate socially or culturally impaired intelligence.

and changing tasks and situations.

But we must not lose sight of the danger inherent in the educational conclusions that can be drawn from such an analysis of the feebleminded mentality. The methods of drill and conditioning, of simplifying the variety of unconnected details and of developing stereotypes, conventional attitudes and reaction-patterns, both in behavior and in judgment, is definitely *counter*indicated in all those cases in which mental retardation is a result of loss of potentials, of decline, under the influence of negative environmental conditions and *not* of innate limitations. We shall come back to this central problem of feeblemindedness in the next chapter, which will deal with problems of causation. But already here we must mention one of the almost unsolvable problems of educating the feebleminded child in his 'learning-phase': How shall we find methods of teaching behaviour and thinking, of helping the child acquire knowledge and skills, of developing proper attitudes towards the tasks with which he is faced—without knowing what these proper attitudes are in each individual case? We may not even know whether he is truly and irreversibly feebleminded and therefore needs methods of conditioning, or whether he is a child whose loss of more or less normal potentials is still reversible and who therefore is capable of reacting to methods of stimulation that require, and aim at strengthening, integrational abilities. The problem is all the more complicated, as both types of children are, as a rule, to be found in one and the same classroom.

True enough: they do resemble each other in their intellectual attitude, both being incapable of polar relationships, of abstract behavior, of resistance to emotional interference, of perseverance. But there can also be found essential differences: the truly feebleminded, unlike the secondarily retarded, shows perseveration more than lack of perseverance, less active distortion of reality (and less fixation to the known) than automatism of reactions; whereas the latter *resists* learning from failure, the feebleminded does not *perceive* failure.

In this last respect, however, there is some resemblance between the resentful attitude of the child whose mental ineffectualness is the result of growing-up under conditions of externalization and the truly feebleminded child in whom suspiciousness prevails as the type-conditioned attitude of determination. This brings us back to the question of the differential role to be ascribed to type-conditions in the development of the feebleminded during the learning-phase.

With the exception of submissiveness all type-peculiarities are liable to prejudice the learning process in the feebleminded child. It is obvious that when we speak of possible impairment of learning —even of learning through drill and conditioning—we have in mind the extreme degree of apathy, aggressiveness or suspiciousness only. Similar attitudes in intellectually normal children can be counteracted by the very learning-process, provided, of course, the teacher is aware of his educational and psychological functions; extreme manifestations of these affective elements in the learning process of the normal child may require the attention of a psychotherapist. They have an altogether different meaning in the education of the feebleminded.

Constitutional apathy, for instance, may require some kind of pharmacotherapy in support, or even in preparation of the educational effort. Nothing would be more futile than to look in such cases for emotional causes or to try out psychotherapeutic methods, such as release therapy, which may be very useful in cases of secondary, symptomatic, apathy. Diagnostically, the two varieties are not always distinguishable, without depth-probing examinations. One of the more characteristic differences, however, is to be found in the very learning process: helplessness and bluntness are typical of the constitutional variety of genuinely feebleminded apathy; the secondary variety is recognized by frequent signs of absentmindedness, day-dreaming and sudden flare-ups of isolated aggressive impulses.

Aggressiveness and suspiciousness are liable to impair the learning processes (*not* the final level of intelligence!) much more radically than apathy, particularly under the influence of those wild phantasies of aggressive mastery, of destructive dominance over a hostile, frustrating environment, or of being victimized by a world of persecutors that we often find in the feebleminded child. *Prima facie*, one could say the educator has to fulfil a similar task here and in the development of the intellectually normal child: that of weakening affectivity for the benefit of rationality and realistic thinking. A closer analysis, however, reveals a decisive difference and contrast between the functions of education in both cases:

Education must help the normal child in his learning-phase to overcome irrational fears and distorting phantasies by building up rational and realistic counterpositions; the feebleminded needs more direct and frequently repeated efforts on the part of all his educators —parents, teachers and environmental chance-figures alike—to alleviate the tensions created by his uncontrolled affects and phantasies, shallow as they may be. There is little hope to achieve this by means of compensatory learning, and thus to stimulate transfer from cognitive to affective areas. Only by providing the feebleminded child, who may be possessed by feelings of hate or by suspiciousness, with consistent experiences of positive relationships, can we hope to liberate him, to some extent at least, from his type-conditioned affects, thus making his, in any way, limited amount of mental energy available for systematic and co-ordinated learning activities.

Since such conditions are, for obvious reasons, unlikely to be found in more than a small minority of the feebleminded children's home environments, we understand why institutional care, if properly planned, usually produces much better results than the school. In this respect, however, the feebleminded differs not only from the normally intelligent child but also from the one who may have lost part of his normal capacities as the result of having been exposed to the externalizing influences of extreme poverty and neglect. The latter needs a more personal contact with his educators and a more variegated and directed contact with the environment than the debilitating and incapacitating conditions of feeblemindedness allow for. In other words: institutional care *per se* has an altogether different, in fact an opposite, meaning for the feebleminded and for the child born with normal intelligence (at least as long as the environmentally caused loss of his potentials is still reversible).

For yet another reason type-conditions are an important factor in the interpretation of the feebleminded child's development during the learning-phase: in the first chapter we have maintained that at least in the two extravert, the aggressive and the submissive types, apperceptivity is relatively intact. This has a direct bearing on the teaching methods. To the extent that the feebleminded is capable of acquiring some mental mobility, awareness of meaning in different contexts and thus polar relationships, in other words: to the extent that he is educable beyond the narrow boundaries of drill and conditioning, this is achieved by using his apperceptive abilities rather than his in any case defective ability to conceptualize.

(In this connection an interesting research question could be asked, that of the correlation between type and degree of feeblemindedness: it may well be that, at least in the phase of development here under discussion, the two extravert (the aggressive and the submissive) types have better chances to maintain a higher level of intellectual functioning than the two introvert types, the suspicious and the apathetic ones; their chances of educational stimulation are smaller because they cannot even rely on a relatively well preserved apperceptivity. On the other hand, we should not forget that aggressiveness is liable to impair the learning-ability (not the intelligence) through the intensity of destructive phantasies that may in this case interfere with the learning processes. In order to test our hypothesis, only children under institutional care should be investigated and compared, that is, only such children whose affectivity can be controlled effectively.)

When speaking of the learning-phase in the development of the feebleminded child we must bear in mind that this phase extends well into sexual maturation (age 16 or above). Although the process of sexual maturation may sometimes be slow, it would be wrong to speak of sexual retardation, since even in such cases full maturity is usually reached in due course of time, whereas the mental functions will *never* even approximate normalcy. On the other hand, we do find not a few cases in which exactly the opposite takes place: a precocious and intensive development of sexual functions. Very little indeed is known about the specific connection between feeblemindedness in its different type-varieties and grades and sexual development. But it is obvious that both, retardation and precocity, are bound to impair social and intellectual learning; retardation—because it is, as a rule, symptom and result of low vitality, precocity—because it is liable to channel almost all available energy in the direction of sexual activities. The apathetic and, to a lesser extent, the submissive types are often undersexed, while the aggressive and, to a lesser extent, the suspicious types are often oversexed.

6 THE FIFTH PHASE

When we call adolescence a phase in personality-development, we have in mind the psychological rather than the physiological aspects of sexual maturation, which marks the beginning of this period (pre-adolescence and pubescence) and which provokes—culturally different—reactions in the boy and the girl passing through this phase. Any attempt to reduce adolescence to its physiological elements and to interpret type- and culture-determined reactions as epiphenomenal only is inadequate: it leaves the question unanswered why the contribution of this phase to personality-development differs not only from individual to individual but also from culture to culture and from one social class to the other.

Anthropological and sociological research of adolescence carried out over the last decades has made the universalistic approach to interpretation untenable (though many clinical psychologists still continue to think of adolescence as if it were identical with its manifestations in the middle-class family of Western culture). At the same time, however, practically no attention has been paid to the question of the different impact feeblemindness has on the lower-class as compared to the middle-class adolescent.

In my study of 'Psychopathy' [21] I have discussed the psychoanalytic theory according to which adolescence is a period of defence against oedipal conflict revival, and partial negation of the parents and of the superego, that offshoot of introjecting the parents, is the central symptom of this defence. I then proposed to define the essential elements of adolescence in the middle-class family as follows: interruption of developmental continuity (in contrast to Erikson's claim that identity is the essential achievement of this period), illusion of staticness and finality, living with principles and the unavoidable experience of deadlock at the end of the phase, an experience that may lead to suicide or psychosis, but in the majority of cases leads to resignation, to some kind of escape into adult conformism. This development was then contrasted with what takes place in lower-class families with their relative absence of emotional closeness and oedipal involvements, hence also of defence-needs in the adolescent. An attempt was made to show how under such conditions adolescence is characterized, on the one hand, by conflict-free transition into adulthood, on the other hand, by a certain radicalization of the values which the adults did not dare to realize in their lives. It is through this radicalization that adolescence helps perpetuate, from generation to generation, what I defined as the externalized behavior patterns [26].

In the development of the feebleminded, adolescence is the period of social failure and over-compensation (by exploiting physical assets). Even though sexual maturation may have started earlier, not later than in the intellectually normal child, the period of tension seldom begins before the age of 16 and extends well into adulthood. The quality of this tension, however, essentially differs, both, from the middle-class variety of defensive discontinuity and 'life with principles' and from the lower-class type of radicalization. To the extent that tension does emerge in this period of development, particularly in the aggressive and the suspicious types, it is as a rule a result and an expression of uncontrolled sex-impulses or reactions to feeling socially rejected.

True enough, we witness delinquent behavior, particularly sexual misdemeanour and aggressiveness, much earlier in the development of the feebleminded child. But it is in adolescence only, that tension accompanies, and intensifies, antisocial behavior-disorders. Girls, and sometimes boys as well, may drift into sexual promiscuity or even into prostitution, when someone knows how to exploit their unrealistic longing for recognition and love. For the same reason they may show off with all sorts of delinquent acts. Tension and restlessness now become increasingly characteristic of their behaviour, so much so indeed, that some may glide deep into perversion, crime, bizarre behavior, until they can no longer be rescued. Others may, for some internal or external reason, be capable of avoiding serious maladjustment, but will, from now on, 'carry' their tension and restlessness with them in all walks of life.

The type-factor becomes now more and more decisive in the life of the feebleminded adolescent and adult.* But systematic education and therapy are nevertheless capable of alleviating tensions and feelings of being rejected and isolated; they also can prevent asocial or antisocial reactions to adolescent strivings, as has been shown convincingly by Sarason [47]. But they may *not* be capable of improving intellectual functioning. It is one of the inherent paradoxes of feeblemindedness that behavioral reactions are much longer accessible and amenable to change through environmental interferences (though of course not *structurally* reversible) than they would be under other pathogenic conditions, particularly of externalization. Lack of structure apparently has not only its liabilities, but also its assets!

There is certainly no need to explain why, in the life of the feebleminded, adolescence cannot be interpreted as the phase of *identity* (in the meaning of the term as used by Erikson): Identity presupposes differentiation and structure. But it is equally obvious why it would be wrong to look in this case for *interruption* of continuity which, as we have maintained, is characteristic of middle-class adolescence: it requires a strong ego-consciousness and a strong oedipal involvement. Sometimes, though by no means in every case, we will find *radicalization* of behavioral symptoms comparable to what we may find in the phase of adolescence under conditions of

* Submissiveness and, to a lesser extent, apathy, for instance, are often quite effective protectors against social maladjustment and even against adolescent tension.

extreme poverty and educational neglect. But the most characteristic symptom of feeblemindedness in adolescence is a *tendency to accept the patterns of the adult environment through imitation and self-subordination.*

This is true even for the aggressive, strongly defiant adolescent: he defies the laws of society and sullenly disregards the adults' condemnation of his misbehavior. However, he does so not because of some deep-rooted hostility or intentional (conscious) rejection of the non-ego, but rather out of a general inability to differentiate and to understand the essentials of a situation. The feebleminded is indeed unable to see the causal and the logical connections between his behavior and the criteria of environmental reactions and judgments. On the other hand, he considers his own sullenness and aggressiveness indicative of strength, of adulthood. In other words: he imitates the—for him—most significant symptom of adulthood, independence, but, of course, in its peripheral manifestations only; he misunderstands and misinterprets this symptom as if it meant independence of norms and rules, freedom from obligations. Hence, there is no contradiction between defiance and imitation of the adult environment: both are expressions of what we would call, in an intellectually normal adolescent, 'egocentricity'.*

This is the feebleminded equivalent of identity. And whereas true identity is essentially dependent on mobility—in fact, can emerge only through the challenge of change—the 'adolescent achievement' of the feebleminded, his seeming egocentricity', is essentially connected with imitation and subordination. Here, imitation does not lead to identification, is not instrumental to growth and development, does not serve the life-tendency towards expansion but, on the contrary, that towards staticness. In other words: in all his imitations and subordinations, the feebleminded remains confined to the narrow boundaries of his unstructured (pseudo-) ego, since he is unable to conceive of the imitated objects in his human environment as of realities in their own rights.

In the first chapter we have said that feeblemindedness is characterized by the co-existence of rigidity (perseverational tendencies, inability to transfer training and learning, inadaptability of habits etc.) and distractibility (yielding to changing stimuli, lack of control,

* The term would again seem inappropriate in a discussion of feeblemindedness, since it presupposes a (conscious or unconscious) intentionality of which the subnormal in incapable, and the existence of an ego-structure, the absence of which is characteristic of feeblemindedness.

impulsiveness, etc.*). We have said that both indicate lack of structure. In a teleological theory, the seeming contradiction between these two main symptoms of feeblemindedness is resolved by explaining distractibility as the basic trait and rigid perseveration as secondary only, as a means for preserving the satisfaction derived from a more or less accidentally found solution of a problem. (Kounin's experiments [35] are often quoted in support of such an interpretation. He claims that, once the feebleminded has mastered an activity, he sticks to it.)

We have warned against the use of teleological concepts in an interpretation of feeblemindedness: they imply intentionally operating forces of inner regulation, in whose weakness or absence we see the essence of feeblemindedness. Differentiation within the ego and within the non-ego and between the ego and the non-ego has not reached a level in the feebleminded at which the establishment of truly polar relationships, this pre-condition of communication and of intentionality, that is of structure, takes place. It is during the phase of adolescence, extending, as it does, well into adulthood, that the mentality of the feebleminded in its specific type-variations finally crystallizes. Aggressiveness, suspiciousness, submissiveness or apathy are the outcome of gradually increasing emphasis on innate dispositions that takes place under the influence of environmental reactions to the adolescent's behavior.

Moreover, we know that it is the attitude of the adult environment towards the feebleminded child and adolescent which determines to no small extent the final level of his intellectual functioning or, better, the extent to which the congenitally given potentialities are going to be used or are allowed to 'go down' through disuse. Here, then, the economic factor becomes decisive. A middle-class parent may have made every possible effort to stimulate his feebleminded child, hoping to see him become normal in due course of time, and may thus have helped him, by the time he reaches adolescence and adulthood, to preserve his—limited—potential. Such changes are much smaller for the feebleminded child of a lower-class family. The latter is also more likely to be placed in an institution not specifically planned for the education of the feebleminded, particularly when he manifests severe behavior-disorders, being of the aggressive or the suspicious type; the really adequate placement

* For an excellent analysis of this co-existence of contradictory attitudes see Th. Abel and E. Kinder: *The Subnormal Adolescent Girl* [1]. Most of the author's findings are, *mutatis mutandis*, applicable to male adolescents as well.

facilities are more likely to be reserved for the feebleminded from middle-class families.

On the other hand, the latter, much more than the former, are exposed to the risk of disappointment when parental protection ceases to be available—which often happens towards the end of their adolescence. By that time, the lower-class feebleminded has already found his place in society: the difference between his social disability and that of the other normally intelligent but socially deprived and externalized, members of his class may have grown smaller by that time, and the varieties of social pathology offer many socially sanctioned (or semi-sanctioned) outlets and activities. The older he grows, the greater becomes the similarity between him, at least when he belongs to the borderline group, and the 'normally externalized' members of the lower-class community at large. Because of this similarity, the transition from adolescence to adulthood is easier for him than it is in middle-class families with their greater frequency and intensity of inner tension and disappointment.

7 ARGUMENTS AGAINST THE CONCEPT OF 'MENTAL AGE'

It will by now be clear why we cannot accept the statistical conception of feeblemindedness according to which the lowest 10-15% of any given population are *defined* as feebleminded, irrespectively of the level of functioning and of achievement reached by the average group. From such a relativistic viewpoint it would follow that, if by biological and educational means the average intelligence of a certain population could be raised to what at present is called the superior group (say: IQ 130-150), there would again be a subnormal group of approximately 10-15% (not including the 'dull normals') with an IQ of, say, under the present 110-mark. But while the members of this 'lower' intelligence group would undoubtedly be less effective *socially* than those of the then average group, they would still be able to act intelligently whereas the truly feebleminded would still have to be sought in the 'below 85' group, although their percentage would be considerably smaller than in what is today a population with a 'normal' intelligence distribution.

The same holds good for the reverse case: in a biologically and educationally 'lowered' population where the average level of functioning and achievement would be the equivalent of what is today, with us, the 70-90 group (comprising 50% of the 'lowered' population), there would, of course, again be a 'low' group comprising 10-15% with a maximum level of approximately 60. But it would be safe to say that the *majority* of the whole population would act and think in a way defineable as 'feebleminded'.

Perceptual acuity, not *per se* but as a precondition and an integral part of observational and apperceptive acuity, again not *per se* but as an integral part of intentionality directed towards memory-retention, combination and communication—these symptoms of intelligent behavior—would, in an hypothetically 'lowered' population, be a rare exception, whereas they would be found present in the majority of an hypothetically 'raised' population. Short-lived, mechanical memory retention derived from isolated perceptions and resulting in non-intentional, associative, quasi-automatic thinking-processes and reactions—these characteristics, according to Burt [6], of intellectual subnormality—would be the rule in the first case. Insight and resourcefulness, foresight and alertness, originality and initiative, creativeness and power of combination—these characteristics, according to Doll [9], of intelligent behavior—would be found even in the lower grades of an hypothetically 'raised' population, while they would be absent even in the average group of a 'lowered' population.

Any attempt to define intelligence and feeblemindedness in absolute terms rather than in relation to observable and calculated averages of achievement, inevitably leads to questioning the justification of the concept of mental age.* Instead of asking, as is customary even today, in what respect the feebleminded resembles a chronologically younger child and answering in the way Terman [53] and most other 'test-psychologists' would do, we reverse the question and ask: In what respects is the younger child of normal intelligence *not* identical with the older feebleminded; to formulate our question still more paradoxically: *why is the young child of normal intelligence not-feebleminded?*

The answer is obvious when we accept a definition of intelligence in absolute terms. The young child, though unable to execute operations that only an older child is capable of carrying out—as the result of maturation, experience and learning—shows the normality of his intellectual activity and behavior through the *quality* of his actions and reactions. He may use primitive, that is, undifferentiated methods of problem-solving, may, for instance, prefer definitions 'by use' to

* Not to speak of the criticism of this concept that is based on purely statistical considerations, such as the criticism voiced by Wechsler [57].

definitions 'by essence' or 'by class', may employ juxtaposition instead of subordination, concretistic identification instead of abstraction, may 'follow' associations instead of 'using' imagination, may show signs of rigidity in his choices and his actions. But it would be an illegitimate analogy-conclusion, were we to identify all these symptoms of immaturity with those of feebleminded ineffectiveness, as it appears in a chronologically older subnormal child. *It is first and foremost the evidence of intentionality directed towards the various tasks of problem-solving and the evidence of polarization between the ego and the non-ego that indicate intellectual normality* already in the younger child: he *seeks* solutions and is happy and satisfied when *he* has found it (and not only when *it* has occurred).

It is therefore the *behavior* of the observed and the tested child and not only the answer he gives that should determine the final evaluation of his intelligence. Obviously, certain functions such as 'comprehension', 'definition', 'recognition of essentials', 'judgmental comparison', 'combination', to mention only the most important ones from the generally accepted measurement scales—allow for such differentiation by observing the child's behavior much better than others, which may be equally important for the so-called objective and comprehensive assessment of his intelligence.

We shall now try to compare certain characteristics of *the* feebleminded mentality with those of normal intelligence in younger children. Such a comparison, to be empirically valid, should refer to different degrees of feeblemindedness at different age levels. Children with an IQ of 75 at the ages of, say, 16, 12 and 8 should be compared with normal children at the ages of 12, 9 and 6 respectively, a child of 16 with an IQ of 50 should be compared with a normal child of 8, a high-grade and a low-grade adult moron—with a normal child of 12 and 8 respectively. The comparisons should be carried out in various functional areas; socio-cultural background, learning experience, sex and type-condition should be taken into consideration as differential factors.* In this way, several hundred varieties of the relationship between feeblemindedness and mental age would have to be discussed.

We propose to confine the present analysis to a comparison of essentials, products of abstraction from all these differentials, as if there existed *the* normally intelligent child and *the* feebleminded. We hope that such an analysis *in abstractis* will help us recognize the fallacy of the concept of mental age more clearly than a clinically oriented

* Not to speak of the difference between congenital and acquired feeblemindedness which will be discussed in the third chapter.

analysis of differentials.

When Piaget speaks of *egocentricity* in the young child, and when the student of feeblemindedness discovers in the answers of the retarded child to his test-question evidence of egocentricity, they both mean something different.

For the young child, egocentricity is an indispensable condition of gradual self-detachment from his unity-relationship with the non-ego, whose independence and separateness he discovers only by experiencing it first as part of the ego. Before, he is so much fascinated with the non-ego that he is unable to detach himself from it. Which is, at the same time, the reason why he is not yet ready for abstract operations; why, according to Piaget [43], egocentricity manifests itself in the use of intuition, concretism, symbolization, analogies and in constant interference of feelings with cognition.

Thus, egocentricity in the young child means that the non-ego (or, better, what later emerges as a separate, objective non-ego) centers in the ego (or, better, in what later emerges as independent ego-pole of relationships). Almost the opposite would seem correct to say about the egocentricity of the older feebleminded: his 'ego' is part of the non-ego, he does not understand the ego but as an object among objects. Thus, his 'egocentricity' is but a form of ego-diffusion, a symptom of non-differentiatedness: he 'is' whatever 'happens to be'.

It would, of course, be wrong to interpret this *non-differentiatedness* in terms of a primary unity-feeling. The latter stems, as we have tried to show in another study [24], from the infant's experience of connectedness with the mother and presupposes a structurally normal ability to experience polarity. The relative absence of this ability explains why we do *not* find in the feebleminded thinking-processes those modalities that characterize the egocentric phase in a normal child's early development (intuition, symbolization, etc.). It also explains why the feebleminded does not feel the same need as a young child for actual and imagined manipulations of the non-ego, for experimenting with the world in order to test its reliability. Where the basic polarization between ego and non-ego is defective, the experience of inner order (and of regulation from within) is defective as well, and, as a result, everything is governed by chance, so that there is no need for experimenting with the non-ego.

This *experience of inner order* which normally prepares the child at the age of 7 or 8 for a more objective understanding of the world never appears in the feebleminded. Hence, even the typical pre-causal tendency of the young child to organize objects and events by *juxta-*

position is not identical with the tendency in the older feebleminded to replace all possible relationships between objects or between events by enumeration of unconnected details. The young child's juxtapositions are usually descriptive and aim at order, although his categories may be inadequate. In the older feebleminded they are non-intentional, chance-dictated and associative and therefore never lead to causal thinking.

Here arises the often discussed question of *whole versus part-perception* in the young child and in the feebleminded respectively. Normally, a syncretistic whole-perception precedes the ability to isolate and perceive meaningful details within that whole; but even the young child is aware of what we may call 'the challenge of the whole', in that it requires analysis and resynthesis of details. It is this vector towards perceiving the constituent parts of a whole that is absent in the feebleminded. In other words: whole perception means something different for the young child and the older feebleminded, insofar as it is more mobile in the former, transcends itself, as it were, both analytically (through isolation of parts) and synthetically (through resynthesis of parts in a new whole and through seeing the whole as part of a wider whole).

Another expression of the same difference is the inability of the feebleminded to *perceive* parts as parts, that is, in their whole-contexts, as against the normal child's inability to *understand* their part-function. The latter inability produces curiosity and tension or at least a feeling that there exists a second level behind the observable phenomenon, a level of meaning, which can be recognized by asking questions; the former inability (of the feebleminded) is both symptom and cause of his rigidity. When the objects of perception have no vectors pointing to something 'hiding' behind their surface, be it their significance within changing whole-contexts, be it their meaning as symptoms of other phenomena, they fail to stimulate or even to set in motion intellectual activity.—No need to add that the very fact of the normal child's curiosity and inquisitiveness safeguards his intellectual development beyond the limits of any given phase. The feebleminded, on the other hand, not only does not genuinely develop beyond the narrow limits of a relatively early phase in his mental development, he is also liable to lose quickly whatever he may have acquired through learning, because he does not see where to inquire, where to ask questions. (This is what we mean by saying that the feebleminded does not use his abilities which, as a result, are bound to deteriorate.)

It is generally agreed, on the one hand, that the focal element of intelligence is *abstraction* and, on the other hand, that the young child is not yet ready for abstraction. No one, however, would call the young child *per se* unintelligent. Does this not mean that abstraction can*not* be considered the focal element of intelligence in the young child? That there exist in his behavior other indicators of intelligence, indicators that are either definable as precursors or as substitutes of abstraction and are to be tested specifically? Are not the numerous inquiries into the nature of the relationship between early and later levels of intelligence in the individual (known also as inquiries into the constancy of intelligence-quotients) meant to answer this control question in any theory of intelligence?*

Here again, it becomes evident that without referring to a definition of abstract thinking such as the one offered by K. Goldstein [29], we cannot hope to find a meaningful answer. We remember that he claims abstraction requires an ability to detach the ego willfully from any given experience or object, to shift from one aspect of a problem to another, while holding in mind the former, to recognize the essentials of a whole and of each detail within this whole, to think in communicable terms ('in terms of others', to quote Piaget). We then understand that abstractive abilities cannot possibly emerge, before the ego is established as a polar counterpart to the world of observable and recognizeable objects, and before it is established so firmly that detaching it from that non-ego would not constitute a threat.

These elements of definition, however, not only allow to answer the question of when abstraction is likely to emerge in the mental development of the child, but also of how to distinguish intelligent from less intelligent behavior even in a young child; in what respect differs the older feebleminded essentially from the intelligent young child?

The latter, though yet unable, for instance, to detach himself freely and intentionally from a given situation, has enough mental energy in reserve to respond to novelty. He will always be less rigid than the feebleminded, says K. Lewin [36]. Although he will not yet be able to keep in mind different aspects of one situation simultaneously,

* Very little attention is given to the *phenomenology* of abstraction in those so-called objective, empirical or inductive studies in which posing a question of essence is considered unscientific metaphysicism! The correlation-coefficient is supposed to 'do the job' of proving that a certain tool is more suitable than others to measure the precursor of abstraction in young children.

he will at least have left enough 'revivable' energy in the first-contemplated aspect, to return to it, to remember it and, in due course of time, even to compare the different aspects—again in clear contradistinction of the older feebleminded.

Although the young child is not capable of thinking in communicable terms, this element of abstraction, too, is, at least potentially, present in his mental activity, if he is intelligent. Normally, the young child thinks in terms of his adults whose presumed omniscience makes communication in language and thought unnecessary, as it were, and is responsible for his heteronomy. It is indeed 'in terms of others' that the young child starts to think. With the dethronement of the adults and the discovery of autonomy in the second phase of development, the need for communicability of thinking grows steadily. It is in this last respect that the feebleminded again differs from the normally intelligent young child: he never learns how to think in communicable terms (his rigidity, says Stoddard [51, p. 287], prevents communication). His heteronomy is not that of an imitating and a learning subject but rather that of an 'impregnated' object. Thinking, for the feebleminded, is never a social function.

This leads us to comparing certain elements in the social development of the feebleminded with those of the young child, at least to the extent that they have a direct or indirect bearing on intellectual functioning.

One of the basic elements in man's social development is social hunger—to use Slavson's term [49]—the need for contact which induces him to *imitate* those who offer security and status, the stronger ones or the adults. Normally, however, imitation is based on a more or less clear awareness of otherness and of changeability, of what 'I am not and yet could be'. In the feebleminded, this awareness is absent and, as a result, imitation, in the proper sense of the word which includes the elements of activity and of anticipation, is replaced by a process of mirroring devoid of intentionality, a mere automatism.

Dialectically, the anticipatory, future- and change-oriented character of imitation is supplemented by the normal child's tendency to seek the 'society of equals', beginning at the age of 5-6, in order to challenge the adults' absolute authority (cf. Piaget's thesis of rule-manipulation and autonomy-growth). The feebleminded never comes to experience *equality*: he seeks the illusion of strength either through imitating older ones or through establishing contact with younger ones whom he may protect or serve, thus indulging in an illusion of superiority. Whereas, at a later stage, the normal adolescent may play at being an adult in order to maintain his illusion of finality [21], the feebleminded passes through this phase into adulthood almost without effort, tension or crisis. There is nothing in the social behavior of the feebleminded adolescent that resembles the behavior of a normal child during his latency period or during pre-adolescence.

In his quest for otherness and sameness, these two objects of social contact, the child learns how to imitate what he is not (and thus to internalize values and concepts), and how to consolidate what he is in the society of his equals. Imitation is an expression of the life-tendency towards expansion, self-consolidation—of that towards staticness. Intelligent behavior, irrespective of age, requires a mutual relatedness of the two; in feeblemindedness the lack of inter-relatedness of the two basic life-tendencies produces an illusion of imitating otherness (=automatic mirroring) and an illusion of equality (=overlooking differences). Closely connected with this first condition of normalcy—hence also of intelligence—is the second one which we have proposed to define as *exchangeability of subject-object positions* [24, p. 34].* Even in the young child, we can discover manifestations of this exchangeability, if he is of normal intelligence; the feebleminded, whatever his age may be, will never be capable of feeling himself to be the subject of mental activity.

It is in the light of this last-mentioned limitation that another essential difference between the young child and the older feebleminded becomes comprehensible: the concepts of *rule and law* are foreign to the mentality of the latter, while the young child of normal intelligence shows the first indication of rule-*consciousness* long before he is capable of *thinking* in terms of rule and law. The earliest experience of sequence and regularity in the primary life-events is the precondition of rule-consciousness; it starts to emerge and to crystallize when the ego becomes involved in this primarily biological experience. In other words: rule is apperceived as ego-related regularity.

We can distinguish between various stages in the genesis of rule-consciousness—from that of extreme heteronomy to that of relative autonomy; but it would still be correct to say that even in the earliest stages of a normal child's development some kind of polarity is present which makes it possible for him 'to tend towards' the non-ego sources

* The determining subject knows itself, in the very act of determination, as *being* determined by the object of his acts; and the determined object is known to determine the subject, is, in fact, a subject of determination while *being* determined.

of experience. In the feebleminded, on the other hand, consciousness of *regularity*, to the extent that it emerges at all, never brings forth consciousness of *rules*, since he is unable to detach himself from the facts underlying a momentary experience of regularity.

It should be obvious that in this way the concepts of inherent law, of temporal, spatial and causal relationships will never emerge in the mental life of the feebleminded. The normal child discovers them through playful manipulation of certain rules of behavior, after he has come to experience mutuality, mutuality between human beings and mutuality between the actor and his fact-creating, revocable or irrevocable, actions. The feebleminded may at best learn laws as expressions of external constraint, laws which, as a result, may be self-contradictory. He will never be able to conceive of himself as of a subject who recognizes laws through being determined by them.

These are a few examples only of the manner in which the feebleminded essentially differs from the younger child of normal intelligence. They can all be reduced to the elements of defective differentiation and absence of polarity between the ego and the non-ego. Here, we are reminded of Stoddard's above-quoted remark (see p. 55) that in the feebleminded, rigidity prevents communication. What he has in mind is, of course, communication with the social non-ego only, with the human environment. But the feebleminded is no less handicapped in his ability to communicate with the *inner* non-ego, the world of phantasy-images and of the unconscious. Is the young child's 'life with the unconscious', his pre-latency intimacy with a world of inner images, characteristic of the older feebleminded as well? The answer clearly is in the negative: in this respect also the feebleminded does not resemble a young child; his phantasies, according to Th. Abel [1], are but elaborations of what he remembers, not of what he 'invents', they draw their material from the external non-ego rather than from the unconscious.

This explains why he is spared the intensive *anxiety* that normally is the inescapable lot of the young child before the latency period. On the other hand, the feebleminded, unlike the young child of normal intelligence, is unable to draw clear dividing lines between the real and the imagined: what he desires and remembers is liable to remain part of his actuality. Hence, an *untrue story* told by a feebleminded has an altogether different meaning from the one told by a young child of normal intelligence. The latter starts out from the presumption that the adult knows the truth so that his lying is a kind of experimenting with adult omniscience. (We are, of course, not including under the concept of lie the child's free phantasies.) When the feebleminded, at a later stage of his development, tells an untrue story, he is usually not aware of the fact that it is untrue, and he certainly has not necessarily the intention of cheating or of testing out his adults.

Finally, a few remarks should be added about the different meaning of the concept of *syncretistic thinking*. Developmental psychology sees in it a pre-causal, associative way of reasoning and understanding, typical of young children, according to Piaget an intermediary link between dream-like condensation or transference and generalization or abstraction. As Piaget rightly says: 'There is nothing unintelligent about these schemes—sooner or later they will be submitted to a vigorous selection and to a mutual reduction which will sharpen them into first-rate instruments of invention in spheres of thought where hypotheses are of use. It is only at the age of the children we have studied that this exuberance hinders adaptation, because it is still too closely connected with autistic imagination' [42, pp. 168f.].

The feebleminded variety of syncretism, on the other hand, does not contain this developmental vector but is a static substitute for genuine thought-processes and remains alive as such in all stages of growth. The element of creativeness is absent, and what remains is inadequacy of solutions.

These few examples may suffice to prove the fallacy of the concept of mental age. Feeblemindedness cannot be understood by comparing it with the younger child's normal mentality but only by using the method of phenomenological analysis of essential elements.

8 SUMMARY

In the following table we summarize the preceding comparisons of the chronologically young child of normal intelligence with the older feebleminded.

The characteristics contained in the table are grouped in two parts; in the first (A) appear those valid for any age-group, in the second (B) those that refer to one specific age-group only.

Table 1 The Young Child as Compared with the Older Feebleminded

The Young	The Feebleminded
A *General Characteristics* (independent of specific phases)	
1. Intentionality	Automatic reactivity
2. Ego-Non-ego polarity	Separation or fusion of Ego and Nonego

The Young	The Feebleminded
3. Exchangeability of subject-object positions	Absence of subject feeling
4. Egocentricity as a means for self-detachment from the Non-ego	Ego diffusion in the Nonego and illusion of egoity
5. Imitation as anticipatory activity	Imitation as automatic mirroring
6. Tendency to experiment with the Non-ego (curiosity)	Tendency to 'handle' the Non-ego blindly
7. Enjoying solutions to the extent that they were found by own activity	Mistaking chance-occurrences for solutions of a problem
8. Whole-perceptions with vectors to the constituent parts	Whole-perceptions, if at all, without awareness of parts
9. Non-understanding of the function of certain parts, leading to curiosity and tension	Non-perception of parts as parts, or mistaking them for wholes, decreasing initiative
10. Responding to novelty and ability to return to the known ('mobility')	Perception of otherness (without apperception of newness) without return to the known.
11. Thinking in communicable terms with the intention to maintain contact (even in the introvert)	'Thinking' the thoughts of others (whether adequately or inadequately), producing an illusion of contact
B *Phase-Specific Characteristics*	
12. Earliest experience of ego-related regularity leading to rule-consciousness	Structural defects, particularly of the memory, preventing experience of regularity, hence also rule-consciousness
13. Mobility of attention in the pre-ego stages as precursor of later abstraction	Structural rigidity, leading to perseverations, preventing devlopment of abstraction
14. Pre-causal juxtaposition aiming at order	Associative enumeration without need for order
15. Prelatency-contacts with the unconscious and intensive anxieties	No contact with the unconscious and little if any anxiety
16. Oedipal identity of the imagined with the real, but maintenance of dividing lines between phantasy and reality	Phantasy being little more than extensions of reality without clear dividing lines between the two
17. Lying as an attempt to test the adult's omniscience	Unawareness of having lied, since lies 'convince' the liar
18. Manipulation of rules in the latency-period helping consolidate autonomy and differentiation	Illusion of strength through imitation of the strong or through caring for the weak leading to further decrease of differentiation

CHAPTER THREE

*Secondary Varieties of Retardation Causes and Patterns**

1 INTRODUCTION

The question of what factors are liable to impair intelligence is not identical with an inquiry into the relative frequency of the various hereditary, traumatic, environmental and emotional factors that may be responsible—either in isolation or in configuration—for individual cases of feeblemindedness. Etiology, in this as in any other field of psychopathology, becomes meaningful only if we include in it an analysis of the essential differences between the outcomes of the various causes.

Thus, A. A. Strauss and H. Werner in their comparative studies of the brain-injured versus the so-called endogenous types [52, 58] (cf. also the bibliography to 47) have made most valuable contributions to the phenomenology of feeblemindedness. But the scope of their analysis is limited by their rather narrow method of classification. They follow the distinction between 'exogenous', meaning brain-injured, and 'endogenous', meaning hereditary, cases. This classification, however, is not only too narrow, (since it leaves no room for cases of environmentally and educationally caused retardation, of emotionally determined pseudo-feeblemindedness or of psychotic distortion); it is also too broad (since each of the two basic groups contains sub-units of feeblemindedness that show essential differences between themselves, so that generalization becomes a liability for the purpose of a phenomenological analysis).

Other comparisons between different outcomes of different causes can be found in psychological studies of pseudo-feeblemindedness; but these are, as a rule, confined to an analysis of the different *test*-responses rather than to an analysis of the differences between the ways of thinking in a genuinely and in a pseudo-feebleminded

* Reprinted, with alterations and additions, from: *Acta Psychologica* **24** (1965), pp. 283-313.

individual. Rarely, if ever, is the latter being compared with a case of secondary, that is, environmentally or educationally determined retardation* as against hereditary and traumatic cases.

Sarason, whose great merit it is to have shown, in his study of subnormality, why the concept of hereditary causes is a fallacy, has collected a wealth of case-material lending itself to a comparative analysis of sub-units, although he himself prefers to describe and analyze each sub-unit as such. It is to him that we owe the recognition of the fact that a potentiality for normal development present at birth may be destroyed by unfavorable environmental conditions [47, p. 106]. Moreover, many normal children of feebleminded parents (supposing we are able to prove irrefutably that they *are* indeed feebleminded) may become retarded in the course of their development because they do not receive adequate stimulations (ibid., pp. 157 ff.); truly feebleminded children who enjoy *favorable* home-conditions are likely to succeed at least in their *social* adjustment to such an extent that they will hardly be recognized as feebleminded (ibid., pp. 113 f.).

Elsewhere in his study (p. 12) he argues against Doll's distinction between feeblemindedness due to constitutional factors and therefore being unalterable, and intellectual retardation due to negative environmental conditions and therefore being reversible. How many, he asks, would prove to belong to the second category, that of the 'retarded only', were they given intensive care and treatment instead of being cast away as 'incurable feebleminded'? Only the lower grades can be diagnosed as 'feebleminded beyond any reasonable doubt'. All the others, among them the many who do improve considerably when given proper care [e.g. 48], are no less genuine cases of feeblemindedness, since *without* such care they would, after a certain time, be as unchangeable as those born with limited capacities.

The question of reversibility is intrinsically connected with that of structurization: what processes lead to *structural* changes in the individual's mental make-up? What environmental and what constitutional factors are conducive to an irreparable loss of congenitally given potentialities for normal intellectual functioning and development? At what age ceases the damage to be reversible? Is this loss one and the same in all areas of thinking, or can we find differences in extent and time required, not only between individuals

---

* The term 'secondary' is used here in a way different from that of Tredgold's well-known distinction between 'primary', meaning hereditary, and 'secondary', meaning traumatic, amentia [57].

but also between functional areas? And finally: what essential differences can be recognized and defined when we compare a case of congenital with one of secondary dysfunctioning, before and after structurization of the loss of potentials has taken place?

2 FACTORS INTERLINKED

The factors that we have in mind when speaking of environmental causes of retardation are: growing up under the externalizing influence of extreme poverty and educational neglect, institutional care or, better, impersonality of primary relationships under conditions of institutional routine, later lack of intellectual stimulation and paleness of the paternal image, emotionally conditioned blockings, regressions or distortions, psychotic personality disruptions, certain types of delinquent behavior.

None of these environmental or personality factors produces retardation, unless it enters into a configuration with other—specific and non-specific—factors. We refer to our analysis of the configurational approach to etiology in other writings [15, 20, 24] and confine ourselves here to a few applications of what has been said there, to the problem of feeblemindedness.

Impersonality of early relationships, lack of stimulation, neurotic, psychotic or delinquent patterns—each of these (and other) causes of secondary retardation requires the support of both, reinforcing and qualitatively modifying factors to be able to destroy a congenitally normal intelligence. Among those reinforcers and modifiers should be mentioned: type-conditions, thresholds of perception and of vulnerability, the congenitally given level of intelligence (the 'starting level'), cerebral and glandular patterns of functioning, but also the time factor, that is, the phase during which negative environmental factors started to operate in the life of the growing child, the degree of their continuity or discontinuity, the total duration of their influence, the availability or non-availability of compensatory factors in the personality structure of the affected individual and in the environment, remedial interventions, spontaneous changes taking place in the child's life, and other structural and environmental factors.

Extravert attitudes, high intelligence, a constitutionally strong power of integration, discontinuity in the process of negative conditioning, all protect the child against the destructive effect of an externalizing environment with its typical impersonality of primary relationships. The same holds good for the protecting effect of these factors where the environment lacks power of stimulation and adequate learning-facilities. A no more than average intelligence, on the other hand, particularly when configurated with a relatively low level of integrational abilities, is much more vulnerable and exposed to the danger of shrinkage, when the environment is not consistently providing stimulation, experience of being protected and adapted teaching methods. (As regards the lower grades of intelligence, the danger is one of disuse rather than of reaction to environmental frustration or starvation which the low-grade feebleminded may not even perceive, let alone comprehend.*)

Certain cerebral and/or glandular conditions may make coordination, motility control, equilibration (return to staticness) problematic. As a result, the thus affected individual may not be able to make use of his perhaps normal abilities and in due course of time will behave and react to his tasks of learning and problem-solving in a truly feebleminded manner. This danger becomes particularly evident, when the environment is unprepared to take his liabilities and peculiarities into consideration and exposes him to normal, unadapted educational methods only because he can not be diagnosed as a clear case of cerebral or glandular disturbances. Even in families in which his behavior-disorder *may* arouse attention, he is liable to be diagnosed wrongly, as a 'case for psychotherapy'; his specific intellectual problems may not be recognized as such but be regarded as epiphenomena to an emotional rather than a somatic disorder.

This raises the question of type-conditions as factors in causal configurations that lead to secondary retardation. We have in mind the four behavioral varieties briefly discussed in the first chapter, the primarily aggressive, the primarily suspicious, the primarily apathetic and the primarily submissive reactions. We maintain (and suggest our hypothesis should be submitted to the test of empirical research), that similar type-conditions operate as differential deter-

* Rigidity, we have said in the first chapter, accounts for the lesser importance of experience in the development of the congenitally feebleminded. This, however, does not mean that the level of parental intelligence is of no importance in this development. The care and consideration, the stimulation and training which intelligent parents may give their feebleminded child (provided, of course, their reactions will not be determined irrationally by unconscious guilt-feelings or by conscious shame) are likely to help preserve the limited intellectual abilities of the feebleminded child. Low parental intelligence, on the other hand, often manifests itself in lack of patience, lack of considerateness, unwise educational demands, unwillingness to recognize the child's specific needs, etc.

minants in the average child as well, when he is exposed to early neglect. Where either aggressive reactions or apathy prevail from early childhood on, irrespectively of whether these reactions-patterns are congenitally given propensities or are the result of early frustration, a no more than average (and perhaps even a higher than average) intelligence is bound to decline and 'wither', particularly when the child grows up under conditions of impersonality and lack of stimulation. We further maintain that reverse type-conditions, which we have described as suspiciousness and submissiveness, and in both of which the material and the social non-ego is experienced as a subject rather than as an object (as in the first two-mentioned types), an at least average intelligence is *not* to the same extent endangered. This holds good even under similar conditions of impersonality and lack of stimulation, although the presence of additional negative reinforcers in the environment or in the structure of the individual are, of course, bound to outweigh the relative protection offered by the first mentioned type-condition.* Such reinforcers are: a long period of maternal deprivation, a very early onset of frustrations, sensory or somatic deficiencies, etc.)

Here we should, though in passing only, mention that the same factors that are liable to affect the development of the congenitally given intelligence (type-conditions, natural endowments and deficiencies, environmental frustration and satisfactions) in similar or in different configurations also determine the personality of the child. The intelligence then may or may not be affected *secondarily* by the thus developing personality. This proves the law of etiology according to which each relative outcome of a causal configuration of partial factors re-enters the etiological equation and becomes in itself a new partial factor. We must always remain aware of the fact that it will be an almost hopeless endeavor to isolate the factors determining the actual level of intellectual functioning in a secondarily retarded individual. Vulnerability, a low level of frustration bearance and similar factors may determine, in configuration with others, the degree of intellectual deterioration and, simultaneously, of personality-restriction; but both, the thus lowered intelligence-level and the thus restricted personality then become factors causally re-inforcing each other. (Which, *inter alia,* comes to prove that both, prevention and cure, must always be multi-functional to be effective: mental *and* intellectual hygiene, therapy

* Extraverts have, as a rule, better chances of resisting the destructive influence of externalization on the congenitally given potentials than introverts [24].

and education; they depend on each other in every field of psychopathology and this all the more so, the more intricately the various factors of the causal configuration are interwoven.)

Another example of the interaction between cause and result in the genesis of functional impairment can be taken from the area of delinquency: There are certain forms, particularly in children and juveniles, that allow for at least a *functional* preservation of the original level of intelligence, though the available intelligence will not be invested adequately in learning-activities, social adjustment or creativeness. We think here first and foremost of the so-called primary behavior-disorder [40] with its conscious negation of the adult world, and of society, because of conscious and unconscious fears of disappointment. This negation, however, requires a fair amount of human understanding and of differentiation between social situations. In most cases, psychopathy too, is not only not injurious to the originally given level of intelligence but may even help develop it. (Here again, as in the case of primary behavior-disorders, the 'support' of intelligence is one-sided only, and rarely if ever will help the individual *use* his intelligence for solving an objective problem in which he may not be specifically and personally involved [21]).

On the other hand, it is well-known that at least one form of juvenile delinquency, the one we have elsewhere described as 'primary waywardness' [14], *causes* deterioration of originally normal intelligence, so that we are not entitled to 'conclude from a low IQ in a wayward child that low intelligence was a cause of his social development' [9]. The latter argument fails to take cognizance of the fact that delinquency *per se* discriminates against test-examinations of intelligence. We do not intend hereby to minimize the importance of the intelligence factor in the etiology of delinquency: it is undoubtedly correct to say that 'the lower a person's intelligence, the lower his power of resistance to negative stimuli and impulses, particularly when he is exposed to conditions of poverty or of cultural crisis'—which happens relatively often in the life of children of low intelligence [18]. But the very passiveness and lack of inner organization that characterize waywardness account for the inadequacy with which even a normally intelligent wayward child will use his potentials. Obviously, he thus risks the danger of deterioration, particularly when certain type-conditions support his passiveness.

The causal effect of symptoms, we have said in the above-quoted paper, becomes particularly evident through an analysis of this form of dissociality: 'To the extent that mental retardation favors the emergence of dissocial behavior, waywardness tends to appear ... waywardness and low intelligence tend to become aggravated as the result of the inductive spread of effect of their symptoms, and this symptom-producing activity of symptoms is the stronger (in both areas) the lower the synthetic power of the ego'. [18, p. 298]. In other words: when we speak of delinquency as of a *cause* of mental retardation, we have in mind primarily this specific form of delinquency called waywardness. Without such clinical differentiation no etiological statement becomes meaningful.

Brief mention should be made here of two other causes of feeblemindedness, cultural confusion and insecurity, and weakness of parental guidance and stimulation. In our time, these are probably the two most potent factors accounting for the large number of socially and intellectually ineffective individuals. Let there be no misunderstanding: we do not wish to claim that the number of mentally subnormal in our time exceeds that of other periods in the tortuous history of men. There have always been at work factors of culture that were detrimental to the full development of intelligence. But each era, we claim, has its *specific* ways of restricting and finally destroying man's spirit, of limiting his ability fully to develop and use what nature has planted in him. Cultural ambiguity and parental insecurity are the forces which in our time are liable to affect negatively the intellectual development of millions of men.

Here, we see again that the two interrelated concepts of structurization and of reversibility must be discussed. Is secondary subnormality (and what Doll, [9] calls 'retardation' as opposed to 'feeblemindedness') the end-product of a long and continuous process of negative conditioning which leads to a mental deficiency as irreversible as a congenitally given low intellectual ability? And let us add already here a question of central importance for the psychologist and the educator: are the recognizable and assessable symptoms of secondary retardation, even though it may prove to be as irreversible as primary feeblemindedness, different from those of the latter? In other words: does the fact that in the beginning of life an individual was of normal intelligence reflect itself in the expression of his later deficiency?

3 STRUCTURIZATION AND REVERSIBILITY*

The concept of 'structurization' has a twofold connotation: it means the developmental process leading to that modality of mental life which we call 'structured', insofar as all its functional and material expressions relate to each other and to the ego as the organizing center of consciousness. This is a process that both presupposes and furthers differentiation, in fact, is almost synonymous with it.

The other meaning of the concept, the one with which we are concerned here, is: transformation of an existing structure under the influence of external factors of determination. Here, we must distinguish between the adequate development of dispositions under the impact of experience ('Geprägte Form, die lebend sich entwickelt', in Goethe's words), that is, a kind of evolution of a pre-existing structure, *according to plan*, as it were, and, on the other hand, radical changes taking place in this structure in *opposition* to the original form.

In its first meaning the concept of transformation refers not only to the gradual emergence of what we later call the individual's character- or personality-structure but also, and even primarily, to the crystalization of what we retrospectively call his 'constitution'. Even in those cases in which this constitution in its final form is, for all practical purposes, identical with its congenitally extant nucleus, it will acquire its full power as a force of selecting the individual's experience—and thus determining his development—only after it has passed through a process of structurization, a process in the course of which the ego and its functions take shape. It would, of course, be a hopeless endeavor later to isolate from each other congenitally given, nuclear elements of constitution, reinforcements of these elements and modifications that may have taken place during the phases of plasticity in infancy and childhood. And the transition from 'modification' to 'radical change' can not be as clearly defined as one would wish to be able for the sake of conceptual exactitude and clinical investigation.

There is no reason to confine the concept of transformation in its second meaning to processes of negative change only, although research is concerned with them more than with positive ones. We

---

* The ideas proposed in this paragraph have been elaborated more fully in the author's book *The Roots of the Ego—a phenomenology of dynamics and of structure* [24, see also 20].

speak, for instance, of the emergence of *psychopathic conditions* under the impact of earliest frustrations on a child born with certain dispositions (such as a relative predominance of the life-tendency towards expansion over that towards staticness and structural weakness of anxiety), [21]. — We speak of the reversal of *congenital type-conditions* (such as extravert or introvert tendencies) under the impact of social or cultural conditions that are not conducive to the unhampered development of these dispositions and tendencies. — We speak of the gradual *decrease of congenitally available qualities* (such as mental and physical vitality and initiative) under the impact of institutional care, leading to irreversible apathy or even feeblemindedness in a child born with normal dispositions. — We speak of *changes in an individual's character-structure* that have taken place in an early phase of his childhood-development, when a deeply frustrating experience forces the child into reactive defences of a neurotic kind; as a result, character-traits may emerge that are no longer amenable to educational or therapeutic treatment, and determine the individual's future development, as if they had been congenitally given propensities.

The fact that we do not hear of opposite changes in structure, *changes from early observable deficiencies into later normalcy,* is understandable enough, since in such cases the early deficiencies are likely to be overlooked and forgotten in the light of the later positive development. But there is, as we have said, no reason to assume that such positive changes do not take place.

Reversibility of such changes or rather, in most cases, of such damages caused to personality-functions, means, so we may claim, that structurization has not yet come to an end. In this case we *define* structurization as irreversible. To the extent that later educational or therapeutic interventions are indicated and meaningful, we should then speak of modification rather than of reversal of the structural changes brought about by the former traumatization. Thus, Ainsworth, in her discussion of the criticism levelled against Bowlby's findings [3], points out that the effects of early separations will make themselves felt in a high degree of vulnerability or in depressive moods, even after improvements have been brought-about educationally or have taken place spontaneously. And she adds that, all partial improvement, i.e. all 'modification' notwithstanding, a more intensive analysis of the individual case will always produce evidence of lasting damage, that is, of irreversibility (in the case of institutionalized children).

Before we try to answer the question of whether or not secondary retardation should be considered a result of negative structurization, a few remarks should be added on the essence of structurization as such. Negative personality changes are reversible to the extent that they did not start very early in life; that the environment places at the disposal of the child educational and therapeutic measures in an atmosphere of personal relationships; that the reversal processes are supported by compensatory factors not only in the environment but also, and primarily, in the child's personality structure.

It is in the light of these conditions of reversibility that the essence of structurization must be understood. We start with those forms of *negative* changes that we know to be irreversible: psychopathic conditions, early type-transformations, vitality loss through institutional care.

What have these changes in common? In each, negative structurization starts at the beginning of life, before the ego-nucleus has had a chance of crystallizing into a center of inner co-ordination. This process of ego-crystallization is one of the main functions of the first months of life (though it is, of course, not completed by the end of this early phase); being exposed to contradictory mother-experiences and being conditioned by them brings about differentiation between ego and non-ego and leads to polarization. After the crystallization of the ego has taken place and the constitution has taken on its final form, experience has the function of eliciting ego-reactions rather than of setting in motion and bringing about processes of structurization.

Thus, we can understand why congenital deficiencies which may manifest themselves in constitutional inability to separate, and keep alive separation, between subject and object and between ego and non-ego (a defect of the schizophrenia-type), or in extreme rigidity (of the feeblemindedness-type) *preclude* structurization.

When the life-tendency towards staticness is too strong, rigidity or an ever ready tendency to relapse into a barely overcome state of non-differentiatedness will make early transformation of experience into structure impossible: *Structurization requires a minimum of structural mobility.*

When the tendency towards staticness is too weak, no systematization, no inner organization, hence also no systematic transformation of experience into structure can take place, and experience fails to make itself felt as a determining factor in the individual's development. *Structurization requires a minimal readiness to systematize.*

When, on the other hand, the opposite life-tendency, that towards expansion, is too weak, processes of structurization will be impeded as well, though for different reasons: in this case, the non-ego is liable to lose its significance as object of incorporation, and the possible scope of experience shrinks so much that there is little need for setting in motion structurization-processes. *Structurization requires a certain intensity of experience.*

An over-*strong* life-tendency towards expansion, on the other hand, makes negative structurization in reaction to early deficiencies in the mother-child relationships necessary, as the emergence of non-congenital cases of psychopathy proves. Here the structurization-process can be interpreted as a kind of defence against the otherwise unbearable 'onslaught' of maternal rejection, indolence, diffusion, disappearance or overindulgence [21]. A prevalence of staticness (whether it is, in turn, due to a basic excess of this life-tendency or to a weakness of the opposite one) offers some sort of structural protection against these earliest onslaughts of disorganizing forces. But such protection must be provided, when the life-tendency towards expansion predominates, and it is provided by the transformation of traumatic experiences—via the infant's reactions—into attitudes, that is, into integral parts of the personality structure. (*Genuine structurization, in contrast, not only does not fulfil such protective functions, it even presupposes their absence.*)

Let us now compare with each other two *environmentally* caused cases of negative structurization: growing up in an institution and the externalizing impact of extreme poverty and educational neglect. It is the element of continuity in an impersonal mode of living that here determines negative structurization, not so much the intensity of educational failure, as the absence of variations and the absence of unambiguous interpersonal relationships. Another condition of negative structurization then becomes comprehensible, the relative absence of communication with the external and the internal non-ego, the human environment and the unconscious. Non-communication between the growing ego and the non-ego is both a cause and one of the major symptoms of those structurization processes that lead to loss of congenitally given potentials in the areas of intellectual and relational functioning.

In other words: structurization in its negative meaning will *not* take place or will in any case *not* produce irreversible damage, when the non-ego acts as an autonomous partner of communication with the ego. Again in other words: it is apparently the experience of being intended by an independent non-ego that prevents shrinkage of intellectual and relational contact-functions during the early stages of development and prevents protective structurization of the thus lowered level of functioning. *Shrinkage of potentials and negative transformation of structure depend on isolation that is, on a basic frustration of the growing child's vital contact-needs and -tendencies. The less radical this frustration, the better are the chances of later reversal* (and vice versa).

This explains, partly at least, why the injury to the child's relational and conceptual functions caused by early separation and institutional care is, *ceteris paribus* (that is, when the factors of congenital assets and liabilities are kept constant), less reversible than the damage caused to these functions by the externalizing conditions of poverty and neglect. For, the frustration of the infant's contact-needs will rarely, if ever, be as radical in the second case as it is liable to be in the first. Character-changes due to later traumatizations, usually of the neurotic or the character-neurotic type, it would then seem to follow, offer still better chances of reversal. And the least irreversible, the most amenable to rehabilitation through social, educational, and therapeutic interventions, should then prove to be those cases in which shrinkage of functions and in particular conceptual impoverishment had resulted, at a later stage of development, from inadequate educational stimulation (without the experience of early isolation).

But we must not overlook the fact that certain results of relative isolation (through institutional care, externalization of the poverty-type, neurotic character-distortions, later inadequacy of educational stimulation) are liable to set in motion processes of *conditioning*, which may then cause irreversible damage even in those cases in which environmental deficiencies make themselves felt in a relatively late phase of development only.

Thus, lack of adequate educational stimulation during the learning phase, following a more or less normal development may bring about certain changes of attitudes in any child of only average intelligence: he may lose part of his intellectual initiative, may forget to ask questions, may become accustomed to external substitute-activities, which not only do not require intelligence but, on the contrary, promise success to the extent that the child learns how to give up his autonomy and how to seek security in groups and other de-individualizing contacts only. Thus, a regressive process of de-differentiation is set in motion, during which conceptual learning is increasingly being replaced by following the lead of external stimulation through chance-occurrences only. Reversibility of the damage caused in this way to the growing child's intelligence depends, it is true, on the degree of intensity and continuity of the factor here under discussion (inadequate stimulation); but the casual importance of conditioning should not be underrated, particularly when the factor itself is auxiliary only to economic deterioration (poverty) or cultural disorientation (immigration), that is, to conditions favorable to de-differentiation and heteronomy.

Another example is that of changes in the character-structure brought about by severe traumatization in one of the childhood phases. Such changes will never be radical and final unless they have been prepared by frustrations in the very beginning of life, that is, by disturbances of the 'basic sense of trust' [11] or the feeling of nearness [24]; but later traumatization, too, may cause lasting damage to the individual's character-structure, if, and to the extent that, the first (defensive or compensatory) reaction of the child to the traumatic event produces attitudes that are in themselves sources of direct or indirect, normal or abnormal satisfaction. After a while, the child will no longer be prepared to live without them, not only because his self-conception may have changed radically, but also because he derives a secondary sense of security from his defences or compensations, from his aggressiveness or his fearfulness, from his apathy or his compulsions.

We now return to the main subject of our discussion, that of the problems of structurization and irreversibility of environmentally caused retardation in its various forms. We shall not consider those cases of pseudo-feeblemindedness that result from emotional disorders not taken care of, or from psychotic personality-disruptions, and shall concentrate on those cases in which mental retardation has been caused by impersonality of early relationships, inadequacy of educational guidance and stimulation, or by externalizing (including delinquent) life-patterns. We suggest the following summary: Secondary retardation is liable to become as irreversible as the congenital variety, when the environmental forces that are responsible for the gradual decrease of the congenitally given level of intellectual (and relational) functioning

1) start operating very early, as a rule before the ego-nucleus has had time to develop into an inner agent of selection and synthesis, that is, in the first six to nine months of life;

2) are supported by certain type-conditions that are conducive to structurization;

3) and by certain processes of conditioning through impersonal reactions (or non-reactions) to the child's behavior;

4) are continuous, that is, are not counteracted by social, educational and therapeutic interventions or by positive changes taking place in the environment, interventions or changes characterized by emphasis on dialogic (polar) relationships;

5) are not compensated by certain factors of constitution, such as a high original level of intelligence, a strong integrational ability.

The last-mentioned ability manifests itself, in the majority of cases in which it is present, in a well-developed 'sense of trust', in basic security and courage. When the earliest child-mother relationships have made possible the emergence of this sense of trust, later inadequacies in the educational environment (such as lack of sufficient stimulation and guidance, value-discrepancies in the life of immigrants, emotional crises, change in the parents' life-orientation following economic crises) will rarely, if ever, cause irreversible damage to the child's conceptual and relational abilities.

To sum up: Contrary to the other results of negative structurization (such as psychopathy or vitality loss through institutional care), secondary retardation will be reversible or irreversible according to the quality of earliest mother-child relationships. Only to the extent that this type of retardation fulfils a protective function in the process of ego-crystallization, should we see in it a case of negative structurization. Only in this case it is irreversible.

4 COMPARISONS BETWEEN PATTERNS OF RETARDATION

It now remains for us to compare the essential characteristics of primary and secondary feeblemindedness. We shall confine this comparison to the so-called endogenous type of congenital feeblemindedness (leaving aside all varieties of exogenous feeblemindedness so thoroughly investigated and described by Strauss, Lehtinen, Werner and others), to the so-called externalization-type as described in the author's study of externalization [20, 26], to the cultural disorientation type and to the non-stimulation-type.

It is relatively easy to distinguish between pseudo-feeblemindedness caused by emotional blocking and genuine, that is, congenitally given feeblemindedness: the discrepancy between normal or even above-normal achievements in certain areas of thinking and problem-solving and utter failure in others is a clear indication of pseudo-feeblemindedness. But the criterion is not a quantitative one: an analysis of the inadequate answers of a thus affected child to his test-or learning tasks reveals their character as isolated failures not only by contrast to his adequate answers but also by his total reaction to the learning situation, by his accessibility to treatment and education and by the clearly discernible evidence of conceptualization.

In other cases of pseudo-feeblemindedness it is the provable connection between seemingly absurd answers and interfering complexes that characterizes this variety of intellectual handicap, or it is the relative weakness of suggestibility and of automatic imitation, the strong admixture of anxiety in the thinking-processes and, sometimes, a compulsion-like concentration on certain operations.

The differences between emotionally caused pseudo-feeblemindedness and partial destruction of intellectual abilities through brain-injuries are well-known and need not be elaborated here. Inability to shift from one mode of operation to another according to the different task-requirements produces inadequate though often highly complicated and intricate thinking-processes in the brain-injured child; the pseudo-feebleminded is helpless in the face of a similar task and may have recourse to absurdly illogical answers, result of uncontrollable associations rather than of any kind of operational activity.

There are indeed many possible comparisons between different varieties of intellectual failure. We shall dwell here on the one between congenital feeblemindedness and the socio-cultural varieties. The fact that the latter respond much more readily to educational intervention than the former, although they may be no less severe in degree, would seem to justify posing the question of differences between the essential characteristics of both varieties. For, attempts at education and therapy, at reconstruction and rehabilitation, in this as in any other field, should be guided by a clear recognition not only of what brought about the pathology to be remedied but also of its essential manifestations (not to speak of the advantage such recognition offers for the purposes of differential diagnosis). *The difference between essentials may here be defined as one between emptiness and illusion, and between inability and distortion.*

In the *congenital* variety we find, for instance, perseverations as expressions of *rigidity*; fixatedness to the moratory area of the known, or what seems to be known (the illusion of knownness) characterizes the thinking-processes of the *socially retarded* child and adult; a tendency to seek solutions to problems of the present through associative referral to the cultural past characterizes the intellectual limitations of the individual who grows up and lives under conditions of *cultural disorientation.*

Imitation occurs in automatic reaction to chance stimuli in the first case, without being directed by any form of intentionality. It is the very lack of structure, in which we have seen the core-symptom of true feeblemindedness, that here produces the tendency to imitate automatically, particularly in the submissive type. On the other hand, where the externalizing conditions of a life in poverty and neglect cause secondary feeblemindedness (that is, loss of potentials), imitation is specifically geared to those who have conditioned the child from his earliest days on, the parents with their typical orientation towards the haveable [20, 26]. Such a child is liable to fail in his thinking and learning tasks, because he is taking over from his significant adults an attitude towards external objects and values that limits both his receptivity to the variety of possible objects of learning and his readiness to separate himself from them in a polar relationship—this precondition of conceptualization.

But growing up under conditions of externalization also means, as we have tried to show, growing up in an atmosphere of impersonality. Being conditioned through such an atmosphere, the child does not learn how to become involved in any of his learning-tasks or, for that matter, in any activity that does not lead to immediate tension-relief and need-satisfaction. This lack of ego-involvement manifests itself in the lack of perseverance, the distractibility, the impulsiveness so characteristic of the externalization-type of retardation. It reflects impatience and shallowness of relationship rather than automatic reactiveness (as in the truly feebleminded).

In the cultural variety, on the other hand, the place of such reactive imitations and that of being conditioned by the parents' external value-orientations is taken by levantine pseudo-adaptability, this mostly unconscious search for identity-through-self-diffusion. In a learning-situation this attitude often deceives the observer and even the teacher; they are liable to mistake it for genuine mobility, until they see the individual in his hopelessly inadequate reactions to an unknown task, trying in vain to solve his problems by meaningless imitations of 'someone-or-something-successful-and-strong'. It is then only that the levantine variety of externalization manifests itself as what it really is—one of the cultural varieties of feeblemindedness.

But it would be wrong to *identify* the cultural variety with levantine pseudo-adaptation. It is only when we compare our three types of intellectual failure, the congenital, the social and the cultural types, under the aspect of *imitation* that levantinism becomes relevant. Cultural disorientation under conditions of change is liable to affect the intellectual functions of the learner, child and adult alike, in other respects as well, and the levantine mentality is not even the most representative form of cultural retardation. We have tried to show, in the above-mentioned analysis of externalization [20, 24, 26], what is liable to happen to primitive man when he comes under the influence of Western (meaning in this case technological and organizational) ideas and values that he cannot assimilate adequately; when cultural isolation causes the values of the past to undergo a process of petrification; when man moves (or is transferred) either from conditions of original primitivity or from cultural isolation to an environment or to an educational system which is governed by ideals of internalization, that is, of rationality, abstraction and individual responsibility.

It is particularly the last mentioned case, that of cultural transition, that allows us to study the emergence of the cultural variety of mental retardation. This is undoubtedly the most important form of secondary impairments, since it affects today many millions of children and adults in the so-called developing countries. It is certainly correct to say that pre-change conditions not only of personality but also of environment, collective experience, tradition (in our case: patterns of 'original primitivity', of 'contaminated primitivity', or of 'cultural isolation', prior to transition from either one of them to modern civilization) specifically determine the emerging patterns of behavior.* But we can nevertheless find and formulate a number of common properties that could serve as further points of comparison between the cultural, the social and the congenital varieties of feeblemindedness. Cultural retardation, whatever its pre-history may have been, is characterized by:

1) a strong tendency towards an illusion of one-ness with the cultural past, elimination of differences, de-individualization—para-

* Eisenstadt [10] has elaborated this point in his analysis of immigration and absorption of immigrants, based on empirical research and not on a phenomenology of differences.

doxically combined with equally strong egocentricity;

2) an inability to recognize the essential differences and similarities between past and present experiences, between different perceptions or concepts of feelings, since such recognition would require giving up the illusion of oneness and accepting, instead, personal responsibility for differentiation;

3) an all-pervading belief that this state of oneness, of being in contact with the environment, of equality, of staticness will occur one day (if it is not felt as being present) without need for active participation and self-involvement;

4) co-existence of ego-emphasis with almost paranoid vulnerability and irrational fears—distorting problem-solving processes through a preference for personifications, emotionally tinged dichotomies and sweeping generalizations;

5) resistance to the recognition of generally valid laws, that is, to the existence of ego-transcending and thought-committing principles of reality;

6) an inability to recognize anything new as such (that is, as requiring not only external adaptation but also, and mainly, inner reorientation), since the separation lines between object and object or even between object and subject, that is, between the non-ego and the ego, are liable to be overlooked under the impact of the above-mentioned illusion of oneness;

7) the use of imitation, manipulation and stereotypes as means of orientation in a fundamentally incomprehensible reality.

We shall now try to compare each of these essentials of the cultural variety of intellectual failure with their counterparts in the social externalization-type of secondary feeblemindedness, on the one hand, and in genuine feeblemindedness, on the other.

The cultural *illusion of oneness* manifests itself in a peculiar insufficiency of the perception of time and cause, the past being experienced as superimposed on, or even as identical with, the present, as what gives the present its meaning. As a result, the dimension of consecutiveness is replaced, in the perception of cause, by the dimension of simultaneity. 'Causing' something presupposes, accordingly, contiguity, and a similar distortion affects, then, the perception of time. We could perhaps speak, in this case, of a shrinkage of the causal and temporal categories.

When we speak of similar categorial deficiencies in the second, the social externalization-type of unintelligent behavior, we should keep in mind that they result in this case from a general lack of differentiation, which, in turn, is rooted in the relative absence of maternal regularity at the beginning of life. The 'illusion of oneness', here, becomes identical with defective differentiation. The world is divided into what is 'wanting' and what is 'haveable', but the two tend to become 'one'. As a result, accidentality takes the place of causality as well as that of sequentiality.

The difference between these two forms of a seemingly identical cognitive deficiency is one between distortion of contents and inability to differentiate resulting from a long process of conditioning. But both differ essentially from the true feebleminded person's inability clearly to distinguish between cause and result or between the dimensions of time. Structural rigidity which explains his limitations, does not characterize even the social variety of retardation: identifying want with the haveable requires more intellectual activity than a true feebleminded will ever be able to mobilize. (It is obvious that these differences have much significance for the methods of education or of therapy to be applied; but we are not concerned here with these aspects.)

But this *inability to recognize essential differences and similarities* between past and present experiences, between different perceptions, or learnable concepts, values or feelings, this concomitant of the illusion of oneness, is also a symptom of ego-weakness. Differentiation requires ego-strength and -activity. What appears, particularly in children and adults from so-called culturally retarded groups within an abstraction- and anonymity-oriented society, as *inability* to differentiate, is often, at least in part, a kind of *escape* from the confusing, disquieting, harassing challenge of those learning-tasks for which their families and cultural groups did not prepare them. Accepting differentiation as a challenge and a task requires, among other things, familiarity with change and growth as life-regulating principles and readiness to face the possibility of failure. In a group for which, reversely, staticness is the culturally established principle of regulation, avoidance of differentiation is a comprehensible defence against the anxiety-arousing experience of ego-loss-in-failure. Non-differentiation here means not only oneness, but also ego-strength, the second being of course as illusory as the first.

In the social variety of secondary deficiency, non-differentiation cannot be interpreted as a defence. It is cause as well as effect of that fixation to the moratory area of the known that characterizes the individual whose life under the externalizing influence of poverty and neglect has conditioned him to an exclusive experience of reality as wanting and haveable. The illusion of oneness, particularly with the collective past, *distorts* the contents of learning and of thinking, but at the same time generates an inner tension that can be used by the educator in his efforts to rehabilitate intelligence; fixation to the moratory area of the known only restricts the scope of learning abilities and makes them shrink.

But in contrast to genuine feeblemindedness, where inability to differentiate originates in an unchangeably short memory-span and in defective cerebral polarization, secondary deficiency even of the externalization-type with its long pre-history of conditioning always remains a possible object of educational intervention, though the chances of reversibility become smaller with increasing age. We have tried to analyze in another place [23] the re-educational functions of comprehensive social work which aims at reconstructing experiences that may be conducive to the emergence of trust, of courage, of initiative and thus of intelligent behavior. In other words: differentiation can here be relearned.

The avoidance-character of non-differentiation in the cultural variety manifests itself, we have said (p. 77, point 2), as *avoidance of personal responsibility*. Differentiation in cognitive, judgmental, relational activities compels man to recognize the fact that oneness does not exist but as a challenge and a task requiring self-involvement and active participation. Where ego-weakness as the result of cultural disorientation and restriction makes such involvement and activity difficult, its place is taken by *passive expectation* of the sudden disappearance of tension and failure, of separateness and insufficiency, the expectation that equality and staticness will be 'there' one day, without causal connection with the present condition.

In this respect the cultural and the social varieties of intellectual insufficiency resemble each other, since passive expectation of changes taking place and of problems finding their solutions automatically is also one of the essential characteristics of externalization. (The genuinely feebleminded differs from both insofar as he is unable to expect any change from the future.) But in spite of this similarity, passive expectation means something different here and there: in an individual belonging to the first group it will often appear with a strong admixture of resentment (as if the lost values of his cultural past owed him a solution of his present problems); in the second case, we would better replace the word 'expectation' by 'chance-addiction':

the socially externalized individual lives in a world that is ruled by chance.

When we compare with each other the learning-activities of the two types, we find this difference reflected in their attitude towards failure: in the first case, of cultural retardation, a very low tolerance of failure produces an ever-ready tendency to rationalize faulty solutions, a tendency which is bound to consume so much mental energy that little is left for objective learning; in the second case, of social retardation, the main criterion of truth and error, of correct and incorrect answers, of adequate and faulty solutions is the amount of immediate need-satisfaction supplied by them. Consequently, intelligence is likely to remain intact in the first case, as a function, even though it will not be freely available for objective learning; whereas its functional level is liable to sink, in the second case, although readiness to learn, at least from total life-situations and in settings of comprehensive care, may remain intact for a relatively long time.

Here we come back to the problem of *egocentricity*, the seemingly paradoxical concomitant of the first symptom of culturally caused failure, which we have proposed to define as the 'illusion of oneness': egocentricity, in this context, means recognition of the changing objects of thinking and learning as determined only by association with some kind of (personal) values of the learner or his groups of identification. As such it is *not* essentially characteristic of the externalization-type of intellectual failure; in an externalized orientation towards the haveable a strong contact with the world of objects is implied, which precludes egocentricity. Although this contact is not accompanied by any objective recognition of the essence of these objects, and having them is all that counts, it would not be justified to speak in this case of egocentricity, since the object and not the ego (the 'haveable' and not the 'haver') stands in the center of consciousness.

Not so in the cultural variety of secondary retardation. Ego-emphasis here indicates ego-weakness. Egocentricity co-exists not only with that culturally conditioned tendency towards an illusion of oneness, but also with excessive vulnerability and irrational fears (see p. 77, point 4), that is, with ego-weakness, which is well-known from socio-psychological studies of cultural changes due to the impact of migration or rapid technological advances. Ego-weakness is also reflected in the *cognitive* characteristics of cultural retardation: preference for personifications, emotionally tinged dichotomies and sweeping generalizations (point 4), resistance to universalities (point

5) and inability to recognize anything new as such (point 6) being its most important manifestations.

It would seem that at the root of all of these symptoms lies defective polarization due, in this case, neither to a constitutional defect (as in psychopathy) nor to individual traumatization (as in certain neurotic developments), but to a culturally conditioned incompleteness of individualization. Both, in cultural isolation and under conditions of transition from so-called primitivity to modern technology, the individual remains—partly—bound to those transindividual forces that, before, prevented the emergence of an independent ego, while he now partly discovers his egoity.

It is this inner contradiction between what could be called cultural fixation and the illusion of oneness (with the transindividual) and the (partial) individuation that here accounts for strongly irrational fears of destruction by even the slightest threat to that precarious egoity, as well as for those above-mentioned cognitive defects, which in reality are but inadequate defences against the threat of egoity.

Thus, preference for *personifications* instead of concepts—inevitably jeopardizing the emergence of intelligent behavior and of adequate problem solving—is a kind of escape from intercourse with concepts and at the same time a kind of naïve experimentation with egoity, an ever repeated attempt to discover the ego outside, in the world of observable objects, rather than inside, in the 'experimenter' himself who would then be forced to give up his illusion of oneness with the transindividual.

Under such conditions, *dichotomization* would seem to be the most suitable way of organizing reality, because it requires neither self-distantiation from the objects of observation, classification or objective evaluation nor ability to differentiate between objects according to their essential qualities. The more radical the dichotomization, the stronger will be the accompanying feeling-tone until it becomes purely affective.

Dividing the world into contradictory parts is often accompanied by false *generalization*, that is, by raising one aspect of an event, a situation, an inner process to the level of essentiality while remaining unaware of the existence of all other aspects. Instead of discriminating essential from non-essential similarities and contrasts betwen observable phenomena and expressing this distinction in the learning-process as abstractive generalization, the culturally retarded individual tends to discover (and to overrate the importance of the recurrence of) a certain trait through the very act of finding opposite, negative cases, that is, phenomena in which that trait is absent. In other words: quality is replaced in his thinking by quantity, essence by existence, individuality by the categories of presence and absence. His generalization is not the fruit of abstraction. On the contrary, it requires a great amount of concretizations.

In each of these cognitive activities, ego emphasis stands out as a sign of ego-weakness. *Personifications* could be interpreted as a constant repetition of egoity, when the ego is actually too weak to take a position opposite the non-ego, as different and separate in its functions of selection, organization and co-ordination. In *dichotomization*, ego emphasis finds its expression in the tendency to identify with the 'positive' part. Hence, the individual's *extreme vulnerability*. The same holds good for *false generalization* with its distinction between 'present' and 'absent': here, too, the ego identifies with what is by chance perceived as present, and ego-weakness expresses itself in the affective rejection of what is 'absent'.

It is almost a tautology to add here that under such conditions man is unable to recognize and comprehend a *law of general validity*, implying, as it does, the ability to subordinate concreteness under the rule of principles. It would seem that, as long as dichotomization of reality is the only concession man is able and ready to make to his illusion of oneness, is his only firm of differentiation, of organization, of abstraction and of generalization—the very concept of general validity is meaningless, since it requires ego-non-ego polarity, the absence of which characterizes cultural retardation.

Again another expression of that same deficiency is the (already mentioned) tendency to relate each *new experience to some group-determined content*, to some traditional stereotype of thinking or of behavior. It again helps maintain the illusion of oneness and escaping responsibility for the thinking- and learning-acts that may be required in the new society.

We now come back once more to comparing these essential characteristics of cultural retardation with similar and yet different elements in the two other varieties we are discussing here, congenital feeblemindedness, on the one hand, and the externalization type of socially conditioned loss of intellectual potentials, on the other.

The cultural variety of mental insufficiency is, in essence, an outcome of that cultural residue that we have proposed to call 'the illusion of oneness'. It does not matter whether it is, in turn, rooted in patterned memories of past contact with transindividual realities, or in traditionally transmitted memories of past greatness (see point

1.) On his way to individuation man is arrested, as it were, through the retracting force of that illusion, and, as a result, his thinking becomes as undifferentiated as it bears the stamp of egocentricity.

This is clearly a different kind of intellectual failure than that of the truly feebleminded individual whose rigidity precludes differentiation, because he has no 'ego-front' with reality. But it also differs from the social variety of mental retardation, in which the illusion of knowness (in essence the outcome of an almost exclusive orientation towards the haveable) provides the externalized individual with a false feeling of security, thus eliminating the motivation and the incentive for differentiation and individuation.

In the cultural variety, weakness of the ego and its extreme vulnerability find cognitive expressions in the tendency to use personification, dichotomization and false generalization (see point 4). The genuinely feebleminded is neither able to mobilize such cognitive defences nor does he need them, since the ego as active center of co-ordination is, in this case, replaced by what can be called a mirror-ego, automatically reflecting, but not truly reacting to, non-ego stimulations. In the social variety, on the other hand, *personalization, dichotomization and generalization,* to the extent that we do find them, have a different meaning altogether: since the externalized individual tends to diffuse, as it were, his ego in outside realities, he is likely to find ego-vestiges in each material or processual part of this non-ego (personification); to the extent that he uses dichotomies as his means of problem-solving and interpreting basically incomprehensible phenomena, it is his orientation towards the haveable that accounts for it, his universe being divided into want and having, into not-having and haveability. But since he experiences what he has not as haveable, dichotomization will never be as sharp as it is in the cultural variety. False generalization, too, is here an outcome of the mind's exclusive concern with the haveable, since differentiation would immediately destroy this specifically externalized illusion, that of haveability (and, in fact, is the means of re-education *par excellence* in this case).

Here, then, is the place to compare the social variety of inability to recognize and comprehend differences with the cultural variety. There, we have said, it is essentially linked with the individual's inability and lack of readiness to undertake personal responsibility for his acts of thinking, as long as he is tied to his illusion of oneness (see point 2). The externalized individual is, of course, no less unable to recognize differences objectively, but not as the result of distorting memories and patterns interfering with his thinking processes; he simply overlooks differences, because he is not interested in the non-ego as such but experiences it as the area in which chance-occurrence is the equalizing, de-differentiating factor. While he has *lack of personal responsibility* for his acts of thinking in common with the former, the cultural variety, it is the basic inability to conceive of the non-ego as of an object of polar-relationship that makes the social variety comparable with genuine feeblemindedness: in the latter, too, recognition of differences is jeopardized by this relational inability.

The relative inability to recognize differences in their objective significance (and thus to organize the perceivable and intelligible universe of facts for the purposes of orientation and adaptation) finds its expression in a similar deficiency, the *inability to recognize newness as such* (see point 6), that is, as a challenge not only to compare or analyze differences but also to try out new attitudes, different mental sets, to experiment with ego-positions. (This is why we suggested that in the cultural variety of intellectual failure it is the illusion of oneness that prevents recognition of newness, since the latter presupposes a clear and unambiguous demarcation line between the ego and the non-ego.)

In the cultural variety inability to recognize newness is indicative of what might be called an *ego-illusion* (the illusion of still being contained in, of still belonging to, a transindividual context which, in reality, has long lost its significance); it is the result of a *non-ego-illusion* in the externalization-type of mental retardation: the illusion that the narrow (moratory) area of living, in which everything recurs monotonously but also foreseeably, represents the non-ego in its entirety and that it is known (and haveable).

For the intellectual development of children who are exposed to one of these two situations, the *difference between a culturally conditioned inability to experiment with ego-positions and a socially conditioned fixation to the narrow area of knownness* is an essential one, in spite of seeming similarities in the failure to solve problems that require cognitive mobility: In the first case we find a tendency to distort new aspects of a phenomenon or the meaning of new phenomena, to interpret them not only in the light of cultural associations, which may be entirely irrelevant, but also out of a rigid self-perception in which self-inflational trends mix with anxieties. In the second case, that of externalizing life-conditions, newness does not provoke tension (in the normative meaning of a challenge to change ego-positions) but simply sets in motion a process (rather than a tendency) aimed at getting hold of the new, at handling it arbitrarily, at 'having' it through the use of available categories and tools of problem-solving.

In this respect, both varieties differ from the *genuinely feeble-minded individual* who is liable simply not to react to a new situation, since his mental activity depends on some sort of automatic reaction, which precludes apperception of newness.

Similarly, the *occurrence-character* of life (point 3) is different in the three varieties. In the *cultural* variety it reflects a deep-rooted irrational belief in the superiority of the past, which, because of its superiority, is bound one day to re-appear as the force that will solve man's problems; it is this belief that in no small measure affects the individual's thinking- and learning-processes and particularly his attitude towards problems of cause and effect, his mental initiative and his reactions to failure.

But whereas occurrence is here conceived of as resulting from some sort of transindividual forces, it means, in the *social* variety of mental retardation, chance-appearance of the haveable, including solutions of day-to-day problems. The effect this conception is bound to have on the externalized individual's thinking and learning is again different from the fore-mentioned, insofar as there will be less distortion in the relevant processes but also less interest, less incentive to think or to learn in general. Comparing with each other the two varieties, it is safe to presume that intelligence will be better preserved in the cultural than in the social variety, where more or less exclusive orientation towards the haveable ('occurring' by chance) dangerously restricts intellectual initiative.

As regards the *genuinely feebleminded*, it would seem more correct to say that his universe is devoid of inner logic and order than that it is a world of chance-occurrences, since in the latter concept expectation of certain defineable events is implied, whereas the feebleminded does not expect anything.

This leads us to the last of the above-mentioned points of comparison: what does *resistance to the recognition of universally valid laws*—as principles of organizing and understanding reality—mean in each of the three varieties? Can we really speak of resistance in each of these cases? In the cultural variety, the illusion of oneness with past transindividuality may indeed produce resistance to the recognition of any empirically and objectively defineable principles of reality-organization (law), since this would almost certainly be in conflict with the binding principles of the cultural past (patterns).

But already in the externalized individual it is doubtful whether we should speak of resistance; it seems more appropriate, in the interpretation of intellectual failure under conditions of externalization, to use purely causal categories and to speak of the negative *effect* that an exclusive orientation towards the haveable is bound to have on the individual's ability to abstract from haveability in order to gain access to an overriding, generally valid principle of organization.

And again, it would seem understandable why, in the cultural variety of intellectual failure, intelligence is, at least functionally, better protected than in the social variety: the feeling of one, essential, principle of orientation and organization being threatened by the social demand for another one (in our case for the principle of universality and anonymity leading to the formulation of generally valid laws) necessitates cognitive efforts which, then, are likely to reflect themselves in the level of intellectual functioning. When, on the other hand, man becomes almost identical with his reactions to external stimuli (of want and haveability), his mental activity, his intellectual intentionality is bound to decrease. Each stimulus-situation being more or less 'closed', he will not be able to perceive the need for postulating, and looking for, generally valid laws meant to bring order and regularity into the multitude of objects and events, let alone to formulate such laws.

Reversibility and modifiability of rules and laws (Piaget) are elements of defining the concept of law; their deficiency is therefore characteristic of every form of intellectual failure, although its manifestations differ from variety to variety: When a *culturally* retarded individual learns how to find his way to discovering and formulating generally valid laws (under the influence of appropriate re-educational methods), his previous fixation to patterns of the past and his illusion of oneness are liable to make themselves felt, even in a rehabilitated, that is intellectually normalized and adapted individual: whenever he finds himself in a concrete situation which contradicts, or seems to contradict, a slowly discovered rule or law, he is liable to feel a similar resistance to reversing or modifying that rule or law as he felt before to the very demand of seeking and finding it as a generally valid instrument of reality-organization. This would seem to justify the presumption that *cultural retardation* as such (before rehabilitation takes place) is *characterized by defensive rigidity*; it finds its expression not only in the above-mentioned resistance to arriving inductively at generally valid laws, but also in the inability to reverse or modify a once established opinion, a once formulated sentence. We could perhaps see in this characteristic a tendency towards secondary patterning, a kind of functionally autonomous return to long-past cultural habits.

In the social variety, on the other hand, we find *inconsistency rather than rigidity*: rules and laws may be found or, better, encountered by chance, as it were, but the individual does not feel himself committed to a certain logical course of thought, to applying these laws to new problems. Reversal and modification are neither the purpose nor the content of intentional ego-activities but, again, the outcome of chance-occurrences only. This is why there are so many fluctuations in the way an externalized individual deals with his tasks and why we may find relatively adequate answers and solutions even on a generally low level of intellectual functioning.

We have already mentioned that the *congenitally feebleminded* differs from the secondary varieties insofar as his *limitations are not determined by distortions or fixations, by escapes and defences, by anxieties or expectations; nor are they influenced by processes of conditioning.* They are the unavoidable and unchangeable *result of structural defects,* of which rigid perseverations, memory-restrictions and unstructured, automatic, reflex-like reactions to external stimuli are the main symptoms. We should not speak in this case of egocentricity, which requires more intentionality than a feebleminded will ever be able to raise, but rather of naïve self-referral which accompanies most of his mental processes (not only in the aggressive and the suspicious, but even in the submissive and the apathetic types). His inability to recognize differences results from the non-differentiatedness of his field of experience rather than from his own fixations or distortions. The same applies, of course, to his encounters with newness: he does not recognize new situations as such, but neither does he associate them with what he believes he knows; he does not react to them, just as we do not react consciously to stimuli that are below our threshold of perception. The absence of generally valid laws in his universe of facts is not the result of resistance or of distortion but simply reflects the prevalence in it of details over whole-contexts.

All these differences should be made intelligible by using properly discriminating measurement- and assessment-tools, though we should add that the presently available intelligence-tests are far from serving such purposes, and it is doubtful whether any factorial and quantitational method can ever be used for the purpose of differentiation.

It would seem that it is one of the central tasks of such discriminating assessment-tools to *diagnose the meaning and the function of imita-*

tion, of the use of stereotypes and of manipulation in each of the three here discussed varieties of feeblemindedness: While they indicate, in a culturally retarded individual, tendencies to distort reality and to indulge in illusions of identity, of knownness and of familiarity with a basically unknown and unintelligible environment, they have a different function (and effect) in the externalization-variety of mental retardation, namely to establish, to support and to maintain the illusion of haveability. In genuine feeblemindedness, finally, they are the quasi-reactive outcome of chance-occurrences, of changing task-situations. To translate these and the other differential characteristics of the here discussed varieties into measurement-tools would indeed seem the most urgently needed practical application of what we have tried to clarify in our comparative analysis.

5 SUMMARY

In the following table, we intend to summarize the comparisons of the preceding paragraph.

When we speak of *social* retardation, we mean that form of intellectual impairment that is due to growing-up under the impact of extreme poverty and of educational neglect. *Cultural* retardation means that variety of impairment that is due to the impact of cultural ambiguity, as it is in evidence particularly when the individual and his group are thrown from undifferentiated, tradition-patterned, so-called primitive life-conditions into the more complex, autonomy-oriented conditions of a modern technologically oriented society.

Table 2 Genuine Feeblemindedness as Compared with Secondary Retardation

Criterion of Comparison	Genuine Feeblemindedness	Social Retardation	Cultural Retardation
1 Ego-weakness	The feebleminded has only a 'mirror-ego', his reactions are unstructured and unselective, he does not use defences. Hence, it would be more correct to speak in this case of 'absence' of the ego as coordinating center of consciousness.	Externalization processes characteristic of this variety produce, among other symptoms, a sort of impersonal generalization of the ego, the tendency to perceive 'ego-vestiges' in every material, human, processional phenomenon. The ego's organizational power is extremely weak (see 12).	Individuation is partial only, insofar as the individual lives in the illusion of communication with his cultural (group) past. Egoity is therefore dangerous since it would mean the end of this illusion of oneness. Hence also the extreme vulnerability.

Criterion of Comparison	Genuine Feeblemindedness	Social Retardation	Cultural Retardation
2 Ecogen-tricity	Since the ego is replaced by a 'mirror-ego' we cannot speak, in this case, of egocentricity.	Since, in this case, the 'haveable' contents of the external reality are in the center of consciousness, we cannot speak, here, of egocentricity.	Egocentricity seems to be contrary to the illusion of oneness with the cultural past and its values. But since the cultural values are, in this case, not experienced as objects of polar relationship but as 'mine', the culturally retarded is nevertheless highly egocentric.
3 Rigidity	Rigidity is here the outcome and the main symptom of a structural defect. Its most characteristic manifestation is perseveration (which must *not* be interpreted as a defense mechanism).	Although the socially retarded is fixated to what he believes is known to him, his orientation to the ever-changing 'haveable' prevents rigidity: he is inconsistent rather than rigid.	The culturally retarded tends to link everything with a (distorted) cultural past and therefore finds it difficult to modify or reverse values and laws, once he has learned them. He learns and thinks in patterns and is therefore extremely rigid in his judgment and behavior.
4 Differentiation-Failure	The structurally weak memory-span of the feebleminded (which is the result of cerebral polarization-defects) makes differentiation almost impossible.	The illusion of knownness in a limited reality-area (which is the result of lack of relational and cognitive initiative and courage) prevents inner tensions and limits the scope of experience. As a result, the ability to differentiate, both in the cognitive and the relational fields, remains undeveloped.	Every task requiring differentiation is experienced as a threat to the illusion of 'oneness' with the cultural past and is therefore avoided even when the intelligence is normal at the start. Non-differentiation here serves as a defence.
5 Relation-ship-Failure	The ability to establish and maintain truly polar relationships with the human environment is structurally weak (although the submissive type	The limited ability to see otherness as requiring polar relationships is in this case due to the weakness of early experience of regularity in the mother-	Fixation to the values of the cultural past and inability to translate them into those of the changed present lead to frequent misunderstandings or

Criterion of Comparison	Genuine Feeblemindedness	Social Retardation	Cultural Retardation
	may give the impression of being capable of positive, the aggressive and the paranoid types of negative relationships).	child relationships. To some extent it can be restored through consistent reconditioning.	even distortions of the human objects of possible relationship. This and the forementioned factors reinforce each other.
6 Expectation of change	Since for the feebleminded everything that occurs is taken for granted and is not ruled by inner logic, changes cannot be expected (this holds good also for the paranoid type who persistently 'expects' being treated injustly).	The socially retarded is 'chance-addicted'. Change is constantly possible, though not as the result of personal initiative. This produces a false feeling of security.	Change, and only to the better, is expected to occur one day, not as the result of active egoparticipation but as the return of the glorious past. Change means disappearance of tension, of failure, of inequality (which, meanwhile, provoke resentment only).
7 Attitudes toward Failure and Success (Learning)	The reactions of the feebleminded are determined by his type-condition rather than by experience: apathy, dependence, impulsive aggressiveness or self-inflation and accusation or suspiciousness. He will not be able to learn from failure or success.	Failure and success are measured by the criteria of immediate satisfaction only. There is no difference for the socially retarded between failure and success caused by chance or by ego-activities. Hence, his intelligence is not challenged by the outcome of his actions. But he is capable of learning the true causal connections if he is given the chance of consistent contact with a meaningful educator.	Failure is rationalized as proof of discrimination by the 'new' environment: success is experienced as proof of the latent superiority of his cultural group. Much energy is wasted in these rationalizations and self-inflations which, then, is not available for meaningful acts of learning.
8 Time-Conception	The present only can be experienced as real, owing to the structurally weak memory-span. Past and future are replications, as it were, of the present.	Although a past can be remembered and a future imagined, as different from the present, the socially retarded will find it difficult to understand the dynamic (causal) connection between past, present and future (see 9).	Here, the 'real time' is that of a quasi-remembered past, whereas the present is experienced as 'temporary' only and therefore as non-committing. The future is experienced as a restituted past and therefore potentially present (see 9).

Criterion of Comparison	Genuine Feeblemindedness	Social Retardation	Cultural Retardation
9 Conception of Cause	Causal links between events and between factors or phenomena are not understood; they may be replaced by type-conditioned modes of interpretation, particularly in the paranoid type.	Every occurrence is accepted as possible. To the extent that the socially retarded feels the need for 'explaining' as occurrence, his causal constructions are based on associations rather than on understanding.	The illusion of temporal oneness (with the past) accounts for distortions of causal connections: certain events 'must' occur 'because' they are felt to have once been realities.
10 Attitude towards the 'new'	The feebleminded is unable to apperceive anything new as such because everything is unknown to him (unfamiliar) whereas newness presupposes awareness of the difference between the familiar and the new.	Since everything is experienced as 'haveable', newness can be eliminated by having. Moreover, the illusion of knownness within the narrow 'moratory' area of the immediate environment also prevents awareness of the 'new' and adequate adaptation to it.	Relating every new experience to some sort of group-determined pattern prevents the culturally retarded from recognizing anything new in its specific context and significance and from reacting to it adequately. Newness disturbs his mind insofar as it is in opposition to his illusion of oneness.
11 Attitude towards Universally Valid Laws	Since everything that occurs is isolated from all other occurrences, the concept of a universally valid law is meaningless.	Here, it is the generalized 'haveability' with its equalizing and de-differentiating effect that makes the conception of universally valid laws impossible.	The culturally retarded resists the social demands for universally valid laws (both in the social and the cognitive sense of the word), since accepting it would mean the end of his illusion of oneness with his cultural past. For him, 'universality' is a given, not a result of abstractions.
12 Personification as Cognitive Modality	He is not structured enough to use personifications, though he does use concretization.	Externalization expressing itself *inter alia* in a kind of ego-diffusion within the non-ego (see 1). he sees everything 'personified', though this modality of perception does not commit him to polar relationships.	Personification here serves as a means to avoid the use of concepts (which would require so much 'retreat' from concrete givens and so much separation and differentiation that the 'illusion of oneness'

Criterion of Comparison	Genuine Feeblemindedness	Social Retardation	Cultural Retardation
			would become questionable). Personification also serves as a means of experimenting with egoity, again by way of avoiding abstraction (perhaps a beginning of projection?).
13 Dichotomization as a Cognitive Modality	He is not differentiated enough even for this primitive way of organizing his experience.	The world is divided into what is available and what is wanting but haveable. All criteria of division are external only.	The divisions of reality are those between 'my own' and 'the stranger' and between 'present' and 'absent' (without qualitative differentiation).
14 Faulty Generalization	Since the reality of the feebleminded is one of disconnected details only, he is incapable of generalization. Every isolated phenomenon is liable to appear to him, under certain (unpredictable) circumstances, as 'general'.	One could call pseudo-generalization what has been described above as the illusion of 'haveability'. It includes the inability objectively to consider individual varieties and variations. As a result, thinking tasks will not arouse his interest or initiative.	Generalization expresses itself in this case as a tendency to isolate one aspect of a given phenomenon and to 'raise' it to the level of 'essential' (general) traits (to the extent that it fits into the cultural patterns). Presence and absence of this 'general' trait are the only valid criteria of application (see 13).
15 Imitation	Since a mirror-ego (see 1) has no intention or initiative, it would not be correct to speak in this case of imitations. Their place is taken by automatic reactions.	Imitation serves (mainly) to *establish* contact with the haveable, as if imitating a person who 'has' something leads to having it.	Imitation here operates on two fronts: the culturally retarded imitates those of his group (thereby learning his cultural pattern) and those in his (alien) environment (thereby establishing the illusion of adaptation).
16 Manipulation	Manipulation of reality too, is replaced by automatic reactions.	Manipulating the universe of environmental objects, figures and chance events *supports* the illusion of haveability.	Manipulation of the environment here serves the purpose of establishing the illusion of *knownness and mastery*.

Criterion of Comparison		Genuine Feeblemindedness	Social Retardation	Cultural Retardation
17	Stereo-typiza-tion	The place of stereo-types is taken, in this case, by persevera-tions	Stereotypes here serve the purpose of *main-taining* the illusion of haveability or even of having something.	Stereotypes here serve the purpose of estab-lishing the illusion of *familiarity* with a basically incomprehen-sible environment.
18	SUMMARY	Structural polariza-tion defects account for rigidity, empti-ness, absence of de-fences, of fixations, of distortions, replace-ment of structuriza-tion by habit-forma-tion and automatic-ness of reactions. No value orientation.	Inconsistency rather than rigidity; chance-addiction, ego-diffu-sion, inadequacy in all cognitive and behavioral areas due to externalization char-acterize this variety of retardation. The cen-tral value is the have-able. Conditioning is responsible for the emergence of attitudes and patterns of behavior.	The culturally re-tarded feels the need to defend his basic illusion of oneness with the cultural past and therefore lives in constant tension. Dis-tortion of reality, rationalization and defences, vulnerability alongside with ego-emphasis make his behavior similar to that of a neurotic.

CHAPTER FOUR

Mixed Types of Secondary Retardation

1 COMBINATION OF ENVIRONMENTAL FACTORS

THE COMPARATIVE TABLE will have made it clear that our analysis so far referred but to ideal types. In reality, these types are represented by *approximations* only to those ideal types. But unfortunately (unfortunately for the sake of conceptual clarity as well as of educational effectiveness), ideal types are represented in reality also by *mixtures* only: in every form of behavior (in our case of the different types of intellectually impaired individuals), symptoms of other units of behavior can be found as well. On the etiological level, we will then find a similar mixture, that is, co-existence of partial causes which, ideally, are held responsible each for one specific behavioral unit only.

Obviously, the definition and formulation of unequivocal and generally applicable educational instructions or of guiding principles for re-educational or therapeutic practice, thus, become almost impossible. This, however, may be an asset rather than a liability: it keeps us aware of the need for individualization of methods, for spontaneity of reactions, whenever we deal with the practical implications of differences in the light of our preceding phenomenological analysis of, and comparison between, ideal types.

Etiological and not only symptomatological considerations are required to understand the intricacies and even the contradictions in each specific behavioral unit or sub-unit. Elsewhere we have maintained that the laws of causal configuration apply primarily to the individual case and not to what is usually called a clinical picture. With regard to the latter, we said, etiology should be concerned with the definition and analysis of *essential* causal elements rather than with discovering in which way partial causes are interlinked with each other and depend on their antecedents and their results [24].

In the preceding chapter, we have applied this statement, to some extent at least, to the problem here discussed, that of the varieties of mental dysfunctioning. Some of the ways in which certain causal elements are responsible for certain manifestations of unintelligent behavior have been mentioned. These are: structural polarization defects, lack of adequate educational stimulation, externalization under conditions of extreme poverty and educational neglect, with its relative impersonality of relationships, fixatedness to the patterns of the cultural past and ambiguity of values and value-clashes in cultural transition. The question of how certain behavioral traits are specifically connected with one or the other of these causal factors requires, of course, a simultaneous discussion of the corresponding question, namely, why they *fail* to appear under other causal conditions.

Such an analysis, however, should serve as an introduction only to our main problem: how the co-existence of characteristics of different behavioral units or sub-units *in an individual case* can be interpreted and understood as the outcome of a corresponding co-existence (and co-operation) of different essential causes, and what this means for education and re-education.

In secondary retardation the cognitive and behavioral picture shows less signs of rigidity, of perseveration and of automatic reactions, those typical symptoms of structural defects in differentiation and polarization. Paucity of environmental stimulation, the poverty-and-neglect variety of externalization, fixation to a cultural past and value ambiguity in periods of cultural transition sometimes operate, it is true, in isolation but more frequently in configuration. As causal factors of secondary retardation, however, they require the cooperation of at least one other variable, that of the impersonality in the primary family relationships.

Impersonality may be characteristic of a *highly stimulating, mobility-oriented family environment within an unequivocal cultural environment*. Obviously, it will then *not* produce secondary retardation; it may be responsible for the emergence of compulsion-like rigidity, particularly in life-situations in which differential feelings are of the essence, but it will not affect the *level* of intellectual functioning. The latter may even be exceptionally high, for instance when it is cultivated, as it were, by the environment and/or by personal ambitions, as an instrument of social mobility and achievement.

Absence of environmental stimulation, on the other hand, will tend to reinforce the negative impact of impersonality on the free development of intellectual capacities, whatever the social or the cultural orientation of the group may be.

When the cultural situation is characterized by *value-ambiguity* and value clashes, impersonality is likely to prevent cultural ambiguity from exercising its destructive influence: a child growing up in an impersonal family-atmosphere is not likely to be affected very deeply by the experience of contradictions between his family's value-orientation and that prevailing in the general culture.

This refers, of course, only to those cases in which impersonality is *not* of the externalization type. A combination of these two factors (*impersonality and externalization through poverty*) makes secondary retardation of the social variety almost unavoidable, as we have tried to show elsewhere [26] when discussing the impact of poverty on the child's development. In this case, the addition of value ambiguity is liable not only to produce what we have analyzed as the cultural variety of retardation but also to re-inforce the destructive effect of poverty and impersonality on primary relationships.

What is liable to happen when externalization and value ambiguity operate either in isolation or in combination without the factor of impersonality in the family relationships being in evidence.

It can, of course, be argued that externalization in its pure form *implies* impersonality and that where the family atmosphere in which a child grows up is one of strong interpersonal relationships, the then inevitable ambivalence-tensions *prevent* the emergence of extreme pathogenic forms of externalized behavior. To the extent that poverty and the parents' orientation towards the haveable do produce some kind of externalized behavior in spite of strong interpersonal relationships, it is likely to be not only less extreme but also more ambiguous. The narrow area of the known may, under such conditions as well, serve as a focus of fixation and refuge, no less than under extreme conditions of impersonality in the family relationships; but it is likely to bear a less illusional and a more realistic character. Relational abilities will remain more differentiated to the extent that the *parents* remain personally identifiable persons. Hence, the chances are better for the child to remain on, or near, the level of his intelligence-potential. Active and meaningful relationships with the parents and the relative security resulting from them will make it easier for such a child to understand the causal and temporal connections between events and between phenomena, to use less personifications (which, we suggest, are an indirect result of early experience of impersonality and relational disability).

Another example of pathogenic constellations in which impersonality may not be a decisive factor is that of the combined impact of poverty and cultural ambiguity in a value-clash situation. To the extent that the parents here 'mean' the child, and the child feels the need for referring to them whatever he learns in terms of contents and values, it is precisely this more or less intimate relationship between the child and the parents that will then account for a frequently observed intensification of personal conflicts within his soul, resulting, in turn, from the experience of value ambiguities. It is as if, under such conditions, the parents felt they must enhance the cultural values of their past in the eyes of the child: in this way they try to remain for them meaningful images of identification. It is as if they felt they must make up for their relative inability to guide the child effectively in his learning experiences (inside and outside the school). They will try to do this by presenting the past as a lost paradise, thus alluding, or even emphasizing that it was (and is) superior to the new culture, in which the child might be able to move and orient himself more easily than they.

The outcome of this combination of factors is liable to be a tendency in the child either to distort his learning contents, under the influence of parental associations, recollections and phantasies, or to waste valuable mental energy on efforts to resist his ineffective parents' conceptions and values. In both cases, intelligence is bound to get lost, though the manifestations of the here-resulting secondary retardation may not be identical with those appearing in our comparative table under the heading of cultural retardation—an ideal type construction which refers to the adult's rather than to the child's patterns of thinking and operating, and to the cultural ambiguity factor in isolation. The two decisive modifiers of this ideal-type syndrome of cultural retardation are:

1) The fact that the developing child is exposed, in each phase of his mental functioning, not only to his parents' value-orientation but at the same time also to the divergent factors of socialization operating in the environment;

2) The impact of the parents' orientation towards the haveable on their reality-distorting tendency to idealize and glorify their cultural past.

Formal and informal, directed and 'occurring' learning-processes within a non-family, or even an anti-family, environment supply the growing child with values and information; they may not only inadequately be received or distorted under the influence of parental patterns and thus produce the syndrome of cultural retardation; they may also help develop at least potentially positive attitudes and more adequate modes of cognitive functioning. To the extent that the *school is aware* of its duty to refer to, and to correct, family-and-culture-induced patterns of thinking and problem-solving in these pupils, to this extent may the family-influence be counteracted, in part at least. The common denominator onto which counteractive influences could be brought, is: a systematic attempt to confront the culturally conditioned patterns of thinking (such as: faulty conceptions of time and cause, faulty attitudes towards change or failure, towards the ego and the non-ego) with their adequate counterparts.* To the extent that the *individual pupil becomes thereby aware* of the essential differences that exist between the two systems of values and patterns, it is this *awareness* that accounts for the modifications of the ideal-type characteristics of cultural retardation (as specified in our comparative table), provided, we must add, the awareness is genuine and not affective, is based on objective confrontation and not on depreciation, shame- and guilt-feelings.

It is self-evident that tension and doubt in this case no longer allow for naïve identification with the values of a cultural past, and that, as a result, the achievements and the failures of the present can no longer be ascribed to transpersonal factors only. A vague feeling of personal responsibility may account for the emergence of inferiority-reactions and shame, obviously to the detriment of simple affect-solutions of one kind or another. Imitative tendencies may, and indeed will, now often result in superficial and frequently changing identifications. The use of magic-like manipulations will tend to be replaced by belief in techniques; resistance to the recognition of universally valid laws (as a means to maintain the illusion of oneness)—by defining law as external connection; inability to conceive of change as of a life-inherent principle—by fear and avoidance of change.

But not only the child's experience of the contradictions between values and patterns that prevail within his parental and his wider environment, also the interaction, in the parent's world, of externalization and cultural fixation determine, as we have pointed out, the special variety of cultural retardation liable to emerge under the impact of poverty, value-ambiguity and some kind of personal relation-

---

* Cf. Chapter VII.

ship between the parents and the child. A few examples may suffice here to make this point clear.

We have said that an orientation towards the haveable is the central characteristic of externalized behavior, as it is liable to emerge under conditions of extreme poverty. This attitude is responsible for that peculiar property-feeling *vis-a-vis* values, which can be noticed in many people who suffer from both, poverty and fixation to the past of their culture, particularly after transition to a new and strange environment. Here, we no longer see naïve pride in the cultural heritage and its often disturbing influence on the perception of the present (as described in our ideal-type construction of cultural retardation), but rather a vague feeling of being in possession of the real values, as if they were something haveable. It is this peculiar symptom of externalization that explains the superficiality of identification and the absence of genuine motivation for learning, recognizing and internalizing the contents not only of the 'foreign' present but of the 'own' past as well. It is this externalized attitude towards the old contents that makes learning of new contents so extremely difficult.

Externalization is characterized, *inter alia,* by the fact that 'having' more or less eliminates newness, or, more exactly, the disquieting effect which confrontation with unaccustomed tasks and situations is liable to have on the individual, both in his practical and his cognitive behavior. The externalized individual therefore feels little need for connecting with each other, and thereby distorting, new contents and old ones (traditionally accepted truths, for instance). This is particularly evident in the so-called levantine pattern in which external mastery ('having') replaces genuine confrontation with any task or situation as a new one. (A fact which seems to be of paramount importance for the teacher who must know that rehabilitating the intelligence in these types of pupils require, first and foremost, a change in their way of perceiving knowledge as something haveable—see later).

This does, of course, not exclude the possible danger of (unconscious, pre-conscious and conscious) interferences of true or imagined cultural recollections with the processes of thinking and problem-solving. But under the externalizing conditions of poverty, such interferences will never be capable of effectively counteracting the basic insecurity that is rooted in the child's regularity-defect, in the weakness of his earliest experience of maternal nearness (although, according to our present assumption, family relationships may not be characterized by a high degree of impersonality). Where this condition of basic insecurity prevails, even the interfering cultural associations are liable to be aroused by personal needs rather than by cultural contents whether learned or spontaneously emerging. Lack of differentiation will then have at least one of its roots in this process of translating, as it were, the personal experience of lack of regularity and nearness into the area of cultural recollections where it appears as lack of clarity, syncretistic or analogistic thinking, etc.

Another root of that same lack of differentiatedness is the typically externalized fixation to the narrow area of the known (or what is believed to be known), whereas, ideally, lack of differentiation and of differentiatedness as a characteristic of cultural retardation can be interpreted as a defense against the threat of losing the illusion of oneness with the cultural past (see p. 79). Where the individual is exposed to a combination of both factors, the poverty-type of externalization, on the one hand, and cultural ambiguity and fixation, on the other, retreat into the known serves as an escape mechanism: it allows for escape from the uncomfortable task of differentiation, as required by the new culture, in so far as 'the area of the known' is, at least in part, identical with that of the cultural past (for instance, in ethnically homogeneous neighborhoods).

This, too, can be interpreted as a defense-mechanism. And although the defensive character of this attitude, like every defense, *prevents* rapid, and final, loss of intellectual functioning, it is nevertheless extremely dangerous, precisely because it no longer serves as a defense for the sake of values (though illusional ones: wholeness, unity), but rather as a defense against objectively justified social demands and pressures. Again, the educational conclusions seem to be self-evident (see later).

Another area of comparison is that of rigidity. This essential symptom of intellectual dysfunctioning appears in genuine feeble-mindedness as an epiphenomenon of structural insufficiency and in so-called cultural retardation—as defensive clinging to certain patterns of thinking and behaving. Rigidity of both types is, as we have pointed out, contrasted by inconsistency in the externalization-variety of secondary retardation. Where the two conditions of cultural ambiguity and externalization meet, we often witness a *prima facie* self-contradictory pattern of rigid adherence to frequently changing principles or to different forms of cognitive behavior—lack of identity combined with sticking to any (more or less accidentally found) position. It is this seemingly self-contradictory pattern that accounts for the superficiality and the non-committal nature of conceptualization in the thinking processes of adults and children when they are exposed to the here discussed pathogenic condition.

Closely connected with inconsistency are certain other symptoms of social retardation, such as chance-addiction, an associative approach to temporal or causal connections and ego-diffusion.

Belief in the omnipotence of chance and the false security resulting from it are bound not only to weaken the individual's initiative and responsibility for success and failure in his practical tasks, they also account for the decisive role of associative thinking in his cognitive behavior. When these attitudes merge with belief in the omnipotence of a cultural past, we often find strong resentments accompanying or directing thinking processes and serious limitations of causal understanding as the result of affective expectations.

All characteristics of secondary retardation operate, under the impact of poverty *and* cultural ambiguity, as impediments of learning: the illusion of being able to have a truth by way of imitation or manipulation (instead of recognizing or finding it); the tendency to divide the universe of factors into two parts and to experience them as present or absent (instead of relating to them as being 'there', independent, objective challenges to the subject's cognitive initiative); the tendency to prevent and to avoid conceptualization by use of ego-diffusion and personifications, that is, by way of eliminating the essential *difference* between subject and object, between the personal and the non-personal. But not only the abstraction type of learning, processes of learning through being conditioned as well are liable to be impaired when naïve reactivity to the multitude of haveable objects is limited by culture-conditioned resentment and by defensive distortion of their reality meaning.

We must not lose sight of the third part of our initial hypothesis, namely, that it is possible to envisage a combination of social and cultural deficiencies with relative intactness of intra-family relationships. This hypothesis seems to contain a *contradictio in adjecto*, insofar as externalization is, by definition, based on weakness of personal relationships between the mother and the infant (and on the resulting lack of early regularity-experience). We should, however, bear in mind that this condition of externalization is present in degrees only (thus accounting for different intensity-degrees of externalization), and that it does not automatically determine later developments. Once we leave the field of ideal-type constructions, we must remain aware of the multitude of individual varieties that are likely to result not only from different causal configurations at the *beginning* of life but also from *later* changes. Intensification of personal relationships between the parents and the growing child, in other words, more or less partial replacement of early impersonality by later emphasis on the intimacy of family relationships is not only imaginable, it is often found; it accounts for those numerous cases in which externalization—particularly when configurated with cultural ambiguity and/or fixation—becomes less decisive for the intellectual development of a child and does not exclude later change in the family atmosphere; it justifies the optimistic belief in the reversibility of intellectual impairments caused by those factors we have had in mind in our present analysis.*

Our initial analysis was therefore incomplete, since it did not sufficiently take into consideration the fact that the cognitive qualities described as the result of externalization and cultural ambiguity may actually appear modified already under the impact of a more personal nature of family-relationships, particularly in the later phases of the child's development. This impact is felt, first and foremost, in the important role of inner tensions that often accompany the individual's inadequate thinking process, as well as in the relatively strong feelings of personal involvement (though they may not arouse initiative or responsibility).

And again, we shall have to bear this factor in mind when analyzing the *individual* varieties of secondary retardation and the methods of educational rehabilitation.

2 INADEQUATE STIMULATION

But before entering this field of 'individual varieties', we must discuss a number of additional combinations of factors. Let us start with an analysis of the factor called 'inadequate educational stimulation by the environment'.

This concept is highly ambiguous and covers a great variety of factors, different from each other in the effect they have on the developing child, not only owing to the degree of intensity and exclusivity at which they operate, but also depending on the child's needs. *The environment may be objectively poor in educational stimuli* and yet adequate, when the cultural expectations are low, as is the case in many isolated cultural sub-groups. The then resulting

* See also Chapter 5.

intellectual retardation differs from the so far discussed forms by its generality and by the absence of cultural tensions and insufficiencies, frustrations and personal sufferings that are inherent elements in all forms of secondary retardation in our culture.—An individual child *may need a particularly high degree of educational stimulation* in order to be able to make adequate use of his potentials, for instance, when he is very passive, either constitutionally or reactively; for him, an otherwise adequate educational stimulation may be insufficient, but the then resulting form of mental retardation will again be different from those we have in mind here, in our analysis of the secondary (socio-cultural) forms.—The educational inadequacy of environmental stimulations may be *compensated by the initiative of the family*, which, in this way, may be capable of preventing socio-cultural retardation, particularly in societies or in historical periods in which the family has not yet entirely surrendered its functions to the institutes of formal education. It goes without saying that in this case the result will *not* be secondary retardation.

In discussing the role of inadequate stimulation in secondary retardation, we have in mind, first and foremost, the child born with normal intellectual potentials who grows up under conditions conducive to the development of a basic sense of trust, to identification with, and internalization of, parental values and to the emergence of relative autonomy, but who, at a later stage of his development, does not receive that amount of educational and cultural stimulation either from his parents or his school that he needs to enlarge his consciousness and to maintain and strengthen his intellectual functions.

These less extreme cases are much more frequently found in so-called developing countries, in countries of immigration or under conditions of poverty than the hitherto described forms of impaired development and functioning. The difference is most clearly evident in the more courageous reactions of the individual to his learning tasks, in his greater ability to bear frustration in the case of failure, to accept his limitations, to adapt himself to changing situations. There is much more family-cohesion manifesting itself in his readiness to share experience, to learn from others and consequently to accept otherness objectively though it may not be comprehensible. There is often a naïve unawareness of generalities and failure to solve a problem that requires abstraction.

A child growing up under such conditions, though bound to fail in school and to be diagnosed as intellectually weak, will not so easily glide into irreversible feeblemindedness as the one who is exposed to the externalizing conditions of a life in poverty and neglect. His inner ties with the family keep alive his relational ability as well as his value-awareness. As a result, he will remain much more responsive to educational and re-educational interventions and will show essential differences in his mental make-up when compared with the ideal or the mixed types of secondary retardation.

Thus, he will be protected, to some degree, against the danger of indiscriminate imitation, since his family-ties provide him with at least the rudiments of an objective value-orientation; on the other hand, the insufficiency and inadequacy of learning-facilities and of guidance that characterize in this case the child's development are responsible for the narrow limits of this orientation.—He will be in a position to recognize differences, to respond to newness and to discover the existence and the intelligibility of objective laws, though only through the medium of associations with his narrow areas of knownness (his family and his neighborhood).—He will be less prone to use dichotomizations and false generalizations as instruments of organizing his reality; he will be capable of seeing and appreciating nuances, though only if properly guided.

On the other hand, he resembles the ideal type of cultural retardation in that he, too, will often use stereotypes, personification and external manipulation instead of concepts and causal categories of interpretation. The intellectual limitation that results from insufficiency of learning and guidance does not allow for adequate differentiation. When faced with tasks of conceptual thinking and learning, he, too, will still prefer belief in a solution occurring from without to individual responsibility for discovering such a solution.

In other words: although his sense of security, his relational ability to accept otherness are, at least potentially, well developed (due to the family-cohesiveness), he is unable freely to use these potentialities when faced with a learning task that requires knowledge, differentiation and abstraction, unless he is consistently supported by an adequate, that is, object-and-family-oriented school-program.

Let us now summarize what we have discussed so far in this part of the fourth chapter. First we have mentioned, though in passing only, the possible effects on intellectual functioning of relative *impersonality* of family relationships, when there exists, and when there does not exist, adequate *stimulation* in the wider environment, or when the family lives under conditions of *cultural ambiguity*, *without* the simultaneous effect of poverty and externalization. Then we asked what was liable to happen to a child's intellectual functions whose parents, though exposed to the impact of *poverty*, had not lost their ability to maintain more or less *personal relationships* with each other and with the child. At some length we then discussed the characteristics of secondary retardation as they are liable to emerge under the *combined impact of externalization and cultural ambiguity*, when family relationships are *not* characterized by extreme impersonality (unlike in the ideal-type constructions of the preceding paragraph). An analysis of the concept of *non-stimulation* and its effects was added, the assumption being that lack of stimulation may operate in isolation, that is, without being reinforced by externalization and/or cultural ambiguity.

3 STRUCTURAL DEFECTS AND SECONDARY RETARDATION

In all our discussions of mixed types of secondary retardation, the factor of structural deficiencies has been neglected, although it undoubtedly represents an important co-determinant of every combination of environmental causes. Whatever the level of family cohesion and of personal relationships in the family, whatever the degree of externalization and/or cultural ambiguity may be, the normality or deficiency of the individual child's structure plays a decisive role in the outcome, both quantitatively and qualitatively.

The concept of structural defect is not synonymous with that of brain injury, although we are more likely to discover some form of cerebral disorder in the more extreme cases of structural defect. The latter concept is wider than that of brain injury, since it covers also those cases in which no physiological corollary of the defective cognitive behavior can be found or shown. In fact, in most cases of genuine congenital feeblemindedness, no such proof can be adduced (so that no more than one out of five cases can be diagnosed definitely and precisely, as the students of these varieties of impaired intelligence tell us—see, e.g., 37, p.2).

But when we call a cognitive defect structural, we nevertheless tend to link it with certain (presumed) deficiencies in the functioning of the brain and particularly in what Rothschild has described as polarization-processes. According to him, it is the relationship and tension between the neural representatives of internal and external reality, of subject and object, of self and world, that makes experience possible. The various disturbances of the normal relationship between opposite poles in the brain-structure are held responsible for a *number* of behavior disorders, each one in a functionally specific way [46]. What characterizes feeblemindedness is the form of the polarization defect, which here results from *non-differentiation in each of the two poles* or cerebral representatives of the inner and the outer world, the ego and the non-ego. In other words: defective polarization is, in this case, due to a primary integrational weakness and impotence of each of the partners of inner relationship and experience rather than—as in other disorders—to a distortion of their partnership.

This is the actual meaning of the causal factor here under discussion. It accounts, as we have elaborated in the first chapter, for the essential characteristics of genuine feeblemindedness: lack of structure and selectivity, automatism of reactions, perseverative rigidity, inability to differentiate and to establish truly polar relationships with the outer or the inner non-ego, with the natural and social environment or the world of phantasies, the unconscious; it accounts for the weakness of the memory-span and the implied inability to see events in their proper time-perspective (the one-dimensionality of time), for the typically feebleminded weakness of causal thinking, of understanding universally valid laws or the meaning of newness; it accounts for the 'relative inability to compare actual with hypothetical or anticipated situations, as a cause of intellectual failure' (p. 15).

The causal connection between structural polarization defects in feeblemindedness and its cognitive and behavioral manifestations is complicated, as we have tried to show, by another structural determinant, that of type-conditioned reaction-patterns. They can be defined as the introvert or the extravert varieties of intensity-constellations between the two life tendencies (towards expansion or staticness). Although the four patterns, described as aggressive, suspicious, submissive and apathetic (see pp. 15 ff.), may be the results of interaction between structural and experimental determinants, it would seem safe to presume that the causal weight of environmental factors and individual reactions to them is in direct proportion to the innate level of intelligence: the lower the intelligence, the more decisive tend to become structural factors of determination such as type-differences, and the less important are experiences in the causal equation of the cognitive and behavioral outcome. In fact, this may be the major contribution of the intelligence level to the causal equations in genuinely feebleminded individuals: that it determines the relative weight of experience and of early structurization—in contradistinction of secondary varieties of impairment and dysfunction, in which structural factors operate as modifiers and qualifiers of experiential causes rather than as primary determinants.

Here, however, the question of the causal role of structural determinants is raised not in a discussion of genuine feeblemindedness but of secondary retardation. How are the typical expressions of that variety which we have analyzed and defined as the result of a combined impact of poverty and cultural ambiguity liable to be modified by a—more or less—defective structure?

This question is far from being a purely academic one; the reversibility of secondary retardation, the chances of rehabilitating an environmentally impaired intelligence and of raising limited potentials to their congenital level, largely depends on the *absence* of such structural defects.

And yet, it is a well-known fact that under conditions of extreme poverty, the birth-hazards and the danger of, at least minor, brain lesions are great. This increased risk is due to socially conditioned impairments of the pregnant woman's health and to often unavoidable irregularities in the birth process. The risk is still more increased by the factor of communication-handicaps under conditions of cultural transition.*

It is therefore not surprising to find in many cases of secondary retardation admixtures of genuine feeblemindedness. How do these admixtures manifest themselves in the cognitive behavior of children and adults? In other words: how are the characteristics of thinking, as we have analyzed them before, modified by those of feeblemindedness due to *structural* polarization defects? Since poverty is the decisive causal factor responsible for the possible increase in traumatic birth risks, we can formulate our question as follows: how are the essential characteristics of the ideal type of social retardation (see column two in our second comparative table) *modified* by those of genuine feeblemindedness (see column one in that table)? In terms of differential diagnosis the question would again be different: how can we distinguish, on the basis of a phenomenological analysis, between purely secondary retardation and cases in which

* Reference is made in this context to the research carried out under the guidance of Prof. Alfred Freedman, New York Medical College.

structural defects add an element of rigidity and automaticness to the manifestations of the former?

We do not suggest one single, quantitative, criterion of differentiation, such as the number of rigidity-symptoms indicating either genuine or secondary retardation. No such quantitative reduction would do justice to the multitude of differences between the various forms of impaired intellectual functioning, as we have tried to analyze them in the preceding paragraphs.

Thus, it is not only the *number* of personifications in the answers given to test-questions but the *type* of personifications that allows for differential diagnosis: when personifications bear the traits of others rather than of the self, the likelihood of genuine feeblemindedness increases.

Similarly, the ego will be emphasized in both, genuine and secondary retardation; but the less 'having' will be emphasized as a value, the more will ego-emphasis indicate genuine feeblemindedness.

Signs of perseverative, but at the same time, non-selective, reaction to changing stimuli of 'haveability' shows feeblemindedness, whereas inconsistency of reactions proves secondary retardation.

To what extent, we should ask, is the retarded child capable of remembering details of his 'area of the known'? To what extent can he learn regularity from his illusions of knownness? The more he *is* able to remember and to learn, the less will his dysfunction indicate genuine feeblemindedness.

Can the child be reconditioned into confidence and, thus, into relationships, we should ask. The answer obviously will be more reliable, when it can be based on observation of behavior in learning —than in practical situations. A higher incidence of type-conditioned reactions will indicate feeblemindedness, with its lower accessibility to reconditioning.

To what extent is chance experienced as enjoyable occurrence and everything is expectable? To what extent serves chance as a 'substitute of logic' as in genuine feeblemindedness?

Can the child learn the difference between outcomes of chance and of ego-activity? Can he learn initiative through consistent contact with meaningful educators? Absence of such learning obviously indicates primary feeblemindedness. The submissive type has better chances than all the others to 'learn' initiative, although even with him it will never be a genuine and reliable learning-process.

To what extent has the child some time-perspective, beyond the dimension of the present? The more understanding he shows for the difference between remembrance, experience and expectation (though he may not be able to feel the causal implications of this difference), the less will a diagnosis of true feeblemindedness be justified.

Causal or quasi-causal thinking is in the feebleminded a function of his type-condition, particularly in the paranoid or the submissive varieties, whereas, in secondary retardation, it is always connected with some sort of (changing) associations and is therefore bound to be less stereotyped, less patterned.

To experience an event or an object or a quality as 'new' will be difficult for anyone of impaired intelligence. However, if we want to find out to what extent structural deficiencies aggravate (and modify) a case of secondary (social) retardation, we should try to find out whether a feeling of unfamiliarity or an illusion of knownness in a moratory area of the 'haveable' accounts for this inability to experience anything as new. Unfamiliarity with the world, as a rule justifies the presumption that there exists some structural defect in the cognitive structure of the individual.

This very feeling of unfamiliarity is closely connected with failure to see reality-phenomena in a context, while seeing them as equally possible objects of having (in the social variety of secondary retardation) creates some kind of connection, illusory as it may be.

And finally, we may say that symptoms of personification, dichotomization, intentional imitation and manipulation, as well as the conscious use of stereotypes indicate relative absence of genuine feeblemindedness, which will manifest itself in concretization, automatic mirroring, lack of initiative and lack of intentionality.

PART TWO

The Function of the School in the Rehabilitation of Intelligence

CHAPTER FIVE

Autonomy and Anonymity

Some Basic Concepts

1 INTRODUCTION

THE IMPORTANCE OF schooling increases in direct proportion to the failure of so many parents to make themselves felt as integrating forces in the development of their children. Society has not yet recognized this fact and has, in any case, failed to provide evidence of its much vaunted respect for the teaching profession by granting its members adequate social status.

For a large proportion of our present-day school population, and in certain social strata or cultural groups even for the majority of the pupils, teaching becomes meaningful only to the extent that it is based on a thorough integration in the teaching methods of: (a) understanding the cultural patterns and the family background which determine the child's associations and reactions, and (b): insight into the thought-processes characteristic of various age-groups in various cultures.

We further maintain that, the vital contribution of mental hygiene in the class-room notwithstanding, the elementary school teacher of our generation—and particularly the one who has to teach children from so-called 'primitive' backgrounds or from socially or culturally under-privileged families—must take cognizance of the intimate connection that exists between the relational (interpersonal) ability, or lack of ability, of the child, and his conceptual ability, or lack of ability. The time has come, so it seems to us, when the mental hygiene movement should be supplemented by what we propose to call an intellectual hygiene movement, to be based on depth-psychology, anthropology, culture analysis, psychology of thinking and a comprehensive theory of teaching methods.

Any definition of what the school is required and expected to achieve, any evaluation of what it actually achieves, any planning, any revision of methods, should start from an analysis of the essential changes that may have taken place in the society in which the school system operates.

When we speak of 'our' society, we have in mind: firstly, the Western countries in Europe and America with their class-differentiated value patterns and their class-conditioned needs for differential methods of instructions; secondly, the many countries in Africa and some parts of Asia which are in a voluntary or enforced—process of Westernization, of assimilation to 'technical' standards and to the ideals of 'modern' civilization. In spite of the essential differences between these two areas of 'our' society, the school's success or failure to achieve its aim depends in both on the parents' attitude towards the school.

The most important cultural factors which the educator of our times must take into consideration when setting out to determine the role of the school, its aims and its methods, are:

a) The democratic ideal of all social strata participating equally in all courses of learning and in all social functions and areas of production.

b) The influence which technical progress has had on our value system, and in particular the preference for impersonal, anonymous and specialized modes of operation and behavior as against the manifestations of individual identity, of emotional involvement, of phantasy or intuition.

c) The inability of many parents, particularly from the lower classes or from 'primitive' cultural groups, and the unwillingness of many others, particularly from the higher and middle classes, to co-operate with the school and to support the teacher's efforts.

Many of the failures of school instruction can be explained as the result of insufficient regard for these three factors. As a rule, our children are being taught as if the school could rely on adequate support by the parents, as if no difference existed between the members of various social classes—or even of 'primitive' and differentiated cultures—in their mentality, their patterns of thinking and their ability to use abstract operations, and as if we still lived in the nineteenth century.

We find this regrettable lack of cultural differentiation among the educators or new and old nations alike.

We find it in countries with no tradition of formal schooling. They face the difficult task of creating an indigenous school system capable of producing an urgently needed leadership as quickly as possible and without drawing too much on foreign, 'colonial', cultures; while the contents of these cultures are being rejected, the methods used in their schools are often taken over with little, if any, modification.

We find it in old cultures, where the educator is called upon to bridge the gap between the traditional values and patterns, on the one hand, and the requirements of technical advance, on the other. (Although he may consider the 'technological' present definitely inferior to the heritage of his cultural past, he still must serve the former, lest his country lose her economic and political freedom.) Here, again, unsuitable methods of instruction are often copied in complete disregard of the intellectual needs of the pupils in their lonely struggle with abstraction and concept formation.

We find a similar inability to revise our methods of instruction in the light of culture changes and their psychological significance when it comes to an evaluation of our own schools. It is only too well known that our schools fail to produce the manpower which is required for the maintenance of leadership capable of keeping ahead of the totalitarian regimes. Here, the vital question arises: Is it at all possible to produce autonomous leaders in an era in which the school cannot, as a rule, rely on co-operation with the parents of its pupils? And is perhaps a social order of heteronomy the inescapable consequence of the 'decline of the parents'?

We intend to add to the many discussions of this issue, in which social and political philosophers have played a leading part, an analysis based on psychological considerations.

2 AUTONOMY DEFICIENCIES

Autonomy (of thinking, judging, and taking a decision on a course of action) is not explained by saying that it characterizes a certain phase of development, or that it is a function or an element of intelligence. Autonomy, as analysed by Piaget, cannot, it is true, be expected before a certain stage in the child's development is reached; but its basis is laid much earlier—in fact, at the beginning of life—and it may be well developed in children of barely average intelligence.

Autonomy is a function of basic security, which, in turn, depends on the experience of regularity in the child's early relationships with his mother. This experience—which we have described in another place [24] as the experience of 'the mother as the near-one, the one-to-be-expected'—is the precondition of that courage which is needed in any act of ego-transcendence, be it an act of establishing an interpersonal relationship, be it an act of abstracting from reality-contexts for the sake of concept formation or of generalization. For, in every such act, the ego must leave its present position, though for a short time only, by way of experiment, as it were.

Lack of basic security and courage, therefore, finds its expression, *inter alia,* in the reluctance, or even in the inability, of the individual to abandon—temporarily and experimentally—his ego positions, for fear of not finding the 'way back'.

This, however, is the case of those children who fail to experience, at the beginning and in the first years of their life, the reliability and nearness of the mother figure. It happens when the mother is too preoccupied with her own ego—the neurotic, the egoistic, mother, or the one who identifies herself too much with her professional functions—or where conditions of extreme poverty exercise an externalizing influence on the mother and on the family environment as a whole. It may also happen under the influence of certain cultural patterns.

It could be argued that the facts seem to disprove our hypothesis: many thousands of intelligent and creative men and women are known to have been born into conditions which, according to our definition, could not but produce in the child feelings of deep insecurity. Against this argument, which we, indeed, hear more and more frequently in the discussion of child development and mental health, we would point out:

a) that a high level of innate intelligence may protect many children against the destructive influence of environmental frustrations;

b) that even a high level of intellectual functioning does not prove autonomy—we should only think of the many highly intelligent neurotics—whereas true autonomy as already mentioned may be found in many people with only average intelligence;

c) that even a basic insecurity, following traumatic childhood experiences, may slowly give way to less rigid, less defensive, more courageous and more productive attitudes under the influence of consistent training in 'abstract behavior'—to use K. Goldstein's term [29]—provided the early traumatization and ensuing personality disorders were not extreme and therefore irreversible;

d) that even an extremely preoccupied or otherwise seemingly 'unsuitable' mother may succeed in giving her child a feeling of security (compensating environmental or constitutional factors in the child being responsible for the 'unexpected' results);

e) that 'autonomy' should be understood only as an ideal and a yardstick with which to measure individual behavior.

On the other hand, there are many cases in which a child whose basic security was well established and who was well on his way towards autonomy, lost his potentialities at a later stage of his development under the impact of negative environmental conditions, such as inadequate schooling.

With this remark we are back at the main subject of our discussion: What is the school's role in view of the ever-growing number of children who, upon entering school:

i) either do not bring with them that feeling of security which, as we said, is the precondition of autonomy and of the ability to form adequate concepts and to use them freely;

ii) or who cannot count on parental support of their learning experience at school?

As we believe that even in the first case the school can still correct or develop what the parents have spoiled or failed to develop, we shall start with an analysis of the second issue. In order to explain what we understand by 'parental support of the learning experience', we propose to discuss briefly a number of social situations. Our first question will be: what happens to the middle-class child when he starts out on his school-career?

Psychoanalysis speaks of the 'passing of the oedipus-complex' [28] at the age of six, the school-entrance age, when the struggle for the parents as libidinal objects is replaced by their introjection and by the crystallization of the superego. This does not mean that the emotional ties between the child and his parents are now loosened, or even replaced by his interest in learning, on the one hand, and in the 'society of equals', on the other. The contents of the child's relationship with his parents, however, do undergo a decisive change: instead of serving primarily as objects of his affective strivings, they are from now on expected to fulfil an additional function—to help him in the process of forming and expanding his spiritual world; they are expected to confirm and to enlarge the area of his learnings. The child is not interested—as he may be at a later stage of his development—in a 'dethronement' of his parents; he does not want a complete separation between the 'agents' of education, that is, the parents and the teacher. On the contrary, he wants his parents to remain the final and highest authority to confirm the truth of what he learns at school. We could perhaps speak of a process of spiritualization of the oedipal images, at least in the development of the middle-class child of 'our' society.

Now, what happens when these parents fail to live up to their child's expectations? They may be unable to do so because of lack of education; they may be unwilling, because of egoistic or neurotic self-involvements, or because of intensive preoccupation with their work functions to accompany the child in his learning experience. The child is left alone with a world of contents which remain 'unconfirmed', as it were, by his parents. The disappointment which he is then bound to feel and the fear of becoming separated from his parents through the very process of learning may have a most disturbing influence on his scholastic achievements, and, even more important, on the internalization of his concepts.

Precisely because introjection of the parental images is one of the main functions of the post-oedipal phase in the development of the middle-class child, class-room learning, to become internalized requires confirmation by the parents. Every concept, it is true, is already the result of a process of internalization; but when a middle-class child, growing up, as he does, in the intimacy of his family group, suddenly or gradually has to forego the emotional support of his parents in one of his most important activities, his learning, the knowledge and the concepts he acquires are liable to remain, as it were, outside the area of his personal responsibility and initiative, taken over from the outside-area of the class-room and the teacher, but not transformed into integral parts of his inner world. At best, the child may go on absorbing new material, but it is doubtful whether he will ever be able to use what he has learned in an autonomous independent and creative way. [24]

This is the fate of many children in our society. The learning processes have become too complicated for most parents to share in their children's experience beyond the first years of elementary school. It would, however, be sufficient to guarantee a continuity in the life of the child from his early years to the pre-adolescent age—when autonomy of thinking and judging, once established, continues to determine the learning processes—if the parents would accompany the child at least during the first years of schooling. But many middle-class parents fail to fulfil even this relatively easy function adequately.

Tensions and anxieties aroused by political dangers, on the one hand, and the (real or imagined) need for constant competition and achievement, on the other, make them forget and neglect their children's spiritual needs, even though they may take more or less adequate care of their physical needs.

This seems to be one of the main reasons for the failure of so many middle-class children of our generation to learn how to think and act autonomously.*

It will probably be argued that a similar tendency on the part of parents to 'abandon' their child to the school may be noticed in other periods and in other cultures as well. It certainly happens in a 'tradition-directed' society—in D. Riesman's terms [44]—at least when this society uses settings of formal education as a means of socialization. It happens in culture-change situations—for instance, in immigrant transition, when the parents' values may clash with those transmitted by the school. And it happens, though for entirely different reasons, in the poverty-stricken family.

The first case, that of the children in traditional societies, does not disprove our thesis. Even when in such a society the parents delegate their educational power to the school and do not co-operate with the teacher in order to make the learning process more meaningful for the child, they nevertheless make themselves felt very strongly in every minute of his life as the guardians of that tradition in whose name the school operates. There is, therefore, at least by implication, very strong parental support of the school's teaching, although the parents may be unable or unwilling to share in the child's learning experience.

On the other hand, the development of autonomy is not considered one of the major functions of the elementary school in a tradition-directed society. We may find differences—individually and group-wise—in the extent of internalization of traditional values and concepts; but autonomy is not the aim of school-education in this type of society; on the contrary, heteronomy can be considered a necessary concomitant of tradition.

Even when the values of tradition are internalized, they are, as a rule, not being used autonomously. Internalization means—here—

* This, however, is a specific variety of autonomy deficiencies in the child's cognitive pattern (one that we shall not analyse here): strong tendencies to internalize parental images and to repress negative feelings operate simultaneously with equally strong tendencies to replace critical ego-judgment by affect-conditioned opinions or by uncritical subordination under the authority of non-parental figures.

conscious identification and ego-involvement, but not individual decision and initiative. It may well be that the difference between internalized and externalized heteronomy in relation to the contents and values of tradition will be found in many cases to reflect a different degree of identification, on the part of the parents, with what the school is doing in order to transmit those values.

That most immigrant parents are unable to participate in the school's activities is a commonplace. The reasons for this inability (loss of status, adjustment and language difficulties, resistance to the new culture, etc.) are too well known to require detailed discussion here. But what we should emphasize is the fact that the immigrant child's chances of scholastic achievement and of advance towards intellectual and social autonomy, including mastery of abstract thinking, improve when his parents feel neither superior nor inferior to the new culture. Only such parents are able to spare their child the crisis of value clash and tension, only they can remain for him representatives of values, objects of identification and internalization, hence also stimulating forces in his mental development. In a way, they do share in his learning experience, to the extent that they supplement his learning meaningfully from their own cultural and personal experience which they do not distort affectively.

When, on the other hand, the former culture has not been differentiated enough to prepare the parents for an understanding of the learning processes in the 'new' culture, the child is liable to grow up in an atmosphere of uncertainty, of lack of orientation, of a value vacuum, and learning is bound to remain externalized, unrelated to the synthesizing activity of the child's ego, because it remains unrelated to the parents' world.

True externalization, however, is the central characteristic of the learning processes in our third case, in the development of the child who grows up under conditions of extreme poverty and parental neglect. We have explained elsewhere [26] the meaning of the concept of externalization by analysing its 'ideal type', the life-patterns of man-in-poverty. We shall therefore content ourselves here with summarizing some of the main points of that analysis, insofar as they are relevant for an understanding of the function which the school should fulfil in the life of the 'externalized' child.

a) It is a well-known fact that the levels of intelligence are distributed unequally among the various sub-groups of a given population. The percentage of 'low-level' children is considerably higher not only in certain culture- or language-groups than in others, but also, and mainly, in the lower-class economic groups, and, in particular, among the town people of Western society. But it is inadequate to point out the causal connection between poverty or certain cultural patterns, on the one hand, and low intelligence, on the other, as if the mere statement of such a connection already included an interpretation. We must try to consider the question of how certain conditions of life are able and liable to destroy the congenitally given potentialities of millions of men. (There is no reason to accept the alternative explanation of an unequal distribution of intelligence, or rather of abstract abilities; namely, that certain groups are biologically inferior [47].)

b) When we speak here of poverty as of a causal factor, we have in mind its mental, its attitudinal, not its economic aspects. Where extreme economic stress in a family weakens the intensity of the child's relationships with his environment, and particularly with his mother, the feeling of basic security, which normally emerges in the first year of life, is liable not to develop properly; its precondition—the experience of the mother as the near-one, whose regular return can be expected—being absent in many cases of extreme poverty. Without this basic security, however, polarization between the ego and the non-ego as equal and independent partners is bound to be defective. Without such polarization, the growing child will lack that courage which is necessary to experiment with separation, as it were, and to venture into the unknown; he will, instead, tend to remain rigidly fixated to any given situation in which he finds himself by chance, or will loose himself in the non-ego.

This courage 'to experiment with separation', finally, is the necessary precondition of differentiation. Hence the relatively large number of individuals growing up under the impact of poverty who are unable to distinguish properly between ego and non-ego; children and adults alike who may tend to identify a phenomenon on the basis of its similarity with another one, believed to be known, or unable to recognize equality or similarity between equal or similar phenomena when they appear in different contexts.

c) This, then, is what we call inability to think in abstract terms, to differentiate, to understand the significance of universally valid laws regulating thinking and behavior, the inability to operate without being determined by quasi-personal contexts. This, in brief, is low intelligence resulting from environmental deprivation.

It is unnecessary to add that under such conditions the individual may not reach a high level of objectivity, or understand the essentials and the laws of anonymity, so that he will be unable to compete successfully with others in their struggle for social progress. His mind may become more and more geared to the external reality of things, from which he will strive to take what he has not. But he will not acquire that inner security that lies at the basis of objectivity, of looking at reality from a distance, of polarization between ego and non-ego as two equal 'partners'. Thus, he will not be able to learn from his observations; he remains fixated to what he believes is known to him, and it is this very fixation which limits his consciousness still more and weakens still further his ability to think in abstract terms.*

These are, today, some of the social and cultural conditions in which the school fails to fulfil its proclaimed functions, because it does not enjoy the parents' support and 'confirmation', whether they are unable or unwilling to give this support.

But the time has passed when learning and the pursuit of knowledge, when guarding the values of society and directing its course, were considered the right and the duty of a few, coming from the small group of the socially privileged or the most intelligent, who, in any case, as we have already pointed out, are less at the mercy of the hazards of inadequate schooling and lack of parental cooperation. During those times when social participation was governed by the principles of selectivity, the fact was more or less taken for granted that most graduates of elementary schools would not take an active and creative part in the life of society, but would remain heteronomous followers (although then, too, lipservice was paid to autonomy as the highest value of education). Today, however, with the spread of 'the democratic ideal of all social strata participating equally in all courses of learning and in all areas of social production', the failure of the school to live up to this ideal becomes a cause of individual and social disorder, of frustration and despair in the life of millions, and a stumbling-block on the road to social advancement.

But should we really make lack of parental support alone responsible for the failure of the school to prepare its students for creative participation in the execution of their social tasks and functions? Moreover, is autonomy really required in order to be successful in modern society? And should it not be possible to develop without

---

* This does not imply, however, that these deficiencies are irreversible. If what we have said about the problem of structurization and reversibility in the third chapter of Part One (pp. 67 ff.).

the support of the parents those qualities that technology enhances—control over personal involvements, objectivity, ability to behave and to think abstractly and to function under conditions of anonymity?

3 AUTONOMY AND LEARNING

Autonomy has been defined as 'inner control', 'inner direction', 'self-determination', but also as 'obeying the commands, the laws, of inner identity'. While in the first definition the ego is conceived of as being the subject of control, direction and determination, it appears in the last definition as the object, though also as the executing organ of some quasi-metaphysical entity and agent called 'identity' or 'self'.*

We believe that any attempt to understand and to define the ego's (relative) autonomy must start from a recognition of the non-ego's (absolute) autonomy. 'True autonomy', we have said in the book previously mentioned, 'does not mean independence of the non-ego, but it does mean awareness of the non-ego's autonomy ... On the other hand, the concept of heteronomy implies not only the ego's dependence on the non-ego, but also the existence and development of the ego as a separate unit of the psychic structure.' And we continued: 'Autonomy means that the ego is capable of guarding its subject position as an object of the autonomous non-ego.... The simultaneity and exchangeability of these subject-object positions is the structural condition of normal development' [24, p. 34].

There can be no doubt that basic insecurity is liable to block the child's path to autonomy. But it would be wrong to relieve the school of its responsibility as a decisive agent in the development of autonomy, only because the parents may have failed to prepare their child adequately for the tasks of effective learning and thinking with which the school is concerned. On the contrary, its responsibility grows with the ever-increasing number of incompetent parents, originating from, and belonging to, all social strata.

The child of immigrant parents, who may be disoriented in the new society; the child from the urban slum-quarter, who grows up under conditions unfavourable to internalization of concepts and values; the frustrated middle-class child—all of them depend on the

* In Jung's psychology [32] this Self is definitely ego-transcending, whereas most other psychologists conceive of it as being almost identical with the ego, the latter being the subject, the former the object, of ego-contemplation, -evaluation and -direction. See for instance [2].

school for that support and stimulation which the parents have failed to give them; they rely on the school to implant in their ego-structure that sense of basic security which is the precondition of autonomy. This is what we have suggested to call 'intellectual hygiene', and which, we believe, is likely to play an increasingly important role in our system of education. It is a kind of 'rehabilitation' of the ego-structure through learning how to think and how to transfer to the areas of relational (personal) behavior experience gained in the areas of thinking and learning.

We have also asked whether, and to what extent, autonomy is a condition of success in a technological era. Is not readiness to accept law and truth as something 'pre-existent', as something to be taken over from 'those who know', is not readiness to follow the lead of others and to display initiative within a functional group only, is not, in one word, heteronomy more likely to secure success under such conditions than autonomy?

It may be argued that the whole question is a specious one, and therefore irrelevant, because the school should not define its function as that of a servant to the individual's social adjustment and success, and determine its curriculum and its methods of instruction accordingly. Maturity, integrity, autonomy may be considered much more important aims of schooling than adjustment and social success at any cost.

The alternative implied in this argument seems, however, rather artificial—no school is allowed to operate in a trans-historical absolutum, as it were; preparation of the child for his future in society is one of its basic functions, whatever the educational philosophy to which it is committed. No school has the right to use methods that would produce graduates with only limited chances of social success. But neither can the school fulfil even this social function without furthering processes of internalization. Even where, as in totalitarian regimes, autonomy is considered a liability rather than an asset, where the influence of the parents is limited or eliminated, in order to make methods of drill and indoctrination more effective—even there the chances of social success grow to the extent that the graduate of the elementary school will have learned to internalize the demands of heteronomy.

This means, as already stated, in our context: conscious confrontation with the truth or the law which is to be accepted as something 'pre-existent'; it means: conscious agreement to fulfil not only the role, but the functions of a 'follower'; it means: conscious participation in functionally defined groups. And consciousness means the ability to use abstract thinking; means objectivity; means control over personal involvements and understanding for the implications of anonymity. These, however, are qualities which can be found in an analysis of autonomy as well.

Thus, we distinguish not only between autonomy and heteronomy, but also between externalized and internalized heteronomy. Whereas we have defined autonomy as the ego's ability to exchange its subject-object position, heteronomy means exclusive identification of the ego with its object position. But whereas in externalized heteronomy the ego ceases to be aware of its object position, and, consequently, may become passive and ineffective in the discharge of its functions, internalization, in autonomy as well as in heteronomy, presupposes not only consciousness and self-awareness of the ego, but also differentiation and analytic abilities. It is the function of elementary school education, whatever the cultural definition of its goals may be, to foster the processes of internalization through its methods of instruction. Whether the school encourages autonomy, in the spirit of individualistic and humanistic ideals, or heteronomy, in the spirit of collectivistic and technological ideals—its primary function is to prepare the child for the solution of tasks which require more and more differentiation. (Methods of drill and indoctrination are inadequate in any social order, at least during the first six years of learning; they are inadequate as means of making the school graduate into an effective citizen even in a totalitarian regime.)

In other words: the smaller the part of the parents in the total process of learning, of the mother as the agent of security and of the father as the agent of differentiation—the more urgent becomes the need for the school to replace the parents (and again we say: in every social order!).

Let us add that we are not dealing here with a problem of social discrimination. It is only too well known that any class-divided society 'allocates' to undeserving sons of wealthy parents an unfair quota of social success, and deprives the sons of the poor of their legitimate chances. But the problem here under discussion is much wider; it extends to all social classes. And it is not identical with the moral aspects of injustice and suffering caused by that injustice.

What we have in mind is the objective failure, resulting from inadequate parental education and schooling, of millions all over the world, in all classes and in all cultures, irrespectively of whether or not some may be considered 'successful' by the external criteria of individualistic evaluation. 'Objective' failure manifests itself in such symptoms as ineffective social behavior, faulty and unproductive thinking, rigidity of the ego, lack of courage, inability to change and to develop. When this failure becomes the fate of millions, it affects the life, and limits the progress of any society, whatever its political order. Abolition of class-divisions and social injustice though undoubtedly capable of improving the individual's chances of objective success, cannot by itself solve the problem of inadequate internalization of learning, or even of autonomy through education and schooling. Such an aim requires a revision of teaching methods in every society.

4 ON ANONYMITY

We shall now try to clarify the meaning of one particularly ambiguous concept which we have used in our discussion, the concept of 'anonymity'. What do we understand by it?

It is one of the characteristics of externalization that its 'representatives' (whom we find under conditions of extreme poverty, among 'primitive' people in cultural transition, among the retarded and others) seek the illusion of knownness. They do not understand trans-individual laws or directions; they do not fulfil functions imposed on them; they recognize moral obligations only to the extent that the reality contexts in which these laws, directions and obligations are present, seem to be 'familiar' to them.

In other words: universality does not mean much to them; at best, they are able to enlarge the area of ego-transcending commitments, so that it includes 'objects' of intimate personal relationship (relatives, neighbors, friends). Rarely, however, will they extend their sense of responsibility to unknown persons, to representatives of anonymous agencies, or to general laws of behavior or thinking. Stereotypes are their (perverted) forms of Man-Bewusstsein, to use K. Bühler's expression. [5]

Here we understand the first aspect of anonymity: behavior and thinking not depending on personal associations. (It is obvious that no man will ever be entirely independent of such associations, when faced with a task demanding ego-transcendence such as subordination under, and acceptance of, a universal law, social or intellectual. But the degree of independence or dependence on personal associations differs, and these differences constitute a continuous scale from extreme disregard for, to genuine understanding of, anonymity.)

But we should not lose sight of a second meaning of the concept under discussion: its negative aspect. By applying the principle of double dichotomy as elaborated by L. Klages [33], we arrive at the following differentiation:

a) We see the positive aspects of an anonymity-orientation in the acceptance of laws of universal validity and applicability, in readiness for abstract thinking, in objectivity.

b) We see its negative aspect in a predominantly mechanistic conception of the social and the physical universe in which Man more and more loses his determining role.

c) The opposite to anonymity-orientation is dependence on personal associations. Its positive aspect is the intensity of feeling and the directness of approach within the narrow limits of possible relationships. Its negative aspects are precisely this narrowness of relationships, the resulting slowness of learning and ineffectiveness, the low rate of achievement and the lack of reliability.

This double antithesis is apt to throw light on the function of the school as an instrument of internalization in a reality in which externalizing factors abound.

Those who see in technological advance an absolute value, tend to overlook the negative aspects of an education towards understanding anonymity, and refuse to accept the positive aspects of the reverse orientation: personalistic attitudes are wrong and unhealthy *per se*, they claim, and impersonality is the ideal. Hence their often contemptuous rejection of humanistic 'speculation'. From among philosophers they may be ready to accept representatives of logicism, of epistomology, methodology and the like, from among sociologists and psychologists—those who limit themselves to methods of quantitation or to the elaboration of functional formulae, imitating, as it were, the mathematical exclusion of content.

As educators they tend to emphasize the superiority of mathematics, physics and chemistry over literature and history, to place methods of measurement and calculation over those requiring empathy or even intuition, preferring observation of the present to the imagination of past and future. Mechanistic elimination of the human being is an asset rather than a liability in the eyes of those who advocate this type of realistic, impersonal education.

At this point, however, it may be asked whether such an educational orientation—though perhaps conducive to the development on intellectual skills or to the expansion of consciousness—is at all likely to foster internalization of learning.

No one will deny that internalization of learning is the *conditio sine qua non* of its effectiveness, both socially and intellectually. We refer to our remarks on the essence of internalization, which, we said, is characterized by conscious confrontation of the learner with the contents of his learning, whereas absence of such a confrontation is one of the main symptoms of externalization (pp. 123). Ability to solve 'from within' one's problems of thinking and learning, of deciding on a course of action, of entering into, and maintaining, personal relationships—this ability requires 'polarization', that is, a dialogic contact between the ego and the non-ego.*

If so, it is the function of the school to help the individual child, from the earliest possible stage of learning onwards to discover himself, not only as an active subject in the process of learning, but also as a receptive subject challenged by the contents of this process, not only to understand his teacher, but also to discover the independent reality of every knowable detail in his universe of learning, and thereby also the limits of knowability. In other words: learning becomes internalized only to the extent that the learner does not lose sight of the non-ego character of his objects of learning.

This internalization of knowledge appears to be, paradoxically, the antithesis to subjectivity: not 'experiencing' the object of learning, but 'looking at it' from the outside, as part of the non-ego, is the pre-condition of internalization and of objectivity. The goal of learning should never be defined solely as 'my' goal (or as that of a personally known environment), but as that of 'all learners'. Behind the veil of subjective experience and of subjective shades of meaning, hides the universality of goals and contents. To make the learner aware of this, means to prepare him towards internalization of learning.

It also means to prepare him for a true understanding of anonymity. For, only to the extent that the individual learner discovers the universality of goals and contents, and thereby becomes part of a 'community of all' only to that extent does he acquire ability and readiness to learn and to function—intellectually as well as socially—

---

* Buber objects to the use of such abstract terms as 'polarization' or 'non-ego', instead of what he calls 'Thou'. The negative term (non-ego) reflects the difference between our psychological and his ontological approach. [25].

without dependence on personal associations and relations.

But is not, it might be asked, anonymity, so defined, identical with objectivity? Does not, then, the concept lose the specificness of its meaning? And can we still maintain that anonymity, so understood, is characteristic of a technological orientation only, and not of a humanistic outlook as well? Is not this type of anonymity the ideal and the aim of every true education, whatever certain representatives of progressive education may say in favour of personalistic attitudes?

There are different answers to the various questions implied here:

a) Anonymity, we have said (p. 126), has two aspects: universality and objectivity, on the one side, mechanistic orientation and impersonality, on the other. It depends on the educator's conception of his function, on his 'philosophy', to what extent the ego of the learner will be emphasized in his educational acts. An educator with a primarily technological orientation may put too strong an emphasis on the non-ego part of the relational equation, and may thus deprive the learner's ego of its active and creative part in the learning process. It is questionable, to say the least, whether in this way true objectivity can ever be achieved, in whatever functional field it may be required.*

b) The humanist, on the other hand, sometimes tends to over-emphasize the ego part of the equation, and thus to neglect objectivity and universality of application. Not only does he not aim at anonymity, on the contrary, he will always endeavour to base understanding of a universal law of recognition on its meaning for the individual. The objectivity at which he aims does not preclude ego-involvement.

c) In the first case, the educator may try to eliminate individuality as a determining force, thereby turning the learner into an almost anonymous factor in an on-going process. In the second case, the educator will—on the contrary—tend to use the learner's identity consciously and intentionally, thereby making him responsible for his learning, as if the production or the attainment of a certain defined result depended on the 'actor' only. Anonymity and identity, these two antithetic values of the educational orientation, here confronted with each other, do not lead to objectivity, unless each is 'tempered' by the other: elimination of individuality—by a conscious readiness on the part of the learner for self-relation, while subordinating his

* Over-emphasis on the non-ego also means lack of polarization, and lack of polarization makes true objectivity impossible.

ego to the mandate of his task; identity—by constant emphasis on the recognition of universality.

These differentiations are of particular importance when we analyse the implication of anonymity for a 'school without parents'. We refer to the different meanings of the concept as an ideal of a technologically oriented education ('impersonality') and as an integral element of each function which the school has to fulfil under conditions of externalization ('universality').

5 THE FUNCTIONS OF THE SCHOOL IN OUR TIME

Relative autonomy, internalization of learning, objectivity, understanding the meaning of universality, avoidance of personal associations 'in the wrong place'—all these are the aims of proper schooling, irrespectively of whether the learner is prepared for them through his early family experience and parental participation or not, and irrespective also of the cultural and social orientation within which the school operates.

But the methods of instruction will be different; they depend on what the majority of the pupils bring with them to the class-situation in terms of prior family experience, intellectual and relational ability (and mobility) and parental support. The kind of activation and challenging of the individual in the class-room, as it is used, for instance, in progressive education, may be suitable for the highly intelligent child. But all the millions whom we have in mind here—children in a situation of rapid cultural change, children of the slums, disappointed middle-class children—do not belong to that category; neither their, at best average, native intelligence (and here it is safe to include IQ's between 80 and 120, that is, at least 80% of all children in these social and cultural situations) nor their relatively low degree of inner security, resulting from lack of consistent parental care in the first years of life, suffice to make them eligible, as it were, for the methods of progressive education. The latter require a relatively high degree of autonomy, of internalization, of objectivity and of understanding universality already available from the start, as a predisposition; whereas the children about whom we are speaking here need the school and its activities so that they may overcome the intellectual handicaps that are implied in their patterns of heteronomy and externalization and in their dependence on the 'illusion of knownness'. Their consciousness cannot expand, their learning will not lead to systematization (through concepts and relational categories), unless the teacher is ready for a considerably higher degree of active intervention and direction than any representative of progressive education would ever regard as legitimate.

This does not mean that we advocate a return of the school to old-time authoritarian methods. We shall try in the next chapter to define in general terms the aims of the school as an instrument of internalization, in the face of that abundance of externalizing factors which is characteristic, on the one hand, of modern technology, and, on the other hand, of our class-divided society, of the poverty-stricken lower class as well as of the tension-laden middle-class family, of culture-change and anomie.

CHAPTER SIX

Learning as a Means of Internalization

1 INTRODUCTION

MODERN MAN'S dependence on the present has been called one of the main symptoms of his cultural pathology. The fate of the individual as well as of the group is determined by anonymous, unidentifiable factors of a political, a social, an economic, a technological order; man therefore becomes less and less capable of changing that fate through the force of his personal initiative. As a result, the future loses its character as the realization of a different, desirable goal, as focus of inner tensions. Hence if we want the dimension of the future to take the form of a determinant of reality, we must bring the individual to a point where he will be able and ready to experience every ego condition, every actuality not only as changeable but also as valuationally inferior to its inherent potentialities, to what is possible, 'future'.*

This, however, means that man must rediscover the dimension of 'the possible', which he had known, in all its attractiveness and in all its threatening danger, when he was a child. Man must rediscover this dimension not only conceptually but through feelings, not only as a category but also as a value, if he wants to find a way out of his immediacy orientation, if he wants to find a way into internalization.

In the externalized style of life, the possible has different meanings. Under conditions of poverty [26], it means haveability; in the value-ambiguity of cultural transition it means: the survival of past clarity in a disappointing present; in the monotony of an impersonal, technologically organized existence, it means: that which may suddenly occur, from without, upon the initiative of machines and without ego-participation; in the fear of perdition it means: the illusion of sudden

* Perhaps an objection will be raised here: what about the person, one may ask, who expects and imagines a future situation of distress? Does not his case contradict the definition here suggested? Is not for him the imagined future *inferior* to the present? But we should not forget that, in this case, the negative, hence perturbing, future is the object of inner preparation only to the extent that is already *implied* in the present.

peace and wholeness. All these, however, are distortions of the possible, distortions that cancel out its effectiveness. It is, therefore, the same when we say that under the externalizing conditions mentioned so far, the category of the possible becomes an illusion, or when we say that it ceases to exist and operate.

What, then, are the instruments of education which we should apply in order to reactivate the category of the possible? How could we make man realize that it is in the growth and enlargement of reality from within rather than in the acquisition of external values, perceived as 'haveable', in which he should come to experience want? Or, when we ask that same question in the context of internalization: What can education, or, more specifically, teaching do in order to transform man's malcontent with his present state into a lever of internalization?

The following is a summary of our answer, which we shall later try to analyze in detail:

a) Teaching aimed at internalization shows the learner how to establish, how to 'create' contexts, rather than to be satisfied with intake of knowledge; it strengthens his power of imagination, and does not content itself with enlarging his *massa apperceptiva*.

b) Teaching aimed at internalization endeavours to protect the learner against the distorting influence of affects and of illegitimate concretizations on his relationship with the human and the social non-ego.

c) Teaching aimed at internalization helps the learner discover his responsibility for his thinking and learning, while recognizing the universality of causal laws. In other words: it brings the learner to a point where he understands that there is no contradiction between genuine relatedness to his ego and genuine relatedness to the non-ego (on the contrary: that they supplement each other).

2 THE USE OF IMAGINATION

As long as the teacher considers it his task to impart knowledge and to help the child develop skills, learning remains more or less irrelevant for the process of internalization. The enlargement of the learner's *massa apperceptiva* undoubtedly facilitates functional development, just as the acquisition of skills strengthens a feeling of mastery and, through it, of security. But as long as the learner remains separated, as it were, from the contents he learns (and unrelated to them), they will never become integral parts of his ego. True learning means *overcoming* the frontiers, the boundaries between what is 'there', to be learned, and the learner who must be active in the process of learning.*

'Activation' has a number of meanings. What we have in mind here is one aspect only: Teaching must become a constantly repeated challenge to discover and mentally to construct contexts, not only, and not primarily, by way of induction (from observable facts to concepts and laws), but rather by way of imagination, of daring. This, however, implies a conception of learning as a means to change not only the *extent* of consciousness but also its *quality*, its mode of functioning.

On the other hand, it is equally true to say that such learning (the ultimate aim of which is activation, discovering and understanding contexts) becomes possible only *on the basis* of a well developed ability to establish relationships. When this ability has remained under-developed, under the influence of externalizing life-conditions, of intellectual retardation or of emotional disorder, the courage to imagine contexts will not develop either [26]. And yet it is precisely such a child who needs an activating type of learning in order to find a way out of his externalized style of life. How can we solve the problem posed by this apparent contradiction?

The teacher must accept the fact that *every* child needs a more or less prolonged pre-stage of learning during which the acquisition of knowledge and skills paves the way for later mobilization of phantasy. But at the same time, he must remain aware of the preparatory character of the phase; only later starts the proper learning process, the one that leads to internalization. The decisive question then to be asked is: how to determine the right proportion between preparatory learning and internalization.

Not only too little or too much of the former may obviate its true function; it is, even more, the teacher's attitude (when he mistakes the preparatory function of his teaching for the essential one) that accounts for his students' frequent failure to internalize their learning. Only when he remains aware of the ultimate function of teaching, will he reach each child individually, even in the 'pre-

* 'Overcoming the boundaries', however, does *not* mean, as we shall try to show later, fusion between the ego and the non-ego, as it is typical of certain extreme pathologies, such as schizophrenia [12], or of reality distortion through egocentric misinterpretations in secondary retardation. It means normal ego involvement and ego relatedness.

paratory stages.* Only then will he be able to give each child the feeling of 'being meant personally', of being challenged. This, however, is the only way by which the pupil may learn to invest his ego in his learning acts, even at those early stages when acquisition of knowledge and skills is the primary function of learning.

(We must not lose sight of the fact that we are speaking here of socially or culturally disadvantaged children only, who because of their ego-weakness and vulnerability need this feeling of 'being meant personally' much more than an ordinary child who may have learned it in other areas of his life experience.)

(Another question, to which we shall return later, is that of the relative advantages and disadvantages of earlier *versus* later mobilization of rehabilitative teaching methods. While no one will deny that it is desirable to introduce adapted teaching methods as early as possible, it is doubtful whether we can conclude from the perhaps astonishingly adequate reactions of many young children that their cognitive structure has indeed changed. Could it be that lasting, structurized changes can take place only at a later stage when the child's ego is already developed enough to operate as a center and an agent of organization, of synthesis, of integration? And this in spite of the fact that the older child's reactions to the teacher's rehabilitative efforts are liable to be much slower and partial?)

We started from the thesis that teaching aimed at internalization must strengthen the pupil's power of imagination and must not content itself with enlarging the learner's consciousness or even with developing his ability to form concepts.

This positive attitude toward imagination in learning implies, of course, the demand that the teacher must be prepared to give his socially or culturally retarded pupils a considerable measure of guidance and control. Not every teacher is up to such a task. Many adults—and the teachers among them certainly are no exception—are afraid of phantasy and see in it a retractive, disintegrating, antirational force. Not only do they react aggressively when manifestations indicating this dangerous 'pathology' emerge in their own behavior, they also react with intolerance and lack of understanding to the appearance of phantasy in their pupils' behavior and thinking, when it is out of place, in their affective opinion. In this way, however, they often make internalization impossible for those of their

* Each new *subject* of learning requires such a preparatory 'stage', even later in the child's development. But the more frequently he may have gone through it, the shorter will be the time required for the preparatory stage.

pupils whose conceptual mobility has remained undeveloped as a result of their externalizing life-conditions.

On the other hand, if a teacher is ready to see in phantasy a legitimate partner and not only a precursor of abstract thinking, it is safe to presume that he will also be able to help his students transform phantasy-images into concepts and concepts into images.

It is questionable whether the intellectualistic tendency of our times to prefer concepts to images furthers internalization (although it may accelerate the development of technological thinking, that is, of a, technologically useful, anonymity-orientation). But when the tendency to internalize concepts, feelings and values is well supported and developed by early parental education and relationships, later emphasis on abstract thinking is not dangerous, may even fulfil an important compensatory function, in phases of a developmental increase in emotional modes of operation. These are the cases in which polarity between the ego and the non-ego, inner conflicts and tensions, repressions, inner confrontation with the environment as well as with the own ego are integral elements of a child's reality. We, however, have in mind those cases in which early parental education did *not* sufficiently support the child's tendency to internalize. What is the function of the school when cultural patterns or individual or social pathologies in the life of the parents prevent them from fulfilling their normative function?

We have already said that in this case the teacher must not content himself with trying to enlarge his pupils' *massa apperceptiva* or simply to teach them certain cognitive techniques. He must also try to achieve, through the very acts of teaching, what the parents have failed to achieve: he must arouse and strengthen in his pupils that very readiness for *inner* confrontation with knowledge.

Such a task requires more than translation of concepts into images and images into concepts; it requires constantly repeated guidance of the pupils in activating their imagination, in order that they 'discover' contexts. It is of particular importance in the education of those children whose consciousness is concentrated, almost exclusively, on external realities, on want and on the haveable. It is they who need their imagination in order to discover 'significance' hiding behind phenomena; externalization not only limits and distorts the child's field of perception, it also leaves undeveloped his readiness to take cognizance of the dimension of meaning, let alone to understand it conceptually.

Now, it is precisely this ability on which every act of internalization is based. Here, however, the question arises that is being asked wherever we try to find a way out of that vicious circle called 'externality of living': can the way to the inner world be opened from the periphery, as it were, through dealing with one of the essential symptoms of that external life-style? Can meaning replace haveability, can the hidden, unclear but discoverable meaning be experienced as that which is wanting? Can the undeveloped ability to internalize through learning be developed by strengthening the child's imagination? Is this perhaps as useful a way as is that of strengthening analytical and conceptual abilities?

Phantasy not only allows the learner to discover new connections between facts and thus activates him; it also allows him to experience the meaning, once he has discovered it, as superior (in value) to the object or the event to which it refers. This, however, is precisely the aim of internalization through learning in the life of an externalized child: to provide him with the experience of value* as connected with that of his cognitive activity.

Why should active imagination† rather than conceptualization provide the externalized child with value experience? We suggest the following, highly speculative, answer.

In concepts, the elements of wholeness and of unity, of connectedness between the subject and the object of cognition, are absent. It is, however, this very connectedness that constitutes value, since it is rooted in the primary connectedness of the infant with the mother, or, better, in the archetype of what we have called elsewhere [24] 'the mother as part'. But we must not forget that *absence* of such a security feeling, of such an experience of wholeness, characterizes life under conditions of externalization (is even responsible for its emergence); hence, no analytical activity (conceptual thinking, for instance), successful as it may be, can ever provide an externalized child with that value-feeling which internalization-through-learning requires. This can be achieved precisely by that non-analytical (synoptic or synthesizing) phantasy-activity which leads to the discovery of connections, that is, of wholeness. (In a child, on the other hand, for whom the basic experience of wholeness and unity is guaranteed through his early relationships with the parents and particularly with the mother, it is acquisition of knowledge and concepts that help differentiate a primary value-consciousness.)

---

* It is obvious that the term 'value' is being used here in its existential and not in its moral meaning.

† The term is, of course, not identical with its meaning in Jungian therapy!

3 THE AFFECTIVE ELEMENTS

But it would be a mistake to conclude from what has been said sofar, that in rehabilitative teaching the emphasis should be on the uncontrollable factors of feeling. On the contrary: learning truly aimed at internalization uses phantasy and imagination in order to make the learner free and independent of the dangerous interference of affects with thinking. The learner who, by way of imagination, tries to connect a newly acquired piece of knowledge with something 'possible', a meaning, for instance, carries out a complicated mental act. This act requires much more objective ego-involvement than connecting such a newly acquired piece of knowledge with some formerly learned contents. Imagination is future-directed, association is past-directed. The more a learner accepts the demand for active ego-involvement as implied in the former, the less will he be exposed to the dangers inherent in the latter: no longer will he run the risk of his personal associations and motives, of his complexes and cultural patterns to determine the direction and results of his thinking and his learning.

We have pointed out that the culturally or the socially disadvantaged child is characterized by lack of readiness for active ego-involvement, by a poorly developed imagination and by strong tendencies towards affective associations. The weaker his ego, the more marked will be his tendency to connect every 'new' content with something known (or thought to be known). Ego weakness explains not only man's relative inability to abstract from a given reality, that is, to think in abstract terms, but also his relative inability to transcend reality with the aid of productive imagination. Externalized man's fixation to the area of the known blocks his ways to an adequate expansion of reality, through conceptual thinking as well as through imagination. Affective ego-relatedness then takes the place of both and distorts the perception of the non-ego as well as the learning processes.

How can the teacher of such a child hope to halt, or even reverse, processes of externalization and affective ego-relatedness precisely through supporting his imagination? Is it not logical to presume that such support will have the opposite effect? That it will only help increase the externalized child's typical readiness to react affectively? Whereas a planned development of conceptual thinking and of a realistic orientation would have a more desirable effect? It is not safe to presume that rational explanations and realistic corrections of false and falsifying ego-relatedness rather than stimulation of phantasy-activities will be capable of allaying undesirable affects?

The answer to these questions is: that developing imagination and using rational explanations are not mutually exclusive and contradictory actions. When we teach children who are secondarily retarded, these methods rather supplement each other, depend on each other. Only in teaching children who grew up under conditions conducive to internalization, do the two methods bear the character of alternatives.

How does the learner discover the 'dimension of the possible'?

—When he understands the regularity inherent in an object or in an event, and he feels his fears subside;

—When he becomes aware, to his surprise, that something unknown can change and become known, and he feels encouraged;

—When he learns that everything is changeable and exchangeable, and his curiosity is aroused;

—When he, courageously, accepts the other as of equal value and is, from then on, able to discover mutuality and causal reciprocity in personal relationships as well as in group contexts;

—When he becomes increasingly ready and able to understand the co-existence and the exchangeability of subject-object positions (see: 24, pp 34 f);

—When he encounters the meaning of a phenomenon and feels committed to it as a thinking and learning subject; when he encounters the motives of an action as distinguished from that action.

In all these forms, the discovery of the dimension of the possible not only enlarges man's consciousness but also liberates him from the shackles of his affective self-relatedness. It is the way towards autonomy that manifests itself in objective thinking and evaluating.

These are the goals of learning, whoever the learner may be, a child growing-up under conditions of externalization or under conditions that may be conducive to internalization. But the teaching *methods* are different in each case. A few examples may illustrate this point:

When the child in his early phases of development has acquired a feeling of basic trust through experiencing the regularity of events in his primary environment, we will usually find in him, when he reaches school age, a readiness to discover rule and law in the multitude of phenomena about which he learns. In this case, the teacher can start from the presumption that his pupils will be stimulated by way of systematically learning their 'facts and figures', how to discover rule and law (provided, of course, their intelligence is normally developed).

Such a presumption is, however, *not* justified when the child failed to acquire that feeling of basic trust and security. In this case, an ever repeated and emphasized *demonstration* of regularity in the multitude of objects, events, processes and relations is often more important than the imparting of additional knowledge. Partiality of knowledge, at least in the early stages of learning, is easily compensated by that affective 'appeasement' that is brought about through perception of regularity or by the accompanying feeling of security. But to the extent that these goals of teaching are achieved, the child will become able and ready to look for regularity, to seek it, that is, to develop initiative towards this aspect of the possible. (In contrast, the non-externalized child usually will show this initiative spontaneously and already in the preceding, the so-called oedipal, stage).

More difficult is the second task of teaching: to help the child realize that the unknown can become known. We understand the difficulties inherent in this task when we remember that fixatedness to the area of the known accounts for two deficiencies: for the tendency to avoid what is new and unknown (not to take cognizance of it), and for the tendency to misinterpret new objects or events in the light of what is already known, and thereby to distort their reality meaning. Overcoming resistance to the unknown could therefore be called the precondition of adequate learning, that is, of the learner's readiness to perceive the unknown as potentially known; but on the other hand, it is also one of the *results* of adequate learning: only through a repeated conscious experience of such transformation (of something unknown into something known) can the affective resistance to the unknown as such be broken, that resistance which stems from the fundamental insecurity of man-in-externalization.

How can the teacher help his pupils get out of the vicious circle of insecurity, anxiety, fixation to the known, avoidance of the unknown, insufficient learning ability and, again, increased insecurity (following social or intellectual failure)? He must provide them, again and again, with the encouraging experience that precisely through learning they can advance the process of transformation. In other words: under conditions of externalization, the expansion of the mind through learning of facts and skills fulfils two different functions simultaneously: not only does it make possible conceptual thinking (as it does in the development of ordinary children); it also supports the experience of knownness being the result of a process and an activity rather than the quality of a statically restricted universe of things. It is through this experience that the growing child can overcome his fixatedness to the area of the known and the weakness of differentiation that goes with it. Learning should make the disadvantaged child skeptical in the face of what he believes to be known, courageous in the face of what is new and unknown.

But we must not forget that fixation to knownness also fulfils an important protective function in the life of the externalized child (and adult): it renders possible the illusion of mastery over all that may happen. Every educational activity, meant to operate *against* tendencies to escape into the area of what is, or seems to be, known, must therefore be capable of providing an at least equally strong feeling of being protected.

It follows that the teacher of socially or culturally disadvantaged and secondarily retarded children has to fulfil an additional function: he must show them, time and again, how a certain phenomenon, how a certain process or event, how a certain action can be replaced by another one; that there is always an alternative, that nothing in this life is final. True enough, the teacher must know how to explain in which ways the alternative, too, is determined by certain describable and defineable factors (a procedure which, again, requires imagination on the part of the teacher as well as of the pupil). Otherwise, the teaching method is likely to aggravate rather than to alleviate anxieties, since the alternative may then be interpreted by the child as arbitrary and as unforseeable only (which would only increase his feeling of insecurity in a basically unreliable world).

But the experience of alternatives, of exchangeability and changeability, will not produce more affective stability, solely through increased understanding of causal connections (between the alternatives and their respective determinants); this effect depends, perhaps even primarily, on the learner's readiness and ability to accept otherness as such, without over-estimating, without underestimating its significance. The learner must come to experience the non-ego as potentially equivalent with his own ego. Such an attitude, which is the basis not only of adequate cognition but also of genuine personal and social relationship, depends lastly on the extent to which the learner understands that every subject-position is at the same time an object position (and *vice versa*).

When externalizing life-conditions restrict the child's mental mobility, it is the teacher's duty to accompany every explanation of otherness and change by comparisons between essential characteristics or between essential differences. Such comparisons, however, cannot rely, in this case, only on analytical thinking or conceptual differentiation; they require constantly repeated perception of wholes whose meaning can be changed radically by changing one of their parts; they require planned development of the learner's ability to perceive himself as well as the other simultaneously as subject and as object.

It is one of the most important functions of the teacher of disadvantaged children to develop in them these abilities through making them participate in processes and activities of change and through relating contents of learning to their own experiences and to those of others. In this way he can hope to counteract the child's lack of initiative and his tendency to use distorting personifications or dichotomizations—these typical symptoms of fixation to knownness and of weak relational abilities under conditions of externalization. *Every* content of learning can be used for the purposes of demonstrating the processes of changing the meaning of a given whole by altering one of its elements.

Such an attitude towards teaching will prepare the learner for the ever renewed task of distantiating himself from the objects of his learning without losing contact with them (see p. 128) or distorting them through too much ego-relatedness. This is the seeming paradox of learning as a means of internalization in the life of externalized children: they must be prepared to relate each content of learning to their personal initiative without letting emotions and affects determine their thinking, without forgetting the objective meaning of these contents; and they must learn how to distantiate themselves from each content of learning without losing sight of its character as a personal challenge. In other words: to recognize the dimension of meaning behind the surface of an object, a process, an event, a relationship, behind a word and a concept—this is the way to internalization-through-learning.

4 COGNITION AND REALIZATION

We could summarize the didactic conclusions to be drawn from our thesis in one sentence: The teacher must make his pupil recognize that he is responsible for his learning. In a child growing up under conditions that are conducive to internalization, such a feeling of responsibility can be aroused and strengthened through using his moral consciousness or his identification needs. In the child we have in mind at present, however, such a feeling must be based on his self-perception as one who is responsible not only for discovering the *laws* of reality and not only for understanding their manifestations, that is, not only for his learning, but also for determining, for choosing the contexts in which to see the contents of his learning—objects, events, processes.

Even a child growing up under conditions that are conducive to internalization, discovers the rules and laws of reality through experimentation and manipulation, that is, through active mobilization of his responsibility for whatever is 'there' or 'happens'. But when the ability to establish polar relationships is normally developed, when ambivalence-tensions and -solutions from the earliest stages on, help transform non-ego contents into freely available ego-contents, such experimentations and manipulations will never lose their 'As-If' character; in this case, the child will remain aware of the fact that his responsibility is primarily one of learning, one of accepting objective givens, one of understanding.

When, on the other hand, the child's ability to internalize has remained undeveloped, perhaps under the impact of externalizing life conditions, it is obvious that this form of responsibility of which we speak here, will remain equally undeveloped. Its place is then liable to be taken by quasi-magic manipulations and by selective learning which will be determined by whatever may seem to be wanting and 'haveable'.

If so, one will rightly ask why precisely in the case of such a child readiness for objective learning and responsibility for learning should be supported concretistically, as it were, by that feeling of being responsible for choosing the contexts in which to see the contents of his learning. Could not thereby genuine responsibility for thinking and learning still more be impaired? May it not be that the child will thus learn to rely still more on magic manipulations? So that his orientation toward the possible, toward the future (in which we saw the ultimate aim of internalization-through-learning) would in the end be restricted still more?

This is undoubtedly a real danger: Patterns of externalization are characterized precisely by lack of ability and readiness in the learner to become objectively involved in the learning process ('objectively' meaning here: as a servant of, not as an arbitrary ruler over, the contents to be learned); externalization is characterized by the learner's preference for manipulations. On the other hand, it is exactly *because* of the existence of such weaknesses and preferences that the teacher must, always again, try to give his disadvantaged and externalized pupils as many opportunities as possible for changing reality contexts in his observational and formal operations. It is in this way that they will learn how to compare with each other, and how to distinguish from each other, true ego-activity and responsibility (with its typical consideration for objective causal connections) and magic-like superstitious manipulations.

When we want to make an externalized child understand a past or present event as the outcome of the activity of man or his groups, it would be insufficient to interpret only the intentions of this man or these groups; we must also try to explain the causal connections existing between intentions and the reality within which they are going to be realized, on the one hand, and the specific acts of realization, on the other. In other words: to show an event as the manifestation and the result of human responsibility means combining teleological, value-related, thinking with causal, fact-related analysis. It is precisely this mode of demonstration that is capable of counteracting the manipulative tendencies in externalized children and put in motion contrary processes, leading, if not to internalization, at least to a weakening of the typically externalized tendencies towards the haveable.

When we wish to enlarge such a child's consciousness which is tied to the narrow area of the known it would be insufficient to refer to the immediate neighborhood, exclusively or even primarily only, as it is frequently suggested by teachers and psychologists: emphasis on the known is liable to prevent rather than to further the necessary enlargement of consciousness. But if the teacher points to the formative and change-inducing actions of human intervention, that is, to man's responsibility for 'his' reality, the opposite is likely to happen: in this case, it is the immediately known neighborhood or the homestead and its natural environment, which then become the area of growth, of change, of expansion and of transition to the new and unknown.

This applies to all subjects of instruction. It is always the first task of the teacher to devest the immediately given of its character of false (illusory) knownness, in order to help the child discover true and reliable knownness; the latter always depends not only on the extent to which the learner has come to understand, through the help of his teacher, the laws governing reality, but also his responsibility for the changeable contexts in which reality appears.

It is generally accepted in modern theories of education that teaching by doing or teaching with the help of audio-visual aids is superior to purely verbal and conceptual methods. But how can a child whose ability to form concepts, whose cognitive mobility is not properly developed, translate percepts into freely available and universally applicable concepts? The question, strangely enough, does not seem to occupy the educator's mind. Their dogmatic lack of critical awareness of the limits to those perceptual methods is indeed astonishing, particularly in the light of their recurrent failure with children who need the teacher's planned activity for the development of their ability to think in abstract terms.

Here we have in mind not only the children of less-than-average intelligence but the many millions of socially and/or culturally disadvantaged and therefore intellectually ineffective children. Again and again, we notice that they are unable to transfer what they perceive and apperceive to a non-perceivable, abstract content of learning, such as a text of history or literature, or a universally valid law. (A child who succeeds in such transfers is, as a rule, not in need of those perceptual 'methods'.)*

In this respect, the functions of the school can be defined as: bringing about transfer from the areas of perception to that of abstraction, through which application of learning to new fields becomes possible. The child must become accustomed to such transfers; it requires activation, responsibility, and again, not only for learning the methods of transfer and abstraction but mainly for *establishing* the contexts, in which reality appears. We maintain that for an unintelligent, a primitive or an externalized child transferability and applicability of percepts is meaningful only to the extent that they are experienced as challenges to acts of realization.

It is precisely in this respect that the mental structure of the child who grows-up under conditions of externalization essentially differs from the mental structure of a child who is brought up, from the first phases of his development on, in the spirit of internalization. Internalization means, among other things, the formation of conceptual representations of the environment. The existence of such conceptual representatives enables the learner to experience his

* It goes without saying that this criticism is not directed against observation as an instrument of teaching, as long as it serves abstraction.

contents of learning as objective, that is, as existing 'there', opposite the ego, and to discover *in* this 'opposite' reality the relationships between the different contents of experience or between them and their meaning. We could even go one step further and say that internalization-through-learning means the development in the learner, of the ability to detach his ego from the learnable reality contents and to make it into an independent, 'opposite' observer (see p. 128 and p. 142).

But the weaker the child's ability to internalize, and the less reality is represented 'within', that is: conceptually, the less will the learner be capable of detaching himself from his objects of cognition and learning. He needs the experience (or—as we can say from the standpoint of internalization and conceptuality—the illusion) of *producing* ('creating') contexts *through* his acts of cognition and learning (just as he needs the illusion of knownness; see p. 141).

It is obvious that we should not *accept* this 'law' of externalization. Producing contexts is viewed in our present context *not* as a symptom of externalization but as a phase on the way from its characteristic preferences (for manipulation, perseveration, imitation and personification) to genuine, reliable thinking and learning: Instead of *manipulating*, arbitrarily and following momentary desires and needs, the ego, in this pre-stage of learning, is already related to, and dependent on, the objectivity of the non-ego. Instead of *perseverating* in areas that provide satisfaction, the experience of realization prepares the child's mind for change and changeability, for self-distantiation from the present with its chance-occurrences. Instead of indulging in feelings of false egoity through *imitation* (in doing and in thinking), the experience that new contexts can be created, is likely to produce genuine ego-involvement in the very act of imitation. Instead of *personifying* the causal factors of occurrences (which in turn, reinforces manipulation and imitation), the learner will become more careful in attributing personal character to reality phenomena, once he feels himself responsible for the realization of contexts.

Stimulating imagination, allaying affects, developing ego-involvement through strengthening responsibility for the realization of contexts—these are the means of teaching towards internalization in the life of the socially or culturally disadvantaged child, when the environment failed to develop his ability to form and to use concepts.

5 CONCLUSIONS

Let us now return to the question from which we set out in our analysis: What can the school do to help the child rediscover the category of the possible, the dimension of the future?

The principles of teaching which we have discussed in the foregoing paragraphs, have one aim in common: to set the learner free from his fixation to the present. Now, it is this very fixation, this very immediacy-orientation that helps man in poverty to cope with his distress, that provides the weak ego with an illusion of adequacy, that protects man in the value crisis of modern times against his existential insecurity and fears (see again page 141). Hence, we can notice that inner tension is liable to appear whenever fixation to the present is loosened, in thinking processes or in relationships.

In other words: in the very restitution of impaired intelligence, destruction of illusory security is implied. Adequate learning, aimed at the formation and formulation of controllable and generally applicable concepts and values requires the experience that man can find what is wanting not only in an external sphere of the haveable and of chance-occurrences, but also in an inner area of the possible which can be realized.

If so, it should be evident that internalization-through-learning depends on the presence of other services as well: comprehensive social care, guidance of the parents and therapy must supplement adapted teaching methods, just as the latter are necessary to make the former into effective tools of internalization.

It is here that the essential difference between the therapeutic treatment of a neurotic child and the educational treatment of an externalized child becomes evident: therapy appeases by making the past 'known', by assimilating unconscious contents and tendencies to consciousness and thus helping overcome neurotic anxieties. In the educational treatment of the externalized child, on the other hand, learning has the function of producing inner tensions by eliminating illusions of knownness, by opening the dimension of the future and the possible.

Therapy, if successful, leads the emotionally disturbed child to reversing false introjections; thus, the child becomes more and more able to perceive the non-ego realistically and to enter into polar ('dialogic') relationships with reality. In the educational treatment of the externalized child, on the other hand, the aim is: growing introjection of the non-ego, through learning and concept-formation, gradual replacement of an almost exclusive orientation towards the haveable by one towards finding the meaning of an event, of an object, of an activity. Self-distantiation means, in this case, correction of *false* ego-relatedness, while in therapy, it means cancellation of false and exaggerated introjections. In therapy, the intellect is embraced in the 'reality of the soul', in learning, the latter becomes an object of the intellect.

For the socially or culturally disadvantaged child, in his secondary retardation, it is the teacher, representing, as he does, the area of the unknown and the unfamiliar, on whom it incumbs to supply the child with an experience of nearness. On the therapist, on the other hand, it incumbs to remain a 'stranger' in order to make possible his transformation into an object of projection and transference. Psychotherapy of the neurotic child is a bilateral relationship; education of the externalized child is a multilateral relationship.

6 CULTURAL DIFFERENCES: INTRODUCTORY REMARKS

In the preceding discussion of learning and teaching methods, no distinction was made between socially and culturally disadvantaged children. We have based our analysis on the presumption that the various forms of deprivation have one element in common: an externalized life orientation. Furthermore, we presumed that the functions of teaching are the same for the child who grows up in the educational crisis of modern technology, in poverty, or in the transition from an undifferentiated ('primitive') life-style to modern technology: in each of these cases it is the school's function to replace the child's fixation to the present by an orientation towards the possible and the future, to correct his false and distorting ego-relatedness, to destroy illusions of being protected in the narrow area of the known.

The following analysis sets out from the opposite question: in which respect *differs* the function of teaching when the pupils belong to the socially disadvantaged groups or grow up in the value ambiguity of cultural transition?

The third chapter of Part One was devoted to a comparative analysis of causes (and symptoms) of secondary retardation under conditions of poverty and of cultural ambiguity, and the modifying influences of personality factors in the causal equation of each of the two patterns was mentioned (pp. 62 ff and pp. 73 ff). In the following, an attempt will be made to draw didactical conclusions from those comparisons.

We refer to what we said above: that ideal types are represented in reality by approximations and mixtures only, so that no generally valid instructions can be given to the teacher. We saw in the limitation an advantage rather than a handicap, since it makes individualization of methods and spontaneity of reaction a necessity. This is true even if we do not take into consideration the individual factors of modification (see pp. 62 ff) but relate the adaptation of teaching methods to the various possible combinations of environmental factors only. These factors are:

1) Impersonality of relationships in the primary environment;
2) Externalized orientation towards the haveable, under conditions of poverty;
3) Inadequate communication and stimulation;
4) Fixation to the values of the cultural past;
5) Ambiguity of values in cultural transition.*

The fate of the child's intellectual development depends on the configuration of these factors, not one of which would by itself be capable of producing secondary retardation in every case. But the educator is concerned primarily with planning differential teaching methods. For him, the question of to what degree the child's intelligence can be impaired by each of the various possible configurations of the above mentioned factors is a theoretical rather than a practical one. For the analysis and the planning of differential adaptations of teaching methods to the needs of the socially and culturally disadvantaged and therefore retarded child, the *qualitative* aspect of the question is of greater importance than the quantitative one. What are the characteristics of secondary retardation, when the configuration of causal factors on which it is based is one of poverty-conditioned externalization of values and culture-conditioned fixation and ambiguity? And to what extent are the patterns of inadequate thinking that may result from this configuration modified by the presence or absence of impersonality in the child's primary relationships and by the presence or absence of adequate channels of communication and educational stimulation in his environment? These are the questions which the teacher will have to ask and answer.

We shall, therefore, try to relate our didactic conclusions to our theoretical remarks on the influence of poverty and cultural

* Cf also Ch. 4 of Part One.

ambiguity *combined* (see pp. 97 ff) rather than on the ideal types of the two factors *separated* (see pp. 73 ff). But before dealing with that issue we propose to analyse and define certain theoretical points of educational policy in regard to the worldwide problem of the so-called disadvantaged child in relation to the school as a whole.

7 CULTURAL DIFFERENCES: HETEROGENEOUS VERSUS HOMOGENEOUS GROUPS

Social history knows of various processes in which the impact of cultural differences on learning becomes evident. Transition of individuals or groups from a 'primitive' non-differentiated way of living to the ambiguity of modern civilization is one of them; incompatibility of contradictory phases in social development as represented by sub-groups is another one.

Transition is characterized by a number of tension factors, such as an intensive orientation towards the future, radical changes in the value system, contradiction between national or racial or religious consciousness and external imitation. Each of these tension factors determines the learning process. An analysis of their impact on the child's patterns of thinking and learning and the conclusions to be drawn from such an analysis as to the necessary adaptations of teaching methods is one of the most important—though hitherto sadly neglected—areas of culture-analysis and sociological research.*

We intend here to deal with another aspect of the problem, that of cultural heterogeneity and its significance for the planning of teaching. We ask: How can the school, operating, as it usually does, in the name of one unambiguous social ideal, teach children from different cultural groups in one class and through one method? How can the teacher hope to lead them to this one, defineable and unambiguous social goal, in spite of the fact that they are exposed to fundamentally different expectations, attitudes and ideals on the part of their parents?

We know well that these parents' expectations and values determine their attitude towards the teacher, towards the child's learning activities and processes, towards his successes and failures. They also determine, directly and indirectly, the *child's* attitude towards his learning tasks, his school and its demands. Not only his objective success, his achievement, but also the evaluation of this achievement through the

* Many excellent studies of culture (descriptive, comparative, phenomenological) are known. But rarely is the wealth of data thus made available used for a differential psychology of thinking and learning or for didactic considerations.

child's family and immediate environment decisively influence his learning processes.

It would be inadequate to approach this problem as if it were one of social education only, as if all we have to do would be: to develop the child's understanding and tolerance for different, unaccustomed forms of living. The basic falsity of this argument can easily be proven: tolerance is always preached to the superior only, to those who are adjusted and successful; they are told that they should show respect for the patterns (of behavior and thinking) that characterize the disadvantaged. But rarely the question is reversed: What do the concepts of 'understanding' and 'tolerance' mean for those who are socially incompetent and retarded? It is difficult to imagine that they could be genuinely tolerant of the competent representatives of society, of the 'rulers', of those who set the tone, instead of either imitating or affectively rejecting their modes of behavior and their values.

If this is the case, however, it should be evident that social education towards tolerance of otherness can never be considered the decisive educational tool in the school's endeavour to bridge the gap between the more advanced and the disadvantaged and retarded sections of the child-population. Coexistence, learning from each other, respecting cultural differences, do not contribute to the development of abstract thinking and of differentiation in children whose intelligence has been impaired by environmental conditions, unless the teacher actively interprets the meaning of those differences.

Can this be achieved in heterogeneous groups? Can the representatives of divergent cultural subgroups be taught in one setting internalization of learning and relative autonomy in the use and the application of contents of learning? Some may try to answer that it depends on the intelligence level of the children concerned, that children of the same or similar intelligence level *can* be taught together and with the help of one and the same method, irrespective of their cultural background (while children of significantly different intelligence can*not* learn together, whether they come from the same or from different cultural backgrounds).

But we should not forget that only the most intelligent children are characterized by that intellectual mobility that makes possible relative cognitive independence of any variety of group-factors, including cultural patterns; only they will be able spontaneously to compare the essentials of their own culture with those of others; only they are capable of benefitting from practically every method of teaching to which they may be exposed.

These few, however, are of little interest to us in our present discussion of educational principles and policies. We have in mind the vast number of average and secondarily retarded children. Their functional intelligence is determined precisely by their dependence on cultural groups. Fixation to the cognitive and evaluational patterns of such a 'sub-group' and to the expectations of its adult members is always prejudicious to an adeqate understanding of 'other', that is, 'culture-alien', contents. We have tried in Part One to draw a picture of the cognitive pattern called secondary retardation of the cultural variety. Its elements all preclude the ability to accept the coexistence of contradictory values, to learn *from* other children and *with* other children.

'Culture' has been defined as 'the recognized, approved, shared, and continuing pattern of the behavior of a group.' The members of an ethnic group, for instance, relate themselves, consciously and unconsciously, to the tradition-transmitted contents of its collective past and give a more or less uniform expression to this relatedness in language, customs, reality perceptions, associations, feelings and values. To what extent do these 'symptoms of culture' determine the learner's behavior, independendly of other group-factors and particularly of the family's economic situation?

It is a well-known fact that such factors of culture are liable to prejudice and impair the families' economic and social status, so that in the end the cultural minority becomes tragically identical with the economically weak and incompetent stratum of the population. It is equally well known that this secondary identity produces feelings of resentment and of being discriminated, produces indolence or aggressiveness in reaction to such feelings. But this secondary identity by no means precludes the fact that both the economically weak and the well developed strata of certain minority groups have in common specific patterns of thinking, just as the economically weak and the strong strata of certain dominant groups have other patterns in common.*

---

* Reference is made here to a study by A. Davis and R. Havighurst [8]; they came to the conclusion that certain 'racial' differences could be observed between American Whites and American Negroes, of the middle-class and the lower-class populations. These differences, the authors claim, are more rigid than class-differences. The 'obstinacy' of certain cultural customs expresses itself precisely in those areas which are decisive for the character formation of the growing child, and reflects unconscious processes. Class-conditioned adaptation of the representatives of different ethnic subgroups to one common social ideal, that of the dominant culture, on the other hand, concerns, as a rule, only the consciously controlled areas of behavior; it leads in the end in many cases to superficial and non-commital imitations only.

It follows that, when we define middle-class as against lower-class patterns of evaluation, when we speak of class-conditioned attitudes, feelings, affects, tendencies, we must abstract from their culture-conditioned variations. These variations, on the other hand, manifest themselves particularly in the parents' attitude towards the infant, hence, explain the transmission and perpetuation of cultural differences in the personality structure. Moreover, there exist value-areas (such as those of the historical perspective, the collective identity, certain religious beliefs) which are, one could almost say: by definition determined by the individual's membership not in social, but in cultural groups.

The culture-conditioned life-patterns and value systems of the parents may, as we have said, advance or hinder the child's social and intellectual development in the new society. Only in the second case, only when they prejudice his development, do we speak of an educational 'problem'. Only then do we ask how the incompatibility between parental value patterns and the child's adaptation to the learning demands of the dominant culture require adjustment of teaching methods. Those characteristics of cultural retardation that we have tried to define in Part One, are in most instances the direct or indirect result of translation of culture-conditioned patterns of thinking and evaluating in the life of the parents into their educational customs and expectations.

As a rule, the dominant culture-group is capable of self-reproduction, that is, of producing a number of individuals sufficiently large to maintain the principles on which it is based. In the Western culture, these are, according to T. Parsons [41], the principles of rationality and universalism. The weak sub-groups, on the other hand, are *not* to the same extent identifiable, either by opposite or any other principles: their very weakness as minorities and 'failure' groups implies ambiguity and ambivalence of values, hence also inability to produce norm-conscious representatives of past values who would be capable of transmitting them.

How, then, can the school succeed in breaking the vicious circle of primitivity? It happens frequently that parents, bound to undifferentiated, 'primitive', cultural life-patterns, sabotage, as it were, knowingly or unknowingly, what the school endeavours to achieve. It happens more frequently in their case than in that of poverty-conditioned and therefore externalized parents: the former, while understanding the aims of the school, often reject them consciously precisely *because* they understand them. In one case, they may prefer seeing the child integrated as an active partner in the family group as quickly as possible, and the 'delaying effect', the moratory character of the school irritates them. In another case, it may be the fact that a woman appears as the authority of culture-transmission, that makes it impossible for them to accept the school and so cooperate with the teacher. Often, it is the seeming lack of reality-relatedness of the curriculum that antagonizes them.

But the decisive factor is the weakness and limitation of the adult's time perception—so typical of every 'primitive' group—that accounts for the school's peculiar difficulties. It is noteworthy that in this respect the economically more advanced and more secure representatives of a less differentiated cultural sub-group are often hardly distinguishable from its economically disadvantaged members: both tend to be 'immediacy-oriented' [44] or to interpret the future simply as a more potent present. Learning as a means to internalize concepts, feelings, knowledge or evaluation is unknown to many of them, irrespectively of their economic condition. Needless to add that, where poverty and primitivity combine, the narrow limits of the parents' time-perception still more impede the child's learning processes.

One of the obvious conclusions to be drawn from this analysis is the importance of interpreting, again and again, the intentions and the methods of the school to the parents in order to secure their cooperation. Social workers and councellors undoubtedly can be of vital help in this respect; but more important still is the teacher's function. We shall come back to this problem in the last chapter, which will deal with the training of teachers for the socially and culturally disadvantaged child. Suffice it here to say that gaining the parents' confidence in the value of what the school is trying to achieve, should be the result of a cognitive, not of an emotional process.*

But the final success of intellectual re-education depends on the teacher's activities in the class-room, on his methods, on the ingenuity of his reactions to the manifold expressions of culture-conditioned cognitive deficiencies in his pupils, and on the manner in which he is

* In this connection those not infrequent cases will undoubtedly be mentioned in which children have successfully completed their school career, although their parents, far from being cooperative, did everything in their power to boycott the school's endeavours. But in the majority of such cases, it can be shown, that an exceptionally high level of intelligence helped those 'successful' children to maintain the cognitive tension required for abstract thinking and differentiation even under the most unfavourable objective conditions. Their success, therefore, does not contradict our claim concerning the close relationship between the child's level of scholastic achievement and his parents' culture-conditioned attitude towards the school and the learning process.

able and ready to integrate their associations with the contents of teaching (within the curriculum). Not only more or less exact knowledge of the cultural background and its possible influence on thinking and learning, not only relative freedom from affects and prejudices are required for the teacher adequately to discharge his functions with regard to the disadvantaged child but also *ability to improvise*. The teacher should know how to use meaningful cultural materials for the purposes of teaching, without being able to rely on well-defined instructions or curricula to guide and limit him in his teaching efforts. Such 'materials' include customs, values, irrational 'opinions', historical or quasi-historical 'reminiscences' of his pupils' culture group or of their family.

But it would not be correct to interpret what we have said so far about the cultural orientation of teaching, as if it meant only a demand to encourage the disadvantaged. Without underestimating the emotional value of encouragement, it would seem problematic or even dangerous to rely on ego-support as a means of cognitive rehabilitation. Like most methods of encouragement, this one, too, is liable to lead to dishonesty: The dominant culture group uses one criterion only for evaluating the success of learning, the individual's ability to think in abstract terms, to differentiate and to internalize. It is therefore utterly inadequate to introduce into the curriculum certain contents of the cultural sub-groups and thus to satisfy the pride of the pupils who belong to these groups. No change will be brought about in the child's cognitive structure by such sentimental manipulations, well-meant as they may be; the teacher must have the courage to compare with each other the culture-conditions which have moulded the pupils' thinking and learning processes.

In every culture, and not only in its 'primitive' sub-groups, we find elements of a-typical, often enough 'culture-alien' patterns of thinking. In every large cultural group co-exist sub-groups which may be characterized by differing yet, at least partially, comparable forms of perception and thinking. But it is precisely this fact of partial conformity, of similarity, which accounts for feelings of being discriminated against, wherever achievement and status prove to be *dis*similar. Here again, the teacher can fulfil an important function by using cognitive clarification for the purposes of social education and the latter for the purposes of strengthening cognitive functions.

Moreover: not only partial equality between differentiated and non-differentiated patterns of behavior and thinking but also their objective comparability prepares the ground for change, development and synthesis: the counterparts of symbols are concepts, of fixation to the known—anonymity, of abstraction—concretization. These equations, however, are reversible. Discovering the counterparts of cultural patterns is the key to equalization and not simply juxtaposing and relativizing the values and patterns of different sub-groups. It may flatter the socially weak representative of so-called primitive sub-groups, when we say to him: 'You, too, have values of which you can be proud, because they are unique and, existentially, not less important than those of the dominant group'. To be accepted in his otherness by the representatives of the dominant culture group is undoubtedly likely to bolster his ego. But in the end, this is nothing but cheap sentimentality. Worse: it is an attempt on the part of overt or covert reactionaries to sacrifice genuine social equality on the altar of cultural relativism. On the other hand, discovering and clearly defining the essential characteristics of different sub-groups may prepare the way to genuine social adaptation and unification without suppressing the cultural identity of the individual who belongs to this or to that sub-group.

Socio-historical, genetic explanation of culture-conditioned differences in the patterns of thinking and perceiving, of feeling and evaluating is not the educationally relevant method—important as it may be scientifically. But looking for the correlates of certain cognitive qualities of the representatives of one group in the mental structure of another one, this method of phenomenological comparison may form the basis of a 'unifying' education, open though it may be to scientific criticism. The educator must know (or at least guess) what in the thinking pattern of the socially and/or the culturally retarded child, takes the place of, let us say, a differential time perspective or relativization or a universalistic conception of cause if he wants to use his teaching methods as tactics of rehabilitating a potentially normal but functionally lowered intelligence.

What then, should be the organization of schooling best suited to attain such aims? Shall we separate between children who come from a 'primitive' and from a differentiated background and teach each group according to different principles and methods? Or shall we teach them in one group, in order to make possible the use of comparisons between essential differences as part of the method of teaching?

The first form is based on the hypothesis and the hope, that adaptation of teaching methods is capable of achieving what the cultural group failed to achieve: to advance a child who, at the age of six, is not sufficiently prepared for the exigencies of formal learning, and to advance him to such an extent that, after several years, he can compete with other better-prepared children in the discharge of learning tasks which require abstract thinking. Adaptation of teaching methods alone obviously does not guarantee successful unification of the different groups after a number of preparatory years. And separation into homogeneous groups certainly does not offer as much opportunity for comparing with each other culture-conditioned differences between thinking patterns, as does the heterogeneous group—a fact which may affect unfavourably the growing child's readiness to overcome prejudices. Homogeneity of the class composition may help strengthen abstract behavior and thinking; lack of opportunity to confront otherness as a reality—is the disadvantage of this method.

In the second case, on the other hand, that of the heterogeneous class, we expose the socially and/or culturally retarded child to the dangers of failure, of externally imitating ego-alien forms of thinking and of evaluating. He is likely to react affectively to the repeated experience of such failures (unless the culturally 'successful' children form a minority only, so that *they* will feel frustrated). Let us not forget that a child who is culturally well prepared for abstract learning, needs neither special exercises nor systematic confrontations with the problem of otherness, in order to develop that ability to differentiate that is an integral element of successful learning.* In a heterogenous class, curriculum and methods will therefore always be determined through those pupils who belong to the culturally advanced group. This in itself is sufficient to act as a factor of discrimination against the culturally disadvantaged.

8 THE DILEMMA OF THE SCHOOL

This is the dilemma of the school in times of cultural contradiction and tension. Paradoxically, the ecological separation between the subgroups of a heterogeneous culture, in itself symptomatic of a dangerous social pathology, reduces the extremity of the dilemma: As a rule, we find relative homogeneity of the school population resulting from the simple fact that socially and culturally weak and insecure families tend to live concentrated in one and the same neighborhood. Hence, the

* Though he does need, as a rule, experience of cultural variety, for the development of desirable social attitudes.

children usually attend one and the same school.

And yet, the dilemma remains: we find many signs of cultural heterogeneity in those schools in which children from middle-class families of various cultural backgrounds meet. More: we find a feeling of being discriminated against among many older pupils, when they come to experience that the school, in spite of its contrary definition of aims and purposes, intensifies rather than eliminates cultural differences. But the more this feeling of being *different* becomes identical with one of being superior or inferior, the less will the school be able to fulfil its functions as a *medium of internalization*.

Is there a way out of this dilemma?

We have in mind in our present discussion children of one and the same age group whose ability to think in abstract terms, to differentiate, to understand the hidden meaning of phenomena is underdeveloped, *not* because they are of congenitally low intelligence but because they are culturally retarded.* In these cases, in which it is the teacher's function to rehabilitate the potentials of his disadvantaged pupils, it does not matter whether he meets them in heterogeneous or in homogeneous classes. In both cases he must help them with the aid of improvized or pre-planned exercises in abstraction an in differentiation.

The *form* of such exercises depends on a number of factors: on the extent to which the socially and culturally disadvantaged are isolated from the members of the dominant culture; on the rigidity of their patterns of living and thinking; on the extent to which their symbols lend themselves to translation into concepts; on the intensity of the child's feeling of belonging in his family; on the individual degree of intelligence; on the proportion between the number of pupils in need of such exercises to the number of others who do *not* need them.

Where children in need of rehabilitation of intelligence form a minority, it will certainly not be easy to integrate those exercises in abstraction with the general curriculum in such a way that the children for whom they are meant should not feel discrimination, precisely *because* of their being in need of special attention. In this case, it will be advisable to plan those exercises simultaneously on different levels of difficulty, though they may serve the same

* Diagnostically this distinction is, of course, more difficult than observationally. We have tried, in Part One, to compare the essentials of congenital *versus* secondary retardation, by way of phenomenological analysis.

purpose, that is, may be *functionally* identical.

Moreover, it will be of particular importance in this case to compare with each other, again and again, thinking in concepts and in symbols, abstraction and concretization, cognitive autonomy and 'tradition-directedness'. Such comparison and explanation will be meaningful to the extent that the teacher will be able to solve his problems of evaluation. All depends on whether the teacher will succeed in making both the culturally developed and the disadvantaged among his pupils aware of the existence of objective advantages and disadvantages inherent in *each* form of cognitive operation. A few examples may help illustrate this point:

Conceptual orientation in its neutrality and objectivity may lack that power of conviction that often characterizes concrete symbols. It is their convincing effect that turns symbols into welcome tools in the teacher's hands to arouse and support processes of internalization. True enough, he must be aware of the shortcomings of a symbolic orientation as well: it limits the extent and quickness of transfer of learning, in clear contrast to conceptual thinking which helps *enlarge* consciousness and accelerates transfer of learning. Another example is fixation to the known: if the teacher understands how to use it properly for the purposes of his teaching, he can, precisely by using the 'area of knownness' in the child's mind, intensify the experiential character of learning; anonymity, on the other hand, includes the danger of lack of realism, of emptiness. But rationality and universality of thinking—these elements and preconditions of successful learning in our times—can hardly be developed as long as the thinking process remains tied up with the known.

Here we can see that the school has better chances with children whose ability to internalize and to differentiate is restricted as the result of growing-up under adverse conditions of culture than it has with children who grew up under the externalizing condition of extreme poverty and neglect (that is socially as against culturally disadvantaged children). The chances to develop the ability to differentiate and to internalize are better in the culturally deprived group. For, the symbols of any, even a 'primitive' cultural group, its historical or quasi-historical tradition, the collectively shared contents of its concretizations—all relate to the individual's conscious mind much more directly and objectively than the way in which, what is wanting and 'haveable', relates to the mind of the child who grows up under conditions of poverty. The fact that culture contents form a reality which the mind of the learner faces as 'objective', makes possible a much more active relationship of the individual child with his learning tasks than the socially deprived and therefore externalized and retarded child will ever be able to achieve.

9 SUMMARY: THE NEEDS OF THE DISADVANTAGED

Let us briefly summarize what we have said so far about the school's rehabilitative function for the culturally and the socially disadvantaged child.

We have defined the functions of the school as an instrument of internalization in the life of the child who grows up under the externalizing conditions of poverty, as follows: to help the learner discover regularity, exchangeability and comparability of reality phenomena, contexts of intention and meaning, that may 'hide' behind these contents; to develop activity, and responsibility in the learner, to bring him to a point where he will be able to distantiate himself from the non-ego. In this way the school may hope to teach the child, and make him experience reality, both in its relational and in its conceptual manifestations, as being based on principles of polarity. The ultimate aim is to make the child ready and able to give up his illusions of knownness, to see, on the contrary, the unknown, the strange, the other, the possible as the fundamental facts of existence and to accept them as challenges. Strengthening the ability for abstraction through adequate exercises and guidance must be supplemented by encouraging imagination if teaching shall ever lead to internalization.

But where the school faces the task of correcting distortions of reality in the spirit of past, 'remembered' cultural residues and associations, where the learner struggles with tensions and contradictions resulting from cultural ambiguity, the school's task is different: Here, discovering regularity and exchangeability is less important than discovering the equivalents of the cultural past in the new present; discovering meanings behind appearances becomes less important than correcting misinterpretations which result from stereotyped symbols; discovering intentionality—less than strengthening causal thinking.

Unlike in teaching *socially* retarded children, who must learn, before all, the laws of polarity and polarization (as a problem of relationships and not of dichotomies!), replacing 'irreal' by 'real' objects of polarization takes the central place in the teaching of *culturally* retarded children. They, too, are bound to what they believe is known to them; but 'the area of knownness' is represented, primarily, by group-traditions (rather than by the ever recurring experience of what is wanting and 'haveable'). Hence, the learner, in this case, must be brought to recognize objectively the limits and the relativity of these traditions ('Want', here, is defined less as 'haveable', that is, as *present*, than it is defined as 'remembered', that is, as *present in the past*).

Here, too, it is the central task of teaching to strengthen and develop the child's ability to think in abstract terms and to use his imagination. But again, there are differences in methods between the two groups: In the first case, abstraction should be strengthened through adequate exercises and instructions; in the second case, this undoubtedly important function must be supplemented by an attempt to adapt to the categories of rationality concepts that may have been determined and impregnated by cultural experiences within and through the family. In the first case, the externalized child must learn to re-discover the dimensions of the future and the possible through activating his imagination (though the teacher must always be prepared to bring the child back, as it were, from contents of phantasy to their conceptual equivalents). In the second case, the teacher must always discuss the pupil's culture-conditioned phantasies, must even anticipate their possible (hypothesized) influence on the learning process, in order to forestall their 'secession' from the rational tasks of learning.

These are some of the dangers to which the child's cognitive behavior is exposed under condition of cultural contradiction, tension, ambiguity: here it is the group-past, anchored in the individual's unconscious psychic layers that may block an adequate approach to the values and concepts, hence also to the expected and required thinking methods of the dominant cultural group and may produce faulty thinking and unsuccessful learning processes.

But since contact with the collective past presupposes some kind of (genuine or seeming) internalization, every attempt to strengthen the child's powers of abstraction and differentiation must take into consideration this past as a spiritual, an intellectual and emotional, reality. Though this does by no means lessen the importance of the first-mentioned methods of strengthening abstract thinking, a different approach is required of the teacher of culturally deprived and retarded children. In the first case, inner tensions must be produced, inner values must be established in the mind of the learner; in the second case, affective tension must be lessened and collective values must be corrected and objectified.

On p. 150 we have mentioned that the didactic conclusions should be drawn from an analysis of causal constellations rather than from ideal-type-constructs. There exist undoubtedly essential differences between the cognitive failures of a socially and a culturally disadvantaged child, which we have tried to define in Part One (see pp. 73 ff.). And undoubtedly, we can (and must) define specific methods of teaching meant to help a child overcome his specific fixation (see the preceding paragraphs). But in the reality of the class-room representatives of the two groups meet, so that the teacher must know how to relate himself and his teaching to all of them differentially at one and the same time. Most children, who can be said to suffer from secondary retardation, are the victims of a combination, or, better, a configuration of conditions, poverty and culture-transition, orientation towards the haveable and value distortion, impersonality of primary education and inadequacy of intellectual stimulation, and each in different degrees of intensity, ranging from near-normality to extreme pathology.

We have tried to show (see pp. 94 ff.) which variations of cognitive defects are likely to result from those causal configurations. Another study will be devoted to a detailed typology in which the sociocultural background of the family, the prevailing educational atmosphere, the child's personality and his cognitive profile will be presented.

Here we shall confine ourselves to an analysis of the 'categories of thinking' and their relevance for the learning processes.

This will then lead to the last chapter dealing with the functions of teacher training in the light of our total analysis.

CHAPTER SEVEN

Categories of Thinking and Rehabilitative Teaching

1 INTRODUCTION

NUMEROUS STUDIES have been published in recent years on the socially and culturally deprived child. They deal with definitions, problems of causation and symptom description of the secondary intellectual retardation, which is the socially most important result of deprivation. Few studies only are devoted to a specifying analysis of teaching methods for the rehabilitation of intelligence. Most authors, it is true, claim that the impairment of intelligence through certain negative environmental constellations should be defined as reversible unless too much time has been lost. But the concept of 'reversibility' is not necessarily identical with that of complete restitution of the—hypothesized—original abilities; we must not forget that these 'original' abilities are potentials only whose development cannot be predicted in any case. Hence, teaching methods are of little interest to these students of intelligence; they are conceived of as being of a non-specific nature, related to the general need for improving the lot of the disadvantaged child, both socially and intellectually; they are not related to the essential characteristics of secondary retardation, since the studies deal with impaired intelligence on a phenotypical (if not descriptive) level only and not on a phenomenological level.

The very concept of 'the disadvantaged child', however, is a pragmatic rather than a sociological or an anthropological one. The studies dealing with the problem are based on the humanitarian demand, that every effort should be made to prevent certain social or cultural factors from playing havoc with man's intellectual potentialities or to restitute (optimally) the abilities that may have been impaired. The equalitarian doctrine of modern democratism is opposed to the injustice implied in the fact that many millions all over the world are doomed to functioning on a low level of achievement, only because they are unfortunate enough to be thrown, by birth or by circumstances, into social and/or cultural conditions detrimental to the preservation and the development of innate abilities.

But this equalitarian philosophy is strangely contrasted by the reactionary attitudes of most educators and social planners: without hesitation they accept the fact that many more representatives of non-abstract thinking, of achievement based on so-called practical abilities only, come from the disadvantaged strata of the population than would be justified by their numerical distribution in the total population. Non-abstractive functions are no less important, they say, for society, than those of the so-called abstract intelligence. Hence, there is nothing wrong in the differentiation of schooling or in the preparation of a small percentage of the school population only for functions implying abstract thinking and operations, if only adequate vocational or similar training is provided for the others.

One question, however, remains unanswered (if it is at all asked). Why should this relatively small percentage be recruited primarily from those strata in which the congenitally given potential of intelligence has better chances of survival? And why should the representatives of 'practical' functions come much more frequently from families in which social and/or cultural conditions are unfavourable to the preservation and development of abstract thinking (cf. p. 121)? To its preservation and development, we say, and not: to its emergence. Biologically, genetically, so we are told, no differences in the congenital level of intelligence can be found *between groups*.* But after a while, such group differences *do* become evident, a fact which the cultural pluralist then tends to accept as a social necessity (without being unduly disturbed by the fact that inequality and discrimination are its unavoidable concomitants).

To justify his indolence, he may use one of two arguments:

—that he is not a politician, that he is helpless, as an educator, in the face of the social order and the uncontrollable forces of culture change and transition through which human functions are liable to be impaired in their free development;

—that nothing can be done against processes of negative structurization which go on in human development under the influence of certain destructive environmental factors, and that the changes then taking place in the mental structure are irreversible.

In other words: the educator who believes in cultural pluralism is liable to lose sight of his responsibility for the rehabilitation of

* Even at the age of ten months examinations with the 'Gesell' scale did not reveal any significant developmental or functional differences between groups of infants born to parents from different socio-economic strata.

environmentally impaired intelligence. Pluralism vindicates, as it were, the principle of irreversibility, so that in the end the only responsibility which the teacher will be ready to accept, is that for preparing different children for different social functions, irrespective of whether the individual difference is the result of congenital or of secondary impairment of functions. In this case, however, the teacher is no longer entitled to speak of rehabilitation.

Moreover, it is doubtful whether vocational or any other so-called practical training is indeed an alternative to abstract thinking, even should we come to the conclusion that secondary retardation is irreversible. Does not such training, so we must ask, require and presuppose, in order to be effective, that very development of abstract thinking which is the essence of cognitive rehabilitation? So that in the end, the aim of teaching would prove to be one, the salvage and regeneration of abstractive abilities, whether within an academically or a practically oriented curriculum?

From what we have said so far, it follows that the concept of secondary retardation implies:

—impairment of an originally normal intelligence potential through the force of certain negative environmental factors;

—the existence of various modes of cognitive functioning, which differ essentially from those of genuine feeblemindedness as well as from each other, according to the essential causes responsible for their emergence and which can be defined by means of a phenomenological analysis (see Part One);

—reversibility through adequate methods of teaching, which should be related to those specific modes of cognitive functioning and their underlying essential causes rather than to the non-specific task of 'improving' the child's ability to think and learn (through simple enrichment programs, for instance);

—non-replaceability of such (inadequate) modes of cognitive functioning and particularly of the child's impaired ability to conceptualize and to think in abstract terms, by other, perhaps *less* impaired or even well-developed functions (in the fields of perception, of body control and motor abilities, of technical understanding, etc.).

Secondary retardation results, as we have tried to show in Part One, from a number of pathogenic conditions. We have summarized them on p. 149 of the present analysis and have added that none of these conditions becomes causally relevant in isolation but only in configuration with others. Not included in our list was 'institutional' care. Although the study of hospitalization and institutional care gave rise to an inquiry into the nature of secondary retardation, it would not seem justified to count the pathological results of institutional care among the varieties of secondary retardation. In another place [26], the present author has tried to compare with each other the essentials of the phases in the development of an institutionalized child, on the one hand, and a child who grows up under the externalizing conditions of poverty, on the other. Without repeating what has been said there, we propose to emphasize one point only, the difference between regularity and routine.

The experience of regularity must be embedded in that of personal relationship with significant persons; 'returning' events must be represented by the intentional 'return' of images in the child's immediate environment, in order to become meaningful for the emergence of what Erikson [11] calls a 'basic sense of trust'. When the child feels the personal involvement of those who take care of him at regular intervals and in response to his personal appeals, he may learn intentionality not only in his *personal* relationships but also in his relationships with the objects of his perception and learning. If, on the other hand, regularity is being experienced as impersonal routine, a process of conditioning is bound to set in, through which the child learns submissiveness, external imitation and indolence.

In the *first* case, the child is ready to accept and to recognize universally valid laws in the different fields of his learning, because he has experienced reliability of relationships and, through it, ever-growing clarity of differentiation between subject and object. (We have said in various contexts that man learns differentiation on the basis of the ever-recurring experience that he is an acting subject at the very moment when he is an object acted upon by others, *and vice versa.*) In the *second* case, he is unable to conceive of such universality because he has come to experience himself as an object only, primarily as an object of manipulation at the hands of his adults.

In the *first* case, the very experience of reliability strengthens the child's readiness to accept changes as possibly temporary, non-final, and passing only, and therefore arousing expectations and tensions, fears or hopes, defences or initiative. It is through such inner tensions that normally a child's time-consciousness grows, when, and to the extent that, he can master courage to leave and give up at least in phantasy an actual situation, in which he may find himself at a given moment (what we have called, following Goldstein [29], the precondition of abstract thinking). In the *second* case, in which the child is exposed to institutional routine, that is, to *im*personal regularity, exactly the opposite is liable to happen: the child may learn how to fear interruption of any given situation in which he finds himself 'by chance', will cling to it in all details and will reject any possible change. When we 'translate' this mental set into cognitive patterns, we are confronted with traits and modalities of thinking such as: rigid clinging to facts learned, without adapting them to changing task-contexts; over-dependence on authority; preference for stereotypes; and, in any case, preferring a remembered concretum to a law which claims universal validity and organizational, regulatory power over a multitude of facts (which, in the very emergence of the universally valid law, lose their concreteness).

This is but one example of the here suggested method of interpretation, which is characterized by two essentials: reducing objective causal factors to their psychological significance and defining cognitive corollaries of emotional and emotional of cognitive elements. Each category of thinking has an emotional meaning; the two levels are, in fact, identical (cf. pp. 176-178). Developmental psychology tends to deal with each of the two functions separately, as if they could be clearly distinguished from each other, cognition on the one hand, feeling and behavior on the other. Lines of influence and reaction are then being drawn, from one so-called functional area to the other and back. These are then defined as the *contents* of psychological research, while actually both areas should be studied as one. Actually, a psychology of thinking and learning becomes significant only to the extent that the emotional equivalents of cognitive categories are discovered; and a psychology of feeling or of—normal and abnormal—behavior derives its meaning from an analysis of psychodynamics and their influence on personality formation on the one hand, and on the formation of cognitive patterns on the other.

2 SOME CATEGORIES OF THINKING

Let us illustrate our claim by an analysis of such categories as: subject, object, boundaries and relationship, time, space and cause. But before entering into such an analysis, a word of warning may be needed: the structural identity of the emotional and the cognitive dimensions should be interpreted as an educational challenge rather than as a norm; normal human development requires a growing readiness and ability in the learner, to separate between the two levels, to control one while freely moving on the other. The less he will succeed in it, the more liable is a process of 'contamination' to set in, through which two things will happen: feeling will lose its spontaneity and degenerate into stereotypes, demonstrated pseudo-intensity or rationalizations; and thinking will be distorted by emotions, by fears, hopes, defences, complexes.

In other words, we should not confuse the structural identity between the elements of feeling and of thinking with the pathological (illegitimate) interference of emotions with thinking or of cognitive with feeling processes. Paradoxically, we may even say that the later, neurotic variety of illegitimate interference of one 'area' with the other indicates both, separation and inadequacy of separation: When a normally intelligent child becomes emotionally insecure as the result of experiencing his parents as ambiguous and tension-provoking, after having become dependent on them, it is this very insecurity that may make him cling to his negative experiences. They belong in this case (of neurotic reaction) almost invariably to the so-called anal or oedipal stages of development, in which some ego-agent of system-formation is already in existence and operates in reaction to the pathogenic experiences.

Reaction, however, presupposes separation that took place at the beginning of life when the infant's encounter with the parental figure was still more or less unambiguous: separation between subject and object, between ego and non-ego (see 24), and, we may add now, also between significant (that is, feeling-provoking) and neutral objects of relationships. As a result, the emotional and the purely cognitive, the personal and the semantic aspects of the categories of thinking (which we shall soon try to analyze) become separated from each other as well. What, then, means 'inadequacy of separation' in the cases of neurotic or character-neurotic development? It means that affective associations connect irrelevant traumatic memories, dating back to early, though not earliest, phases of development, with a specific cognitive task and thus revive, in part at least, the experiential equivalents (and roots) of the categories of thinking as well. It would be incorrect to speak in this case of secondary retardation (although learning will be impeded and/or distorted): separation between the emotional and the cognitive levels of the categories of thinking, which had taken place at the beginning of life, remains intact, at least potentially, so that a conscious confrontation (perhaps with the help of a therapist) between emotion and cognition remains possible.

But when a child *fails* to experience his parents as sources of regularity, polar relationships and differentiation (due to the conditioning influence of externalization in poverty and neglect or in cultural transition), separation between the two levels is liable *not* to take place in the first instance. The child may then continue to think in categories contaminated by, or even identical with, the external representatives, the occurrence-elements of his earliest experiences. Since these experiences are predominantly negative (experiences of want, lack of regularity and lack of consistently personal relationships), the categories, too, will bear the character of affect-charged negations, devoid of all relational qualities. This, however, means that they cannot be used adequately for cognitive tasks which require complete separation of the 'universals' from experiential particulars. This is man's handicap in secondary retardation: he is so much conditioned and bound to the universe of affectively charged occurrences that he cannot move freely in the area of anonymous laws. His categories are themselves distorted by feeling elements.

We shall now analyze a number of interrelated categories of thinking in order to show how the cognitive and the emotional levels of meaning are interwoven and how inadequacy of separation between the two levels becomes the essential element of defining secondary retardation.

Intentionality, we have said elsewhere [24], is an ego-modality. It, therefore, lends ego-character also to a non-ego, in which it appears as change-tendency, while in the ego, intentionality aims at system-formation. 'Intending' implies 'being intended'; the category of 'subject' implies that of 'object'. But both require the category of 'boundaries', meaning: delineation, between separate and interrelated areas of existence meaning structural organization *and* transcendence: Only when boundaries exist, change can take place through transcending them, systems can emerge within the limits of these boundaries.

Thus, the concepts of reality, process, action, reaction are intrinsically connected with that of intentionality. This, however, means that cognitive operations in which these concepts are of the essence require a basic feeling of security, which, in turn, results from the experience of consistent intentionality in the early phases of the individual's relationships with his environment, from the experience of being an intending and intended subject in polar relationship with an intending and intended object. Thus far the normative and structural interdependence of the emotional and the cognitive aspects of the categories of thinking. Transition from this stage to that in which the cognitive aspect dominates, means that the individual has learned how to use the concepts of 'subject' and of 'object' as anonymous instruments of semantics, independent of all personal associations and connotations.

The same applies to the category of 'boundaries'. Its emotional roots lie in the individual's experience that the environment imposes limitations, and that the individual's isolation (behind boundaries, as it were) can be eliminated by help coming from beyond these boundaries. If the environment consistently provides the experience that boundaries are a challenge to the child's initiative and that they are there to be overcome through such initiative, the category of 'boundaries' becomes universally applicable in cognitive operations. In this way, it can even be said to become the precondition of thinking as an active operation (in contrast to associative processes): differentiation, problem-solving, concept-formation, internalization of knowledge—all these and other cognitive activities require the existence of boundaries between the subject and the object, as resistance to be overcome and as a principle of organization.

In secondary retardation, the child continues to see objects as parts of his universe of the haveable only and in any case as being absolutely separate and not as intentionally related to the subject. Being a subject, then, means: waiting for solutions to occur, rather than developing initiative in finding solutions. 'Boundaries', then, mean something negative only, sources of frustration to be eliminated by ignoring them or by rejecting them forcefully. And cognition becomes arbitrary manipulation. Hence, the importance of reinterpreting the category of 'boundaries', if we want to rehabilitate the lost potentials of intelligence.

We have so far related only the category of 'boundaries', in its organizational and its dynamic meaning, to the categories of 'subject' and 'object'. Similarly, that of 'relationships' could and should be related to them. With the concept of boundaries, separation, with the concept of relationships—connectedness and unity are associated.

Transcending boundaries leads to relationships between an ego and its objects; establishing genuine relationships presupposes as well as strengthens the independence of their partners, that is, the existence of boundaries.

How are the emotional and the cognitive levels of meaning interwoven with each other in this category? In developmental, social and personality psychology, the concept of relationships is usually employed to connote normal and abnormal varieties of association between the individual and his human environment. In the psychology of thinking it refers to spatial order, temporal sequences and causal connections. In its first meaning the concept is positive *and* negative, in the second it is neither one nor the other. But to the extent that personal relationships contaminate, as it were, cognitive relations, it does not make any difference whether the former are of a positive or of a negative nature: in both cases, spatial, temporal or causal connections are liable to be distorted through the impact of personal associations.

We repeat what we have said above (p. 168): that we do *not* have in mind here later interference of emotions with thinking, in our case, the impact of a traumatic relationship experience on the perception of spatial, temporal or causal relations in a specific task of thinking and learning, at a later stage of ego-development. We deal here with a much more fundamental and at the same time much more complex problem: how the cognitive category of relations emerges in the child's mind through the mediation of primary experiences; how the evaluation of spatial distances, of temporal intervals, of possible causal effects is patterned by the child's evaluative reactions to the distance and the interval at which his 'primary figures' appear or to his earliest experience of the connection between his own actions and his environment's reactions.

'The dimensions of space and of time are—structurally given conditions of experience', we have said elsewhere [24], 'and as such are parts of man's inner non-ego ... Although (they) would never produce experience without ... the medium of empirical occurrences ... the latter would never produce the dimensions of space and time as organizational forms of experience but can only transform them into dynamic forces of development and ego-formation.'

'Thus, the category of space is represented in the inner non-ego through the images of "near and far", of "contained and alone", of "contact and emptiness", the category of time, through the images of "staticness and movement", of "halt and flux". In other words, the categories of experience are relational categories from the very first second of life on. Hence they enable the organism to experience the external environment as a likeness, a replica, of the inner non-ego, even though the environment may not always supply sufficient confirmative experience. We suggest that the categories of time and of space are primarily one, and that they are split into separate categories in the course of development only, through the actual life-process. It is the very contradictoriness of human existence that produces the separation of space from time.

'... Were there nearness, containedness, contact only, were there farness, isolation, emptiness only, there would be no time-experience (which requires the element of change). Were there halt only, staticness only, space would become meaningless, since tridimensionality presupposes movement. It would be correct to say the same, however, if there were movement only, since placeability, this second element of space, requires limitations' (24, pp. 12 f).

This quotation comes to support three claims:

a) that the categories of space and of time have their experiential equivalents (*not* their origin!) in early child-mother relationships, whose changing forms are accompanied by contradictory feelings;

b) that they are interdependent;

c) that it is the very contradictoriness of feelings that makes the categories into a dynamic reality.

Cognitive development and maturation of the individual means: gradual separation of each of the two categories from its experiential equivalents, thus setting them free of any personal association, making them into abstract, hence freely available instruments of organization. It also means: gradual separation of one category from the other. Thirdly, it means: gradual transformation of contradictoriness from being a dynamic tension factor into a cognitive stimulus: towards ever increased relativization and objectivization.

All we have said about the experiential equivalents of the categories of time and of space, or about their gradual separation from those emotionally charged equivalents, applies to the category of cause as well. In the case of the first-mentioned category (space) these equivalents are dialectic reflections on the conditions of the child in his relationships with the primary environment. The second category (time) reflects the dialectic basis of life-processes in general. In the third category, that of cause, the emotional as well as the existential elements of contradictoriness are being bridged. So interpreted, it supplements the before-mentioned categories of 'boundaries' and of 'relationships'. We said that transcending boundaries leads to relationships, and that the establishment of relationships increases the importance of boundaries as a principle of organization.

Both categories, however, imply the existence of subject- and object-poles as separated units, facing each other from beyond the boundaries or entering into relationships. The category of 'cause', on the other hand (implying, as it does, 'effect'), no longer leaves subject and object in their separateness, no longer requires the presumption of boundaries or even of relationships; essentially, it means that the power of determination is vested in one (human or material) factor. Thus, it is the category of cause, through which, paradoxically, autonomy is being experienced, first on the level of determining *non*-ego factors, later, to the extent that learning leads to internalization, on the ego level.

But it is precisely this undifferentiated conception of cause through which we can show again, that, and how the cognitive and the emotional levels of thinking are interwoven.

Determination means both, action and process. As action it elicits emotional reactions much more easily than as process, since action is associated with force, hence also with threat to personal freedom. Process, being less intentional, less ego-rooted, is less predictable, hence also less final and less threatening. For the same reason, process is less 'promising' than action. Thus, we see how the emotional components of the category of cause are essentially linked with its actional rather than with its processual meaning.

In the socially or culturally disadvantaged child, however, earliest frustrations of his relational needs support tendencies to mistrust *processes* (of development, of change, of determination); this child's causal thinking becomes, instead, dependent on actions expected to come (though as a rule unintelligibly) from the environment, actions which then, inevitably, evoke positive or negative emotions. Hence, causal thinking in the disadvantaged and therefore retarded child tends to be externalized and manipulative.

(Corrective and rehabilitative teaching should then try to develop the child's understanding for the meaning of cause in processes which lead from one condition to another, as against the concretistic conception of cause being a force of change.)

Not only are the categories represented in the human mind by images of a relational character, almost all of them appear as opposites. Identity and variety, the known and the unknown, whole and partial, protection and threat, intake and output, openness and closedness—all these and many other opposites are the basic categories of man's thinking and not only the ways in which he experiences his world and the events in his life.

But in order to fulfil its function as instrument of cognitive organization each category must be seen *balanced by its opposite.* Just, as, biologically, life is based on the laws of homeostasis, cognition normally depends on mutual relatedness between opposite experiences and between opposite categories. None should be seen as being of absolute validity, each should be seen as limited by its opposite one. Affective and irrational judgements are the inevitable concomitants of isolating one quality, one characteristic of reality, one experience, one category only and raising it to the level of absolute validity. The earlier in life such processes of isolation take place, whether for reasons of structural or constitutional defects or of negative experience, the smaller will be the chances for the child to learn through differentiation.

'Differentiation' has at least three connotations. It means:

a) recognition of the differences between phenomena, between events, between qualities, between feelings;

b) recognition of the fact that the validity of any statement is limited by its opposite (that and how contradictions co-exist);

c) recognition of the fact that opposites appear in many different forms.

The socially and culturally disadvantaged and therefore retarded child shows his underdeveloped ability to differentiate in each of these three meanings. Not only does he often fail adequately to differentiate between partially identical (that is, similar) facts or to identify partially identical elements; he also tends to dichotomize, as we have pointed out on several occasions already, to see opposites as two equally valid ends of one alternative rather than as interrelated factors of mutual limitation and relativization. Moreover, secondary retardation manifests itself in an extreme shrinkage of the multitude of possible opposites, until, in the end, the only remaining pair is that between 'mine' and 'not-mine'. All that is 'mine' is identical with 'present'; all that is 'not mine' is identical with 'absent'.

In other words: qualitative differentiation is being replaced, in the child whose intelligence is socially or culturally impaired, by the existential statement that something or someone is present or absent (cf pp. 82 ff). Whatever cognitive task he may face, will lose its qualitative specificness, when the sole mode of experience and the sole approach to solving a problem is by way of seeing a certain content matter as present or as absent. It is obvious—that relating facts or concepts to each other—this precondition of differentiation—thus becomes impossible.*

Does not our analysis of defective differentiation in the socially or culturally retarded child contradict what we have said before about his tendency to isolate one quality from all others and to overemphasize its importance? Overlooking differences certainly does not contradict dichotomization, since the latter is but a method preferred by the insecure to create the *illusion* of differences and thus to organize the intelligible universe of objects and events. But reducing the multitude of possible dichotomies to one pair of opposites, that of presence *versus* absence, actually goes beyond the principle of dichotomization, as which it is classified from a formal point of view only. In dichotomy 'black' is the opposite, not the absence of 'white'. Interpreting reality according to the principle of presence or absence of a certain trait or phenomenon, may even be called the opposite to dichotomization, since, in contrast to the latter, it is devoid of all value-emphasis.

And yet the two operations are closely connected with each other: while dichotomization is an attempt to restitute differentiation in the thinking process of a secondarily retarded child, the tendency to think only in terms of presence or absence supplements and vindicates that other tendency to isolate one trait or one quality from

---

* To give a few examples: Whereas, normally, man experiences *nearness as approximation* to presence, as a kind of preliminary stage, the socially retarded does not feel committed to nearness, since he recognizes presence only. *To be in contact* with something or with someone means nothing to him, since it implies the relative autonomy of two equal partners, hence also the co-existence or the alternation of presence and absence. *Every state, every condition* is conceived of as being 'final', not having either a beginning or an end, just being there or *not* being there. *Change* in a subject or in an object is hardly conceivable, as long as presence and absence are the only valid categories of thinking.

all others. The two patterns, far from being mutually exclusive, in fact co-exist. Both dichotomization and interpretation by presence or absence (of 'isolated' traits), lead to rigid clinging to what seems, at a certain moment at least, to be known and 'true'.

3 REHABILITATION THROUGH TEACHING

What can the teacher do in order to restore the child's intellectual abilities through the use of appropriate methods of instruction? This will be the subject of the following analysis of methods and the accompanying discussion of class events. It would seem, there are at least four types of corrective teaching actions, bearing in mind all we have said in both parts of the present study about cognitive deficiencies in secondary retardation. Each of these didactic interventions is meant to protect the pupils against the dangers inherent in their thinking patterns which are characterized by insufficient separation between the cognitive and the emotional elements in the basic categories of thinking: *

a) The teacher should try to develop in his pupils rational thinking *not* in order to weaken but in order to organize their phantasy-life; he should try to help them use imagination as a tool of discovering the dimensions of the possible, not as something opposed to reality, but as its supplementation. Above all, however, his pupils need rationality as a defence against their irrational dependence on chance associations or on concrete realities which they prefer to concepts.

b) The teacher should develop his pupils' readiness and ability to differentiate instead of using stereotypes, dichotomizations, misunderstood analogies, or other means of distorting simplification.

c) He should try to increase their readiness and ability to take upon themselves responsibility for their acts of thinking and learning instead of relying on chance solutions, manipulative pseudo-operations or on the authority of sources (books) or of teachers.

d) He should endeavor to help them operate on two levels of

---

* The following is an elaboration of what has been said in Chapter 6, translated into a rationale of didactics.

thinking simultaneously, whether the task be one of perceiving two aspects of one problem or one of carrying out two cognitive directives at one and the same time.

None of these types of intervention is exclusively applicable to a specific learning-and-teaching situation or, better, to a specific faulty pattern of thinking. Rationality requires differentiation and *vice versa.* The pupil will become responsible for his acts of thinking and learning to the extent that he is able to think rationally and to differentiate, and, on the other hand, he will learn rationality and differentiation through feeling responsible. Operating on two levels simultaneously presupposes the three other cognitive modalities. The emphasis, however, is different in each type of intervention, and the didactic methods will differ accordingly, as we shall try to show on the following pages.

In every case, however, the teacher must be prepared to assume that the experiential elements of the basic categories of thinking are responsible for his pupils' wrong answers, whatever their place in the here suggested classification may be. He must therefore relate every explanation of the meaning, the function and the factual basis of a concept simultaneously to the level of its (possible) experiential equivalents and to that of logic. This is one of the ways to deprive the emotional concomitants of thinking of their distorting impact on learning.

We shall try to apply these remarks to a number of basic categories, which we have discussed on the preceding pages (subject, object, space, time, cause and relationships):

a) The teacher should emphasize the formal, grammatical significance of the concepts of *subject and object* as against the personal associations which are liable to be evoked by them. Socially or culturally retarded children tend to see in every subject and object bearers of intentions directed towards them. Hence, their attention is concentrated more on the *content* of subject, action and object than on the *relations* between them. This, then, gives rise to what might be called personalistic thinking, and many of the cognitive peculiarities mentioned later, particularly in the third group, are rooted in this structural deficiency (f.i. dependence on authority, misunderstanding causality as the product of manipulation, personification, but also: preference for concrete data or symbols to concepts). In formal, grammatical thinking, on the other hand, content is unimportant and can be exchanged without affecting the meaning of the sentence.

b) The teacher should try, again and again, to weaken the unconscious associations connected with the category of *space*, from the beginning of life on: fear of what is liable to approach and injure or of what is liable to vanish and leave you isolated; feeling alleviated at the approach of help and rescue or at the disappearance of threats. The teacher must try to replace these primary feelings (of which the child is certainly not aware!) by an adequate understanding of the dimensions of space, which allow for comparison and measurement. Space must be conceived of as a category of orientation, free of all personal feelings of fear or hope, of all irrelevant associations.

c) The emotional components of the category of *time* stem from the infant's experience of the regularity in the rhythm of adult interventions with his existence as a dependent being. To separate the emotional components of time from its purely cognitive elements means: understanding time as the regulating principle of events, also, and particularly, when they are not connected with each other in a relationship of meaningful continuity; it means: understanding time, 'within which' certain events take place that are not necessarily connected by links of cause and effect.

d) The teacher of disadvantaged and therefore retarded children must try to replace their conceptions of *cause* as something dependent on their manipulations by an understanding for the universality of laws, laws binding everyone alike. The child must learn to see 'cause' as an intrinsic quality of events rather than as the result of his more or less arbitrary activities.

e) The teacher must teach the child how to perceive *relationships* not only in their personal, but also in their formal meaning. Here again, grammatical explanations and exercises may help develop formal understanding of 'relationships', f.i. by way of comparing with each other the significance of different prepositions and by analyzing their impact on contexts of meaning.

The aim common to all these didactic interventions is, as we have already pointed out: to help the child separate more effectively the cognitive elements of concepts from their emotional counterparts or their earliest experiential roots. Each of the methods explained on the following pages offers opportunities for such interventions. In other words: correcting a faulty conception of the basic categories of thinking, which we have mentioned here does not require *specific* interventions (though they do not exclude them either), but must be chanelled through each didactic activity meant to bring about more rationality, more differentiation, more responsibility for the learning acts.

It may be argued that faulty attitudes or conceptions, rooted in the earliest phases of development and experience cannot be corrected since they form part of the child's structure (reference is made to Chapter V of the author's book *The Roots of the Ego* which deals with the complex problem of structurization and reversibility, a problem which has also been dealt with at some length in the present study—see pp. 67 ff). Suffice it here to point out that, whatever the chances of complete reversal of structurized attitudes and conceptions may be, the teacher of underprivileged and therefore retarded children must remain aware of the fact that powerful affective tendencies are liable to distort his thinking; he must accept this fact and relate to it in each of his teaching actions, irrespective of whether or not he can prove the presence of such, mostly unconscious, influences.

We shall now deal with a number of faulty patterns in the cognitive structure of the socially or culturally retarded child and shall suggest some didactic interventions specifically related to each of these patterns. (We repeat what we have already said: every pattern can be classified differently as well, and the methods suggested as counter-measures against one may be useful as counter-measures against the other patterns as well.)

A Strengthening Rational Thinking

(a) *Irrelevant associations*

Rational thinking is often jeopardized by the interference of autonomous reality factors represented by associations. *Irrelevant associations* are those that spontaneously establish connections between a specific task of problem-solving or of learning and memories of previous experiences, without passing through the control of conscious selection, that is, without being submitted to the mind's activity. Relevant are those associations that are being recognized as essential to the specific cognitive task.

Irrelevant associations should be distinguished from what we propose to call 'unstructured phantasies.' They, too, appear spontaneously and autonomously; they, too, are uncontrolled. But they are rooted in an inner world of mental processes, more often than not pathological in nature, rather than in previous chance recalled experiences. Unlike 'ordinary', that is, structured phantasies, they are not fed or directed by forces and contents of the unconscious, they are devoid of all inner logic. The extreme character and even their absurdity are, strangely enough, sources of satisfaction and substitutes for thinking. Their emergence indicates not only ego-weakness in cognitive functions but also emotional disturbance, particularly in a child who has passed that early phase of development in which such an indifferentiated life with phantasies is natural.

In other words: we should distinguish between 'irrelevant associations' and a process of passively being drawn into wild and unstructured phantasies which appear automatically, as it were, and are frequently followed by others, no less unstructured, phantasies that are little more than responses to intrapsychic processes of unknown origin. While they characterize the thinking processes of severely disturbed youngsters (and adults), they are *not* to be counted among the essential characteristics of socially or culturally retarded children, most of whom remain unaffected in their emotional reactions.

Whenever a teacher of s.r. children* encounters cases in which intrapsychic disorders operate simultaneously with secondary retardation he may try to counteract their symptoms of ego-weakness by using cognitive means and thus *prevent* further deterioration.† In this case, the teacher should constantly try to confront the child with the dimensions of the possible as intrinsically *connected* with defineable givens, as a kind of logical and rational enlargement of reality. He should show the child in which ways this conception of the 'possible' differs from the one in which the 'possible' is nothing but an arbitrary, completely unrealistic 'appendix' to reality.

These methods meant to strengthen thinking in s.r. children are of greater importance as strategies of prevention than as means of rehabilitation. It is a well-known fact that growing-up under conditions of extreme poverty and educational neglect, or, as we would prefer to say, under conditions of externalization, are conducive not only to secondary retardation but also to inadequate separation

* In the following the abbreviation 's.r. children' will be used to connote secondarily, that is socially or culturally retarded children.

† Although he may have to call for the help of a case-worker or even a therapist, should the case be extreme.

between the ego and the non-ego. This inadequacy, in turn, is responsible for partial replacement of reality by phantasies, even in later phases of development, when ordinarily the distinction between inner and outer reality is fairly well established. Hence the relative frequency of psychotic diseases in lower class families. (30a)* Hence the decisive importance of the teacher's corrective interventions as means of preventing escalation into quasi-psychotic withdrawal. Unstructured phantasies should also be interrupted as quickly and as radically as possible for the sake of other, less disturbed children in the class who can easily be brought to imitate the wild phantasy production of one disturbed child. (Needless to add that any discussion of the possibly underlying personal experiences of a child must be avoided under all circumstances in the presence of other children.)

But we must now return to analyzing *irrelevant* associations as against those wild and unstructured phantasies which we have discussed so far.

Irrelevant associations may be of a cognitive or of an emotional order, may have their sources in something learned before,† in emotionally charged personal experiences or in social or cultural patterns. They are distinguished from both, the above-mentioned experiential elements of categories and what we have called unstructured phantasies. The experiential elements of categories are always intrinsically connected with a specific concept, and their distorting influence on cognitive processes goes through the emotional reactions that are liable to be aroused at the time this specific concept is used. Irrelevant associations, on the other hand, are rooted in *later* experiences of the child, *not* connected with a specific concept and therefore liable to appear 'at their own discretion', as it were. But insofar as they are rooted in some kind of *past* experience, they are essentially different also from unstructured phantasies, the latter being connected with some *immediately* acting, internal stimulus only. It is true that some irrelevant associations may be due to stimulus contiguity as well; but then they differ from unstructured phantasies by the absence of all affective intensity.

To counteract associations, the teacher must try to refer to such —possibly interfering—experiences (though he must be careful not to glide-off, while doing so, into pseudo-therapeutic discussions). He

---

* The fact is often overlooked that psychotic disorders resulting from structural defects are more frequent in these strata than neuroses resulting from drive repression.

† Unless they are elicited simply by external stimuli, such as sounds or words, or by the preceding answer of another child.

also must have recourse to methods meant to strengthen the learner's sense of responsibility for his acts of thinking and learning.

We may even go one step further and say that the 'autonomous' interference of associations with the child's thinking process necessitates permanent awareness and readiness on the part of the teacher to examine even those associations that may seem to be 'correct' and, in any case, may have produced correct answers. The teacher must never rely on the regulating power of a s.r. child's associations. It may, of course, happen in the thinking processes of an ordinary child as well, that associations, without being essentially connected with the problem to be solved, produce correct answers. But the weaker the child's ego is and the less reliable its functions of organization and co-ordination are, the more important become the teacher's critical controls and interventions, meant for instance, to demonstrate to the child where and why his associations are inadequate for the solution of a certain learning-problem.

In a regular class, where most of the pupils have a relatively well developed power of integration, the teacher's function is made much easier: he can rely on the children's ability to 'select' associations. In other words: normally, the learner's integrational and selective power prevents the emergence of rigid connections between certain chance-conditioned associations and certain trends of thinking. Not so in the s.r. child: for him, regulation and selection are the teacher's functions.

So far, no distinction has been made between associations of an emotional and a cognitive order, between associations the roots of which lie in some personal experience and others rooted in cultural patterns. True enough, their negative and distorting influence on thinking processes may be equal irrespectively of their origin. But from the teacher's point-of-view, the difference is one of the essence: it is relatively easier to sever the ties between a s.r. child's faulty thinking-pattern and associations of cognitive than of emotional origin, since the degree of ego-involvement tends to be lower in the first case. The same applies to personally as against culturally conditioned associations: while personal experience and the associations accompanying them change frequently, culture-conditioned associations are considerably more obstinate and, therefore, require much more intensive intervention on the part of the teacher.

In other words: the more the intervening associations are determined by unconscious forces and contents, the more difficult and comprehensive become the functions of rehabilitative teaching. The stronger the interference of associations with cognitive processes are being felt (although they may not always be clearly defineable), the more must the teacher be ready to rely on guesses and presumptions when working with s.r. children.

(b) *Concretizations*

It has been stated, time and again, that s.r. children 'prefer' concrete realities to abstractions. Their basic insecurity finds its most dangerous expression in this preference (of examples to formulae or laws, of specific concepts in which as many elements of qualification are preserved to more general and more comprehensive concepts). An ordinary child is courageous enough to leave the universe of concrete givens for the security of general laws and concepts; he knows that it is precisely this generality that allows for regulation of, and mastery over, that bewildering multitude of ever-changing, hence unreliable, phenomena which we call 'reality'.

It may sound strange when we speak of 'preferences' while dealing with problems of concept-formation and abstraction. But this is exactly the issue under discussion: the s.r. child is, we have said, unable effectively to separate, and keep apart from each other, the area of feelings and preferences and the area of purely conceptual and formal operations. No need to point out again what we tried to make clear at some length in the preceding paragraph (see pp. 167 ff) and in the examples analysed on pp. 176 ff: that this 'contamination' of the cognitive by the emotional fields is *not* the result of interferences of later, emotionally charged, experiences or associations with thinking processes (such as we know from the study of so-called emotional blockings or of pseudo-feeblemindedness due to pre-oedipal and oedipal conflicts). It dates back to the first stages in the child's development and to the lack of differentiation that characterizes these phases in the life of a s.r. child.

The faulty cognitive patterns, of which the above-mentioned remarks on cause, space, time etc. (see pp. 176) are but a few examples, manifest themselves not only in those basic categories of thinking but also in a general preference of concrete givens to concepts. Their distorting influence on cognitive processes, it is true, 'goes through' those categories (which is the reason why we cannot always isolate them in specific learning situations); but to the extent that insufficient separation of the cognitive from the emotional fields leads to the here-discussed 'preference' of concrete data of reality to the unreality of concepts, the *result* should be classified as a manifestation of irrationality. The teacher must try to expose the s.r. child, again and again, to the need of giving up his universe of examples and of data for the benefit of concepts and of laws; in other words: he must try to correct this faulty pattern of thinking by repeated 'experiments with courage'.

It may be asked why we do not include the pattern in group B (Differentiation). In structural terms it is undoubtedly proof of incomplete differentiation between the stimulus-sending object world and the actively reacting and synthesizing subject. Irrationality, however, is the *outcome* of precisely this lack of structural differentiation. Strengthening differentiation would not be sufficient to combat the here-discussed 'preference' of concrete data; the teacher must also try to weaken the s.r. child's tendency passively to react to chance-stimuli coming from reality and to make him feel more 'at home' with general concepts and laws. This, however, is what we call 'strengthening rationality': to loosen the s.r. child's fixation to those modes of operation that are characterized by irrational escape from abstraction into the (equally irrational) 'security' of concrete realities.

As a matter of fact, we could mention in this connection all those signs of externalized behavior and thinking that we have analyzed in detail elsewhere (f.i. 26): identifying social or moral values with their material manifestations; replacing inner tensions or conflicts by their external corollaries; fixation to what seems to be known as a means to avoid adequate differentiation and recognition of what is new and objectively unknown (see also B!); overlooking interpersonal relationships and their specific causal connections under the impact of external facts. In all these or other symptoms of externalization, concretization replaces abstraction.

(c) *Symbols instead of concepts*

Strengthening rational modes of cognitive operation is a useful instrument in the hands of the teacher when trying to protect a s.r. child not only against distorting phantasies and associations but also against his tendency to prefer symbols to concepts. It will be remembered what we have said in the sixth chapter (pp. 133 ff) about the vital need for developing the s.r. child's power of imagination and phantasy. We have emphasized there the value of seeing 'wholeness', precisely for a child growing-up without a basic sense of trust, which normally provides that experience of wholeness (and therefore prepares for differentiation). In another place (p. 156), we have mentioned the *positive* functions of symbols as against the relative weakness of conceptualization in the child whose intelligence is impaired. It would be, indeed, a grave mistake to underestimate symbols in an effort to strengthen rational attitudes, since symbols stimulate thinking. This, however, is not contradicted by our present claim: the contents and the expressive intentions of symbols must be understood rationally if we want to rehabilitate impaired intelligence.

When we speak here of symbols, we have in mind neither the literary nor the mathematical variety. In the first case, the aim of the symbol is: to enlarge and to deepen our understanding of the symbolized content, to open the reader's eyes for allusions. It means: strengthening our ability to experience what is concealed, while, at the same time, keeping in mind the connection between the concealed and reality. Man's ability to distantiate himself wilfully from the world of symbols is one of their essential elements (and one of the reasons why he can enjoy them).

We need not discuss, here, the symbol in its mathematical meaning: the latter represents but an abbreviation of complex thinking-processes, particularly of thinking about spatial or quantitative relations. In this respect, there is no essential difference between the teacher's functions in an ordinary class and his function with socially or culturally retarded children. In both cases, he must try to translate the symbols into their relational meaning.

But here, we have in mind the symbol as a *substitute* for concepts in the cognitive pattern of a s.r. child. We could speak here of a symbol taking the place of meaning, and not necessarily of what is meant by the symbol, but rather of the meaning of the problem under discussion in the class-situation (the problem to be learned or to be solved). In his thinking, the symbol, any symbol, may replace the most different answers that he may be expected to give. In other words: in this case, it is precisely the use of symbols in which lack of differentiation and lack of rational thinking find their expression. Hence, it is through analyzing the contents and intentions of the symbol that it will lose its irrational meaning and its affective impact on the s.r. child's ways of thinking. It is only through such rationalization that the symbol can be recognized as what it really is: a product of man-in-history, rather than a pre-existing part of reality. (And we may add the seeming paradox that it is through such rationalization that the symbol will become more strongly representative of wholeness and unity—though on a plane of cognition and no longer on a plane of reality).

B Developing the Ability to Differentiate

(d) *Inability to comprehend differences and similarities*

To the extent that lack of differentiation manifests itself in the child's failure to recognize differences between similar phenomena and similarities between different phenomena (personal qualities or events or objects), the teacher's function is obvious; its is, in fact, common to all teaching methods. But the teacher of s.r. children must know that, at least in the beginning stages of his rehabilitative teaching, he must always be prepared for finding expressions of defective differentiation in his pupils and should therefore offer corrective explanations as frequently as possible. For this purpose, he must refer to the observable facts of reality, rather than to phantasies, associations, symbols or analogies; it is through the medium of such facts that similarities and differences should be 'learned', before differentiation can be applied to more complex issues (such as understanding the essence of analogies, recognition of relativity, of nuances, of personal versus cognitive problems, of differences between points on the scale of the time-continuum etc.).

(e) *Analogy as identity*

In secondary retardation, we are often faced with distortions of reality contexts and cognitive tasks resulting from a confusion of analogy with identity. The dimension of the 'As If' is unknown to the s.r. child. Although we could include this kind of faulty pattern in the first-mentioned group as well (since it always contains an element of irrationality) it would seem to be much more meaningful to ask what type of 'exercises in *differentiation*' are required to sensitize the s.r. child to recognizing the essence of analogies.

They aim at answering questions such as: 'What is the function of analogies as against that of direct statements of facts?' 'When does partial similarity allow for the use of analogies?' These could also be called 'exercises in hypothetical thinking'.

As a rule, we see the importance of analogies in that they help enlarge man's horizon, stimulate his imagination and develop synthesis and differentiation at one and the same time. But analogies will fulfil these functions only when those who use them remain aware of the element of comparison contained in them. On this condition, two, apparently, contradictory, tendencies can be satisfied: the tendency to perceive connections between the innumerable and always different phenomena of this world, and the tendency to differentiate between them and not to lose one's sense of orientation within the diversity of facts.

There can always be found children who will oppose the use of analogies precisely because their extreme need for accuracy may be offended by the 'As If' character of analogies. Others will tend to escape from differentiation and accuracy into 'unifying' analogies. The socially or culturally retarded child does not belong to either group: he does not escape into analogies, but is liable to be drawn into them, as long as the teacher has not succeeded in teaching him the rules and the value of accurate differentiation between facts and analogies. But he does not escape from analogies either, since his power of imagination is not sufficiently developed. It is precisely for this reason that explaining the functions of analogy, the conditions under which its use may be legitimate, and its differences from reality-facts, is of vital importance in the instruction of socially or culturally retarded children.

(f) *Dichotomization*

Simplifying variety by dichotomies is one of the main symptoms of externalization and secondary retardation. The teacher must, therefore, use every attempt by his pupils to 'organize reality' to show them the falsity and futility of absolutistic statements and to make them familiar with the ways of relativization and objectivity. True enough, much security can be found in the pseudo-systematization of 'Either-Or', and much encouragement is needed to 'leave' this security. But once the s.r. child will have understood that the world becomes more interesting and more reliable precisely through the discovery of alternatives and of relativity (in accordance with a variety of possible criteria), this may become a turning-point on his way to regaining his lost intellectual abilities.

Dissolving false dichotomies can, of course, also be seen as one of the methods of strengthening rational thinking or the child's sense of responsibility for his thinking. This is far from being a problem of semantics or of classification. We are interested, primarily, in the question of didactic conclusions to be drawn from the different ways of classifying the teacher's attempts to act against dichotomization:

When we regard these attempts as means to develop differentiation, we emphasize the *informational* aspects of the learner's sensitivity to differences which exclude dichotomization.

When we regard them as means to strengthen rational thinking, we have in mind *replacing the learner's false feeling of security* (rooted, as it is, in irrational, mostly unconscious, motives) by readiness to live with, and to face, the bewildering multitude of facts without escaping into simplifying schemes of 'organizing' them.

When we regard them as means to develop the learner's responsibility for his thinking and learning, we think of the need to cause the s.r. child to become *involved in his cognitive tasks*; when the child is not allowed to think schematically (and dichotomization is only one variety of such schematic thinking), his involvement is likely to grow: thinking becomes more difficult, more complicated, hence also more responsible, once the way out into dichotomization is blocked.

One and the same didactic action can fulfil the functions simultaneously; but the teacher must nevertheless remain aware of their difference and must give expression to each of them.

(g) *Presence and absence*

Dichotomization recognizes only contradiction between two opposites. Both are realities, the one of positive, the other of negative value. Thus, every phenomenon is defined as being the negation of its opposite rather than through its own essence.

Different from, though closely connected with, this tendency is another one, as we have already mentioned (pp. 174 ff), the tendency to see reality as an 'extension' only of one specific phenomenon accidentally perceived, whether it is an object, a quality, behavior or event. We could speak here of a simplifying and distorting monism, a limitation of reality through identifying an accidentally perceived part of this reality with the whole. Here, we find no value element, in contradiction of dichotomization.

It may perhaps be argued that, in comparison with this form of defective thinking, even dichotomization is preferable. Could we not see in it an attempt to overcome the accidentality and the simplification inherent in that distorting 'monism', a precondition of relativity?

It is true that the tendency simply to see reality in the light of an accidentally perceived (or non-perceived) 'present' (or 'absent') phenomenon indicates a lesser ability for cognitive organization than dichotomization; for, partial perception means the exclusion of many reality-parts; dichotomization means the exclusion of nuances in whatever reality-part may be perceived. But it would be a mistake to draw the conclusion that a tendency to use dichotomies could counteract, as it were, that other more 'primitive', tendency here discussed. On the contrary: it is easy for the child to glide from the tendency to identify reality with what happens to be there at a given moment, into dichotomization. But this certainly does not help him to think more adequately. In both cases the teacher must try to enlarge the child's consciousness, through developing his perception of as many reality-parts as possible, or through explaining the meaning of nuances. The child must learn that the simple existence of a certain phenomenon does not exclude the existence of others, different from the first one and not necessarily its opposites. The child must learn that even an 'opposite' phenomenon is but one alternative among many; and that it cannot be defined or properly recognized by negating it but, on the contrary, only by accepting it as another form of existence.

To sum-up: perceiving reality as an extension of an accidentally perceived phenomenon—which may be 'present' at a given moment and 'absent' at another—results in a much more dangerous limitation of reality than using dichotomies. In the first case, reality becomes dependent on the accidentality of our perception and subsequent concentration on a phenomenon. Only what happens by chance to enter our conscious mind, 'exists'; all the rest remains 'outside'. This is a way of thinking devoid of all principles of regulation and organization (in clear contradistinction of dichotomies).

It may perhaps be claimed that we are dealing here with a restriction of perceptive abilities as a cause, but not as a symptom of defective thinking. And it will perhaps be added that this deficiency is characteristic of genuine feeblemindedness rather than of secondary retardation. But then, we should bear in mind that restricted perception may be, both, a cause and an expression of faulty thinking, and that it means something different in each case. It is true that, in the first case it is characteristic of genuine feeblemindedness, while in the second case it is a symptom of secondary retardation: in the first case, a general tendency to simplify reality is one of the expressions of structural rigidity (and as such causes the feebleminded person's faulty thinking); in secondary retardation, on the other hand, restricted perception is the—reversible—result of a process of conditioning.

It can be maintained that some of the categorial deficiencies mentioned above (see pp. 176 ff) are reflected in the here-discussed tendency to interpret reality in terms of presence and absence: their prototype and its roots may be seen in the child's earliest experience that his significant environmental figures are either 'present' or 'absent', but that no understandable or foreseeable connection and continuity exists between the two states.

(h) *Stereotypes*

The same restriction of reality which finds its expression in the two last-mentioned tendencies results also from the use of stereotypes. Absence of differentiation is common to the three modes of faulty thinking, but the latter is the most obstinate one: the quasi-autonomy of stereotypes and their culture-conditioned contents endow them with authority comparable to that of the 'book' or the teacher. They are attractive because they offer ready-made answers, sanctioned by tradition, and they are often rooted in the trans-personal areas of the unconscious.

Counteracting stereotypes is, therefore, one of the most complex tasks in the art of teaching socially or culturally retarded children. We must not forget that giving up a stereotype often means giving up the protective belief in the parents' authority. Hence it would be futile to base rehabilitative efforts on purely rational operations without simultaneously dealing with the child's irrational attachement to his culture and family. The teacher must beware of belittling those cultural roots of stereotypes. They cannot be eliminated effectively, unless adequate measures are taken to strengthen the child's sense of security through non-cognitive as *well* as cognitive interventions.

These interventions require, of course, constant readiness to develop the learner's ability to differentiate. At the same time, however, we could include them in the group of didactical measures meant to strengthen his feeling of being responsible for his thinking and learning or his rationality. It can be maintained that the two last-mentioned groups are *included* in the first, at least insofar as responsibility and rationality *presuppose* differentiation. But for the teaching process it makes indeed a difference to which of the three groups we relate the didactical attempts to eliminate stereotypes.

When we see in them means of developing differentiation, we have in mind, first and foremost, making the learner aware of the limits of a 'truth' expressed by stereotypes; making him see the exceptions in the light of which the stereotype is bound to become dubious; in other words: making him skeptical as to the validity of the stereotype.

When we see in them means of strengthening rational thinking, we have in mind helping the learner overcome his irrational attachment to his family and his culture through which he has 'learned' his stereotypes, and overcome his tendency to replace thinking by believing in an absolute truth and to feel attracted by it.

When we emphasize the learner's responsibility and personal initiative, we have in mind counter-acting his tendency to escape into passive dependence on what claims to be 'facts'. This dependence is not identical with blind belief in the absolute truth: such belief presupposes acceptance of something 'known' to be true, whereas dependence means passiveness.

([illegible]) *Indiscriminate use of 'scientific' terms*

Different from the preference for culturally conditioned stereotypes is the *indiscriminate use of scientific terms* in contexts of learning or problem-solving in which that term is inadequate or even meaningless.

This pattern can be interpreted as manifestation of an externalized value-system: terminology is attractive because it makes possible the illusion of intelligent reactions and of equality with the sophisticated masters of knowledge and understanding. Neither a normally intelligent nor a truly retarded child show similar tendencies: critical self-evaluation, one of the characteristics of intelligent behavior, precludes readiness to indulge in that illusion; the feebleminded is unable to conceive of the symbolic significance of terminology. We can therefore define the pattern here under discussion as a different indicator of externalization and secondary retardation.

The question then arises what didactic steps the teacher should take to counteract such a tendency to use terminology indiscriminately and inadequately. One may feel tempted to include the interventions to be used against it among those meant to develop rationality: the externalized belief in that magic power of words and the affective element of satisfaction gained through the use of empty terminology certainly preclude rational attitudes towards a cognitive task. But, on the other hand, it would be a mistake to believe that actions meant to *prove* the irrationality underlying that pattern could effectively counteract it. On the contrary: they are more likely to provoke an affective chain-reaction (of shame and withdrawal or of stubborn insistence and reinforcement), at least when the teacher uses them in class, that is, in the presence of others.

Some teachers may then draw the conclusion that the best way of counteracting this faulty pattern is—simply to ignore it; others may prefer explaining *why* a specific term used by the pupil is inadequate or irrelevant in the context of the problem-to-be-solved. But all will agree that didactic interventions meant to develop differentiation are more effective than actions implying reference to the irrationality of the pattern.

On the other hand, strengthening the ability to differentiate may not have the desired effect of rehabilitating impaired intellectual potentials, if we fail to take into account the personality factors of ego weakness and avoidance patterns, of passiveness and irrationality. In the re-education of s.r. children, differentiation has not only its immediate cognitive function, but should, at the same time, be seen as a factor contributing to a growing feeling of security and ego-strength. Only then will the child become ready to give up his dependence needs, his concretistic preferences, his modes of simplification, his quasi-magic belief in words as well as all those other faulty modes of operation which we are going to discuss.

(j) *Cognitive versus personal problems*

It is difficult for s.r. children to distinguish between the two meanings of the concept of 'problem'. The teacher uses the term when he tries to teach his pupils how to find a solution in one of the subject-matters of learning. The child, however, encounters 'problems' every day in their practical and personal significance, problems that usually *cannot* be solved. A cognitive problem is closed, as it were, when it is solved; the personal problem, on the other hand, remains open, At best, its intensity decreases for some time, owing to some chance occurrences or even to a day-dream only. But even then, the underprivileged learns from his bitter experience that the personal problem returns every day anew and demands from him always renewed efforts to solve it.

In other words: the underprivileged is necessarily much more involved in the personal problems of his environment and of himself than he will ever be in his problems of thinking and learning. The latter 'have' a solution, so he feels, and the teacher who knows this solution, must transmit it to him. But once he has learned (that is, received) it, be it through mechanical, be it through active learning, this problem ceases to be one in his eyes; his thinking is then free not to invest itself any longer in this area. The child no longer considers it necessary to renew cognitive contact with that problem and thereby to let it become a recurrent topic of his thinking and learning. Nor is he ready to put himself in the place of someone who once had to face that problem and solve it. The mere fact that it has been solved makes it into something given alongside other givens, no longer representing a challenge to his thinking.

We can understand this tendency in a socially or culturally retarded child, when we consider how limited his freely available cognitive energy is, and how many thinking tasks are imposed on him. He therefore must be economical, and he cannot afford wasting energy on tasks of 'thinking for the sake of thinking', on some sort of cognitive games with solved problems that have long become facts.

From a didactical point-of-view, the question is far from being a purely semantic one, and it is not enough for the teacher simply to explain to his pupils the difference between the two meanings of the concept, the personal and the cognitive one. It is more important for the child to accept the existence of these two kinds of problems, so not to allow the area of the first ones to distort the meaning of learning assignments. Emotional associations that usually accompany personal problems should not interfere with thinking processes aimed at finding the right solution to a learning-task.

But it is only at this point that the process of differentiation starts. Its aim will be achieved, when the learner will be able to relate himself differently to the *facts* that are at the basis of personal and those that are at the basis of cognitive 'problems'. In the first instance, 'facts' co-exist with the difficulty caused by them, and finding an, at least temporary, way-out of it depends on changing these facts. In the second case, 'facts' exist independently of the problem which actually comes into existence only through the one who formulates it and uses the facts for its solution, whenever he decides to do so.

Here, strengthening the child's ability to differentiate serves as a means of rehabilitative teaching insofar as he must learn how to change, his attitude to problem-solving: *not* through *changing* facts (as in the area of his personal experience), *but* through neutrally *accepting* facts as a basis of drawing conclusions or confirming claims; *not* through *identifying* facts with problems *but* through *separating* between them; *not* through becoming *emotionally* involved in facts and problems, *but* through *keeping apart*, as much as possible, cognitive concentration on a problem and its solution, from feelings. The child we have in mind here should come to know that there exist always a number of ways leading to the solution of a problem, and that a problem 'remains' as such, independently of its solution.

To attain this goal, the teachers should compare with each other different learning assignments (questions), different formulations of the same question, different approaches to answering that question. In this way, the child becomes more elastic and more mobile in his learning; this, in turn, will help protect the learner against the danger of investing personal feelings in his approach to his thinking —and learning-tasks, where such feelings are out of place and are only liable to distort the perception of a problem and its solution.

We have already mentioned the essential difference that exists between the principles of rehabilitative teaching and those of progressive education (see p. 130 and p. 145). The latter is based on the presumption that the child's emotional involvement in his learning strongly stimulates the process of thinking and learning; their meaningfulness and their effectiveness increases to the extent that the child invests in these processes his whole personality, his emotions. Should this personal involvement produce personal disturbances (particularly in a child coming from a problem-family), the *psychologist* may have to intervene, but not the teacher in his classroom activities. Should this involvement jeopardize a child's capacity of abstract thinking and learning, this may not be altogether an indication of failure; on the contrary: in one case, the manifestation of the conflict in the child's 'personal' way of learning may serve as a basis for sublimation or for the development of 'substitute' skills; in another case, it may even be decided to leave the child alone with his personal problems.

Those, however, who will derive the optimal benefit from progressive education are the intellectually gifted and highly differentiated children whose abilities will also, as a rule, help them overcome their personality difficulties, at least in the area of learning. But the socially or culturally deprived and retarded child is different: in his case, the primary and decisive function of teaching is developing his capacity for abstract thinking and for differentiation. He, too, must be involved in his learning, but this involvement means something different, almost the opposite of what it means in progressive education: ego-emphasis, for him, means—becoming the bearer, the subject, of responsibility for his learning, placing himself opposite the universe of objective facts, decreasing the relative weight of personal *experience* as against that of personal *initiative*.*

(k) *Narrow time-consciousness*

When we include the enlargement of a limited time-consciousness in the group of didactic interventions meant to develop and to strengthen the child's ability to differentiate, we have in mind the following facts:

a) the child must learn that the past cannot be understood adequately as long as we try to interpret it in the light of our present experience. Nor can the future be imagined adequately, if we regard it as a repetition or a perpetuation of the present.

b) the child should learn that continuity between past, present and future does not mean that they are identical. Something or someone may develop from phase to phase and may continue to develop, and this something or this someone may be self-identical in each of these phases. But their remembered past and their imagined future are not identical with that past or that future as objective time-periods through which they may pass. The child must be taught to recognize the objective and essential differences between phases of development in their historical and in their personal meaning. Through such differentiation the distorting perception of past and future as identical with the present may be avoided.

c) Enlarging the child's time-span also means: making him capable of distinguishing between processuality and causation, between a developing subject and the factors responsible for his or its development and change, irrespectively of whether these causal factors are internal or external.

We have already said that weakness of causal thinking and limitations of the child's historical perspective (these two main expressions

* This is the reason why didactic measures meant to develop the child's ability to differentiate between the two aspects of a problem-to-be-solved can also be included in the next following group of interventions, aimed at developing the pupil's responsibility for his acts of thinking and learning, or, more specifically, for keeping in mind the problem-character of a problem already solved before.

of a limited time-span), are the unavoidable results (and epiphenomena) of ego-weakness. This weakness is responsible not only for the personality defects in socially or culturally retarded children (their vulnerability, their resentments, their fears, their aggressiveness), but also for their cognitive limitations. It follows, then, that the teacher cannot hope to enlarge their time-span solely by enriching their *massa apperceptiva*; he must try to supplement whatever methods of teaching he may decide to apply, by strengthening their courage. Courage will then find its expression in increased readiness to abandon a static and one-dimensional orientation towards the present for the benefit of a multi-dimensional perception of happenings as the outcome of an interplay between actions and reactions (within a time-continuum).

C Developing Responsibility for Thinking and Learning

(1) *Dependence on authority*

The child's dependence on the teacher's authority is a common characteristic of all cases of secondary retardation. Knowledge of facts, knowing the answer to a problem, knowing solutions is identical, in the mind of a child whose intelligence has been impaired by adverse social or cultural conditions, with 'taking it', 'receiving it' from a *source* of knowledge, a text or a teacher or a tradition. Paradoxically, their dependence on authority does not indicate trust in the teacher as a person, as a subject, but rather a perception of the teacher as an impersonal, hence exchangeable object of manipulation: the learner simply has to adopt a certain passive and imitative attitude in order to 'bring about' the process of knowledge, since answers or solutions are 'being given'.

Such an impersonal and mechanical approach to learning (see also point p: Imitation) does by no means prevent the child from becoming emotionally attached to a teacher and finding deep satisfaction in such attachment. But it remains without cognitive significance. It may be that a socially or culturally deprived and retarded child will even be ready to show increased steadiness and perseverance in his learning activities, it may well be that he will make strong efforts to succeed 'for the sake' of a beloved teacher. But this does *not* necessarily lead to internalization of contents or to a new conception of learning as an activity which requires from the learner responsibility for each of the learning phases and for their results. The emotional area, in which such a child may be capable of strong attachment to a certain teacher, is here disconnected from the cognitive area, in which he continues to expect results, called 'knowledge' or 'skill', to be given to him. We can even say that it is precisely this process of becoming more and more attached to a teacher (when it happens), that supports belief in the processuality of learning. Not once we witness a child's deep disappointment when he sees that his learning progress remains limited, although he did succeed in establishing personal ties with his teacher (as he feels).

Here, the teacher faces a particular difficulty: he must beware of interpreting a child's personal attachment to him as proof of cognitive progress; it is by no means easy to resist this dangerous misinterpretation. The teacher must make his pupils rely on him as a subject of guidance, while, at the same time, seeing their own role in the learning process as one of active subjects.

The way to bring about this change goes through two phases: the teacher must set out from explaining the content, the meaning and the function of a law or a sentence and then encourage his pupils to find its application in various empirical fields. In other words: he cannot rely on methods of inductive thinking since the latter presupposes trust in the regularity and meaningfulness of facts and recurring events. It is, however, precisely the *absence* of such trust that is one of the main causes, and symptoms, of externalization and secondary retardation. The use of *deductive* methods, on the other hand, can satisfy both the child's needs for dependence (though only on the basis of rational operations), as well as the objective need for developing activity and responsibility in the learner (through correct application of laws learned to various fields and facts). Reliance on the teacher, it is hoped, will result from the very fact of his activity in offering 'useful' interpretations. The need for applying the laws thus learned (under the teacher's guidance) will counteract this child's blind belief in authority, whether represented by teachers or by texts.

(m) *Causation and manipulation*

Our demand for responsibility is not contradicted by that very principle of interpretation according to which causal connections become reliable only to the extent that we understand each factor of determination as being determined by other factors. On the contrary:

the child becomes responsible for his thinking and learning only when he accepts processuality rather than action as the basis of causal connections, when he feels himself standing opposite that infinite process and gives up all illusion that causality can be 'manipulated'. The danger of identifying causal connections with those between acts and their results is particularly evident, when we analyze the cognitive structure of the s.r. child who tends to associate every 'activity' with 'manipulation'; and 'manipulation' implies disregard for the existence of objective connections between facts, in history or in nature.

Manipulation is the *opposite* of responsibility in which we see one of the main factors of rehabilitating intelligence. True cognitive activity and true responsibility for thinking is based on a clear separation between the learning ego and the universe of facts-to-be learned; it is based on the laws inherent in these facts which become manifest precisely through this cognitive activity. Manipulation, on the other hand, is based on seeing facts as epiphenomena only of the manipulating ego, as dependent on the ego's arbitrary decisions.

Thus, rehabilitative teaching *must* emphasize processuality rather than action as the basis of understanding causality. The s.r. child must learn to follow the results of a defineable factor from a distance, as it were (the results of a force, of an act, of an event). Objectivity and neutrality in the learner's attitude towards facts are better guaranteed in this case, than when he follows the results of actions, since 'action' is liable to arouse in him affects, anxiety or aggressiveness. Thus, 'action', too, must be understood to be conditioned, to be connected with factors preceding and following it.

In this way, it would seem, the dependence of such a child on the authority of teachers, texts, or other 'sources' of truth and knowledge may decrease, and his readiness to see in his teacher, as well as in himself, a subject, will grow.

(n) *Personifications*

Absence of personal responsibility of the learner for his learning finds its expression not only in his excessive dependence on the authority of teachers and traditions, but also in his tendency to use personifications. Usually, we see in this tendency the expression of a weak ego's attempt to compensate its weakness by attributing 'egoity' to objects. When his ego becomes stronger, man will as a rule, hesitate to distribute egoity so 'generously' to dead objects or to processes.

But we should also ask: what connection exists between personifications and lack or relative weakness of autonomy? Why should the tendency to use personifications become weaker when the child feels himself responsible for his thinking and learning, instead of relying on sources of authority?

The answer seems to be closely connected with our first interpretation: responsibility for thinking and learning becomes possible only when the learner feels himself anchored and focused in his own ego, when he knows that 'egoity' separates between himself and the objects of his learning in their constant change. True enough: a feeling of egoity not only *does not contradict* a feeling of dependence on forces of determination within or without, that is, on the non-ego, but even *presupposes* such consciousness of dependence. But the first condition of ego-feeling is awareness of the essential difference between that ego and the universe of objects of relationships. Man learns responsibility to the extent that he can see himself as ego; and *weakness* of egoity supports, as we have said, the tendency to 'diffuse' egoity, that is, to use personifications.

The latter also indicates, paradoxically, a strong tendency in the learner to relate the contents of his learning to himself, instead of relating himself to these contents. Paradoxically, we say, since that tendency seems to be indicative of ego-strength; but actually it is a substitute only for genuine ego-feelings, a kind of illusion; genuine ego-feeling excludes egocentricity; it manifests itself precisely in the ego's directedness towards the non-ego, which is an essential condition of objectivity. (We are not dealing here with the complex problem of egocentricity in feelings and interpersonal relationships, but with the cognitive aspects only.)

What didactical conclusions can be drawn from the present analysis? The teacher must prepare his pupils for a more adequate differentiation between the personal and the material areas of reality. He must explain, in various contexts, in different learning-situations, the essential difference that exists between a tendency *of* somebody and a tendency *in* something. The aim of such clarifications is *not* a better understanding of analysis, but first and foremost: helping the learner towards a better understanding of the difference between an ego-world of intentions and intentionality and a world of processes. The more successful the teacher will be in these endeavors, the more effectively will the tendency to use personifications be blocked, while the learner's responsibility for his thinking- and learning-acts will thereby be strengthened.

(o) *Non-recognition of universal laws*

We have already mentioned the influence of emotional associations on thinking processes (see point a). Here we come back to the same problem from another angle: if it is correct to say that passive drifting into chance solutions (by the force of associations) is characteristic of ego-weakness in secondary retardation, one didactical conclusion becomes imperative: the teacher cannot hope to strengthen his pupils' feeling of responsibility for their thinking processes, which we are discussing here, unless he helps them find a selective counter-force against the chance influence of chance associations. Such a counter-force is the universally valid law, which can be discovered only when the learner feels himself responsible for its discovery, instead of expecting its emergence as the result of isolated facts associating with each other (cf. also pp. 126 ff where we discussed the connection between universality and anonymity).

Discovering a law of universal validity, which determines the significance of isolated facts and regulates the relationship between them, is also one of the most effective *means* of developing cognitive responsibility. But it is precisely through such discovery that the socially or culturally retarded child comes to know that his very responsibility for the act of discovery—*limits* his responsibility and activity. The latter can be 'learned' only, if the learner is ready to limit himself through the findings of his objective thinking.

(p) *Imitation*

'On his way' to activity and responsibility an externalized and retarded child is liable to find a substitute for activity—imitation of temporary or permanent authority figures. Both, his tendency to *depend* on authority figures and his tendency to believe that truth or solutions to a problem can be 'taken' (see point l), support this tendency: to imitate the external expressions of the teaching act and mistake them for the contents that are being transmitted by this act.

There exist perfectly legitimate forms of imitation in the learning activities of every ordinary child: imitation in deep identification with a teacher, which may find an expression in the learner's endeavor to apply the teacher's explanations to new learning tasks and in critical thinking; imitation in order to become free for new and, at least subjectively, more important thinking-tasks; 'experimental' imitation, that is, imitation of the teacher's ways of thinking to find out whether they are 'worthwhile'; imitation of a certain method of interpretation, which is liable to produce rigid dependence on this method, without, however, necessarily restricting the learner's ability to differentiate. In the present context we have in mind only the following two, negative, forms of imitation: imitation in order to please the teacher; and external imitation, without readiness or ability to internalize the contents of instruction and certainly without ability to transfer learning to new areas of knowledge.

The socially or culturally retarded child is liable to imitate the teacher's way of explaining things (and not only his behavior), he is liable to use the teacher's expressions; he may remain completely unaware of the difference between the *way* of explanation or expression and the explained or expressed *content* (cf. also point j). Moreover: he may be unable to understand the essential difference between the teacher, who explains, and himself, the pupil who learns. External imitation prevents understanding.

What are the didactical means at the teacher's disposal, when he wants to weaken this tendency towards external imitation? He must try, again and again, to establish relationships between himself and his pupils, in which each of them can be experienced by the other as a subject. He must be aware of the many expressions of external imitation in his pupils. He must ask questions to which he himself does *not* know the answers, in order not to appear in the eyes of his pupils as the bearer of the mask of omniscience. In this way, the child may cease to see his teacher as absolute authority; his very tendency to imitate the teacher is then likely to change his expectations and his attitude towards the actual learning-process: when the teacher is ready to admit the limits of his competence, the child may feel encouraged to see knowledge as something that he can 'build' only through his own efforts, but that cannot be 'taken' 'ready-made', as it were.

Another didactical means against external imitation is to show the socially or culturally retarded child that no solution is final, that every result may be changed, that there exist always and everywhere alternatives (cf. p. 141). When the tendency to imitate appears together with rigid preference of certain 'absolute' answers to the teacher's question, he must try to strengthen his pupil's responsibility for his thinking- and learning-tasks by counter-acting this rigidity: the laws of reversibility in arithmetics, for instance, are a good example; the child should understand that no solution 'exists', as it were, metaphysically. Learning is essentially connected with making a choice.

On the other hand, this way of teaching alternatives requires protection by the teacher against the dangers of arbitrariness. Without such protection, the child is liable to return to manipulative modes of thinking (see point m), well-known from the study of externalization. This may then be his reaction to the bewildering multitude of methods and of answers.

D Simultaneity of Two Aspects or Two Directives

(q) *Two aspects*

Whenever intelligence is impaired, one of the most salient symptoms of retardation is the individual's *inability to see different aspects of a certain phenomenon or of a certain problem at one and the same time*. K. Goldstein [29] speaks of the inability to shift from one aspect to another, while holding in mind the former aspect. We start from the presumption that in secondary retardation this inability is reversible. The teacher must therefore use the contents of learning to show the co-existence of different aspects of one and the same problem. He must show that, and how, these aspects become visible when we use different criteria of judgement or look at a certain problem or fact from different points-of-view. This means not only less rigidity and more mobility, but also increased responsibility for thinking-as-action, increased ability to differentiate and to think rationally.

The learner's inability to shift from one aspect of a certain phenomenon to another aspect, means, among other things, that the total phenomenon is perceived as identical with one of its aspects; it is a *qualitative* statement on the phenomenon as such. The perception of reality as an 'extension' of one accidentally perceived phenomenon only, on the other hand (see point g), is an *existential* statement on reality as such. The question raised *here*, of shifting from one aspect to another, actually becomes meaningful only after the phenomenon has been perceived as *part* of reality only, as existent in its own rights.

Let us add here that there exists an essential difference between 'shifting from one aspect to another' and simultaneous perception of the two aspects as co-existent. It is a difference between changing positions and intuitive perception of a whole, before it is recognized as a configuration of parts. But both *presuppose mobility and help develop mobility* and, through it, the learner's responsibility for making a cognitive choice. It is obvious that in the humanities it is easier to discover co-existence of different meanings of a statement or a 'truth' to be learned. But it is precisely in the *non*-humanistic subject-matters that using a variety of criteria or points-of-view becomes most important for making the thinking-processes and activities more elastic.

(Here, it will be remembered what we have said on p. 137 about the importance of developing imagination and phantasy, in the rehabilitation of intelligence: it provides an experience of wholeness which a s.r. child badly needs; in fact, he needs it much more than an ordinary child, since the latter has much better chances of having made the experience through his intimate family relationships. In the present context, intuitive perception of wholes appears as the precondition of the learner's ability to see the co-existence of different aspects of a problem. It may be argued that absence of the basic experiences of regularity, of trust, of wholeness, which characterizes the earliest life conditions of the s.r. child, impairs precisely this ability intuitively to conceive of wholeness, hence also the ability to conceive of several aspects as co-existent and that this constitutes an almost irreparable damage in the cognitive structure of many s.r. children.)

(r) *Two directives*

Rational, differentiated, responsible thinking and learning requires yet another kind of mobility: that of *following two directives* or two instructions given by the teacher (or implied in a specific learning assignment) and of operating accordingly on two planes at one and the same time. This means more than strengthening the learner's memory (to 'keep in mind' the two directions); it means planned development of configurational thinking, that is, of the *ability to relate each of the two directives to the other.*

We have said above (p. 197) that in the cognitive rehabilitation of s.r. children, the deductive method of teaching, when followed by applications to different problem areas is preferable to inductive thought-stimulation. But it would seem that understanding the simultaneity of two directions, more than any other pattern mentioned on the preceding pages, can be advanced precisely by opposite, that is, inductive teaching methods. In other words: the s.r. child will not be able to learn operations which imply configurational thinking, unless he is being led, step by step, from concentration on one directive only, to seeing two directives as alternatives or as 'subsequent', as following one another, and from there to discovering the principle of two directives being interrelated, being in fact one.

It may be argued that if s.r. children can be made to benefit from inductive teaching methods in *this* case, it may be possible, and would be preferable, in *every* case; the *kind* of problem to be solved or the *type* of faulty thinking to be corrected should not make any difference.

But this is exactly the point under discussion: as a rule, we have claimed, the inductive way of teaching is *counter*indicated in the rehabilitation of the s.r. child's impaired intelligence: Not only does he not bring with him to his learning tasks that sense of security and that courage that are needed to benefit from induction; the latter also requires much more time than would seem to be justifiable to spend on it, in the light of the s.r. child's need for cognitive guidance during his class hours.

But 'awareness' of what is implied in following two directives simultaneously, that is, in configurational thinking (even more than perceiving two aspects as co-existent, that is, whole perception) *cannot* be produced by offering explanations of these directives or their interrelatedness, and then applying what has been explained to other learning-tasks. Here are required cognitive activity and experience of being able to *discover* simultaneity as essentially different from each of the directives given and even from their sum total.

E SUMMARY

It is obvious that teaching methods alone will never be sufficient to restitute a socially or culturally disadvantaged child's impaired intelligence. No less important are, as we have said (see p. 147), physical and social care, adequate organization of the child's leisure-time activities, stimulation of his creativity, vocational guidance and preparation, councelling in crisis situations, guidance of his parent. On the other hand, it would be a dangerous illusion to believe that with the help of such interventions a child's intellectual effectiveness could ever be raised. They will undoubtedly improve his physical and mental health and may, thereby, in some cases at least, also improve the level of his intellectual functioning. But if we want to attack the problem of secondary retardation as one of social pathology affecting millions of children everywhere in the world, the planning of adequate cognitive interventions is of the essence. Even the fruitfulness of physical, social, recreational, vocational and therapeutic measures depends on the adequacy of these cognitive measures.

Let us now try to summarize what we have said so far about teaching methods in the service of intellectual rehabilitation.

Discovering the emotional elements of a concept means: translating them into the language of cognitive relations, through analysis, classification and differentiation; and it means: suggesting to the child possible associative connections between the emotionally charged elements of his experiences and his (faulty) thinking processes. If he wants to use such a method, the teacher must be familiar with at least the elements of psychodynamic psychology. Just as a psychotherapist, who offers his patient interpretations of dreams, phantasies or symptoms, learns only through the latter's reactions whether his interpretations had been correct, so must the teacher of secondarily retarded children be prepared to offer his pupils interpretations without knowing beforehand whether or not they are 'objectively' correct.

On the other hand, however, he should not discuss in the classroom the emotional experiences of a pupil's private life. This is dangerous not only when the child is emotionally disturbed (in addition to being socially or culturally handicapped and retarded); it is counterindicated in every instance. The level on which emotionally charged experiences that may determine irrelevant phantasies or associations or other faulty patterns of thinking can be discussed, should always be one of anonymity and generalities.

There is no contradiction between the teacher's endeavors to strengthen the child's ability to differentiate and to think rationally and his attempts to refer to irrational strata in the child's mind. To give up dichotomization or the use of stereotypes, preference of concrete data (to concepts) or magic belief in words—to mention only a few examples—requires courage and a sense of security, which, in turn, result from ever-repeated confrontations of the child's consciousness with the dimensions of the possible, of alternatives, of otherness. This, however, means mobilization of non-rational functions such as imagination, phantasy, intuition, together with increased rationality.

Ordinarily, activation of the learner is seen either as a problem of techniques or as a means to increase motivation. But when dealing with secondary retardation in its different aspects, activation has an altogether different meaning: here, a fundamental change of relationship between subject and object is required before. We must not forget that conditions of externalization which are responsible for the impairment of intelligence means, among other things, absence of polar relationships between an autonomous subject and an object with its intrinsic constitution. Hence, the child must be taught how to recognize the essentials of a knowable object (or event, or process), and thus (that is, through accepting the separateness of the object), to become ego-involved. This way differs from that of the ordinary child who is being activated in and through his learning; for him, learning through activation may mean: almost personal contact with the fact or phenomenon to be learned and *not* separation between subject and object.

It may seem paradoxical when we now add that developing the secondarily retarded child's responsibility for his learning activities not only does not contradict, but in fact requires deductive methods of teaching.* Not finding but applying laws to a variety of reality areas, is the method through which the disadvantaged and retarded child will learn that laws are not arbitrary inventions of his teacher, not manifestations of the latter's authority, but are 'qualities' of reality which can be demonstrated and can be proven to apply meaningfully to an ever-changing variety of phenomena.

The most valuable achievement in the restitution of cognitive functions, however, is the recognition that nothing empirical is final, that only the regularity of recurring phenomena or the inner law of regulation to which a certain phenomenon obeys, can be called absolute. To the extent that the learner becomes capable of accepting this truth, he will also be able to think in alternatives and his cognitive mobility will be restored.

---

* See, however, our remarks on the limits of deductive methods on p. 204.

Appendix to Chapter Seven

(*Examples of Faulty Patterns of Thinking*)

1 Irrelevant Associations

(a) *Due to word similarity*

The word 'rhythm' was explained by a girl as 'a kind of dance', apparently under the influence of the association 'eurhythmics'.

'Personal Bonds' were interpreted as implying preferential treatment, since the words evoked the association 'personnel', and the members of the staff were known to be treated preferentially in the clinics in which they worked.

'Straightforward' was identified with the straight line. As a result, its opposite, 'dishonest' lost its moral connotation and was identified with certain physical qualities.

(b) *Due to previous learning*

What is the work done by a man who pushes a wall with a strength of 10 Kg?' was the question. Instead of answering: 'Nil, because the wall does not move,' a girl answered:

'We don't know, because we don't know that the wall moves.' To this another girl reacted:

'When we say simply: a wall, we cannot know the answer. But when we say: *the* wall, we can know everything, since in this case, the wall is known to us.' Here, an explanation of the meaning and the function of the article, given in a preceding syntax lesson, had interfered.

(c) *Due to emotional factors*

A story told of a woman who, in a state of depression, refused to eat. When the teacher later asked the pupils to characterize this woman, one boy described her as 'obstinate', evidently under the influence of an emotionally significant association: he himself used refusal to eat as a weapon against his mother when he was in opposition to her. This association determined the boy's thinking more effectively than the text read (although he remembered it well).

When asked what changes had been brought about in the life of primitive man when he gave up his cave dwellings and started building huts, a first suggestion was: 'Insecurity and fear: wild bears and elephants now could attack him.'

When the difference between zero and both positive and negative numbers was discussed, a pupil identified 'zero' with 'non-existence', hence with something negative. As a result, negative numbers became identical with 'zero'.

The fact that subtracting a negative number results in an increase of the positive number was called by a boy to indicate 'discrimination' in favor of the positive number, obviously the result of emotional associations interfering with cognition.

The younger the child, the less disguised will be the influence of emotional associations: when the children learned of certain reptiles laying their eggs in the sand, a child's spontaneous reaction was: 'Do they not care for their children?'

(d) *Due to social experience*

A story was told of people streaming from all over the country into the large temple precincts to pray there for long overdue rains. One (younger) girl explained: 'They went there to find protection, since rain does not fall on holy places.' For her, the idea of rain pouring down without mercy on weak roofs was so frightening that she forgot the situation described in the story, that of dearth.

Another child found it difficult to understand the causal connection between dearth and famine: The first remained associated with 'lack of rain', the second with 'lack of money'. The child's social experience here produced irrelevant associations interfering with causal thinking.

(e) *Due to cultural patterns*

The Bible (Samuel I) tells the story of Elkana who was married to Pnina, mother of several children, and to Hanna, the barren woman whom he preferred. However, one boy declared it was obvious that he preferred Pnina since she had given him sons—an indisputable merit according to the boy's cultural value system. Thus, he was obviously unable to understand the essentials of the Bible story which enhances individualized relationships.

2 Concretizations

'Justice' was defined as 'power to determine right and wrong'. 'Law' was identified with 'imprisonment'. 'Giving up a right' was felt to be identical with 'objective decrease in substance'. 'Pride' as an inner quality was not understood since the hero of the story which dealt with that problem had nothing 'to pride himself of', neither wealth nor status, neither knowledge nor influence.

When the continuum of positive numbers was discussed, a boy asked: 'what is $\frac{1}{2}$? One half of what? It cannot be one half of zero!'

When the rhomboid was discussed as a combination of two triangles with a common basis, the latter was counted twice so that the total number of sides was said to be six.

Some pupils rejected the concept of negative numbers, since they could not relate it to concrete givens.

3 Symbols Instead of Concepts

When discussing a certain underground movement, the fact was mentioned that the fighters literally went underground by hiding in mountain caves. The cave, however, became a symbol of independence and withdrawal, of absolute freedom from all danger of oppression. The children were therefore unable to accept the fact that the freedom fighters, once victory was achieved, left the caves. The concept of freedom was replaced by the symbol of withdrawal.

The varieties of light were classified, according to source, distance, intensity, etc. The pupils were asked to give examples: One boy suggested: 'The light of the Bible'. For him light as a symbol of holiness (of which everyone could be a partner without conceptual activity) was much more attractive than all those complicated and ego-alien physical phenomena and concepts which the teacher had mentioned.

Among younger children, much more naïve examples can be found: 'Organic' was defined as 'green', thought to be the symbol of fertile not of low-lying lands on geographical maps. Moral badness was said to be 'black' or 'ugly'.

(The dangerous connection between symbols and stereotypes—see 8—is evident.)

4 Inability to Comprehend Differences and Similarities

The concept of 'natural catastrophes' was defined as including wars solely because both had one element in common, men's helplessness when they happen to befall them.

Two stories were said to deal with the same topic because in both two women appeared though in different contexts. Thus the differences of meaning and essentials was overlooked. On the other hand, the essential identity of a number of natural phenomena and their belonging to the same class could not be understood by a number of children who insisted on their being basically different phenomena because of their difference in size, weight, frequency of occurrence. Thus, the concept of 'class' could not be made clear (see also what has been said about concretization as against concept formation).

5 Analogy as Identity

When the development of plants was discussed, the bud of a flower was said *to be* its foetus. Negative numbers were said to be the same as fractions because both become 'smaller' with the increase of the absolute number and the denominator.

When on a picture a contemporary soldier was shown together with one of the 'glorious ancient times' (to enhance the present-day army), a pupil considered this a distortion of history, since he could not grasp the As-if character of the analogy. When the central point of a problem was called, by analogy, its 'center of gravity', a girl brought up the association of Archimedes and became confused by the seeming identity of two areas of knowledge.

6 Dichotomization

When discussing the meaning and the function of the zero, a pupil suggested that there should be a $+0$ and -0, since every positive number had a negative corollary.

The Either-Or character of moral judgement and chauvinistic dichotomization are found no less frequently in normally intelligent and retarded children.

The differences between spoken and written language were discussed. A boy decided that the two were opposites: 'spoken' was the language of the streets, 'written' was the language ... spoken at school only. (Here, the dichotomous pattern proved also to be a warning signal, since school values seemed, in the case of this boy at least, not to be internalized.)

7 Presence and Absence

When discussing the transformation of water into steam and of one energy into another, it was difficult for some of the children to comprehend the terms of 'latent existence' or of 'existence by implication': what was no longer present ceased to exist.

The words 'dictionary to Hebrew and general literature' were interpreted as meaning: 'dictionary of Hebrew words used in literature and in the commonly spoken language'. It simply did not enter the mind of the child that 'general' might mean something more comprehensive than 'my' language.

'Present' is only what can be recognized by its external manifestations. This is one of the symptoms of externalization in a s.r. child. A phenomenon once recognized as 'present' will never be considered 'partially present'. Hence, the here-discussed category of faulty thinking is almost identical with an All or Nothing attitude.

8 Stereotypes

'What was the reason of the military and political success of Napoleon?' was the teacher's question after he had analyzed the historical contexts in great detail. 'The Lord was with him,' was the answer given by a (non-religious!) student.

After a lengthy discussion of leadership qualities, the teacher's question, what made a man into a leader, was answered by a pupil who simply said 'His greatness'.

The life and art of cave-man were discussed and their impressive drawings were shown. When later, various art-periods were compared with each other from the point-of-view of tri-dimensionality, some children did not hesitate to prefer the Sumeric art by saying: 'The cave man was much too primitive to know how to paint'.

9 Indiscriminate Use of 'Scientific' Terms

'Scientific' terms such as 'criterion', 'profile', 'developmental stage', 'reference' frequently appear in the class-records as quasi-magic tools to solve a problem and to cover up lack of knowledge.

10 Cognitive Versus Personal Problems

Galilei's problem was: how to avoid the inquisition, said a boy, not: how to prove that the earth revolves around the sun. For, the latter is *known* to be true. How should it then be a problem? A 'real' problem is only a practical one: how to repay debts, how to live with new neighbors, how to avoid quarrels, etc.

11 Narrow Time-Consciousness

Anachronistic thinking is its best-known example, particularly in younger age-groups. Later, it often clashes with rational knowledge. But a hero of the past may still be experienced as present, and a hero of the present may still be allowed to bear the traits of past images. This is so, particularly when thinking patterns are determined by religious tradition. As a result, historical understanding is bound to be impaired. Co-existence of times is more 'real' than sequence of time. Nothing distorts the time perspective as effectively as affects projected onto the past. (Medieval Arabs were said, by an Arab child, to have fought against—the Zionists.)

History teachers of s.r. children often face the task of making them aware of the proper time perspective. S.r. pupils resemble in this respect young children for whom everything that happened before their birth belongs to a far remote past, as remote as a thousand years ago.

12 Dependence and Authority

When asked to think of an alternative way of proving a law in geometry, a pupil said: 'You have already proven the truth of the law. How can there be another solution?' When the teacher showed the alternative, the pupil's reaction was one of fear: 'Do you mean to say,' he asked, 'that you can choose from among various truths?'

On another occasion, a pupil asked the teacher: 'Are you sure that you did not invent this solution?' Another pupil asked: 'Where did you find this solution?' He was satisfied when the teacher showed him the place in the text book where it was printed.

Two different essays on the essence of a certain type of poetry were analyzed. When the class was asked, in the end, to compare with each other these two views, one pupil said: 'Since both essays have been published, both must be true. Therefore, they cannot be compared with each other.'

13 Manipulation and Causation

A teacher asked: 'What causes phototropy in plants?' Some answers were: 'The sun's magnetic force'. 'The light which is stronger than the plant'. One boy suggested: 'We should strengthen the plant's power of resistance' (apparently considering phototropy a pathology, which could be changed by manipulation).

Economic and political factors were explained that led up to a certain historical event. 'Everything could have happened differently,' said a girl, 'if they had killed the king in due time,' (according to the principle that man makes history, not history man).

14 Personifications

The changes in the content and structure of a certain story, when being transmitted from one culture to another were discussed. A girl called these changes 'adjustment difficulties comparable to those of a new immigrant'.

A sheet of black paper was used in an experiment with plant seeds, in order to make the process better visible. When the class was asked why black paper was used, a pupil answered: 'The seeds need darkness to rest before the experiment starts.'

15 Non-recognition of Universal Laws (and Concepts)

Orientation to the 'haveable' and the 'known' operates against the recognition of universally valid laws. (The cognitive faults mentioned under 1, 8, 9, 10 and 12 could be quoted here as well.) When discussing the generality and specificness of statements (f.i.: 'Children breaking windows' as against 'The children breaking the windows'), some pupils called the undetermined form of the sentence irrelevant, since there we knew neither the children nor the windows. Determination, they felt, implied personal contact: only when we know the individual subject and the individual object of a statement, does the latter become meaningful. Paradoxically, then, universal validity depends on knownness and specificness.

In the younger age groups, this tendency has a dangerously restrictive influence on concept-formation. 'When is your birthday'?, a young girl was asked. She answered that she no longer had birthdays —meaning birthday parties. The universality of the concept obviously was meaningless to her.

16 Imitations

A class was asked about the essential differences between democracy and oligarchy in ancient Greece. The question could be answered, some pupils said, only after analyzing their leaders' motivations. It was obvious that they blindly imitated their teacher's emphasis on motivation (as against that of another teacher who emphasized the 'central idea' and a third one whose accent was on the ethical conclusions to be drawn from a story). The pupils obviously failed to understand the problem which was one of objective description rather than of psychological analysis.

In another lesson, a pupil of that same (motivation-oriented) teacher answered questions about positive and negative numbers by saying they had 'mutually exclusive tendencies'. On the other hand, students of the third-mentioned teacher (with his ethical orientation) spoke about the benefit migrating birds bring to the southern countries which are their winter homes.

Many s.r. children mistake blind imitation of a teacher's style of interpreting facts or of expressing himself for internalization of contents of knowledge.

17 Inability to See Two Aspects Simultaneously

The 'collective noun' was defined as denoting a whole composed of many individuals. To the question in which form the verb would appear in this case, some pupils answered: 'In the plural, of course, since it is composed of many individuals.' They failed to keep in mind the second aspect, that of wholeness.

In a lesson where English was taught as a foreign language, a pupil said: 'My shoes is brown'. The teacher corrected: '*are* brown'. The pupil objected by saying: 'But it is *my* shoes'. In other words: He was unable to keep in mind the two aspects of the problem, the plurality of the object and the singularity of the owner, while at the same time relating the verb to the object only.

18 Inability to Follow Two Directives Simultaneously

'Can you imagine an angle whose two sides have more than one point in common?' the teacher asked. One of the pupils drew on the blackboard first one line, then drew the same line again, on the former, thus showing that he had understood the problem. But then he branched off, adding to the identical line—an angle. Thus he split the task that contained two directives to be followed simultaneously into two actions one coming after the other (a: two sides of an angle having more than one point in common, b: an angle).

In a syntax lesson, the teacher asked the pupils to construct a sentence according to a number of directives. It proved to be too difficult for them; everyone forgot a number of directives and thus 'simplified' the task.

CHAPTER EIGHT

Teacher Training

1 SOME PRELIMINARY QUESTIONS

How can the teacher be trained to become sensitive to the intellectual needs of the socially or culturally retarded child? Are the principles of such training essentially different depending on the pupil's age level? Or can we find certain elements of attitude training that are common to the elementary *and* the secondary school teacher, irrespective of the obvious differences in subject matters to be taught?

Here, the question of reversibility will undoubtedly be raised again. Is it not too late at the age of, let us say, 14 years to acquire those cognitive habits (of abstraction, for instance, or of learning for the sake of learning, or of persistent attention and concentration) that are the prerequisites of successful learning at the secondary school level?

It is often considered a foregone conclusion that the chances of reversal decrease with age. Although it will be added that the initial intelligence level and the degree of damage inflicted on it by adverse socio-economic conditions are differential factors of no less weight than age. In other words: when speaking of 'impairment' or of 'reversal' (of 'rehabilitation'), we have in mind partial impairment or reversal only.*

Reversibility does not exclude irreversibility. It is a fact well-known from other areas of pathology that damage to mental or to somatic functions caused by environmental factors may *cease* to be reversible if left untreated too long.† This finding applies to secondary retardation as well. The teacher of underprivileged children must be pre-

* It will be remembered that we have included in the definition of secondary retardation its reversibility. Any so-called empirical research of causes or methods 'proving' its irreversibility must therefore be considered irrelevant, that is unrelated to the subject under discussion, since it relates to something irreversible. *Unsuccessful* rehabilitation of socially or culturally impaired intelligence only proves that the methods employed were inadequate and should be revised. Such revision of methods may, or may not, require a prior, or parallel, revision of the underlying theory.

† Cf. What we have said before (pp. 67 ff.) about negative structurization.

pared for such cases within each class. Not only too many years of neglect, of lack of training and stimulation, of repeated failure and disappointment may account for such a pupil's inability to react to rehabilitative teaching; there are structural factors at work as well that determine his reactions: the initial level of intelligence, type-conditioned expectations and preferences, thresholds of perception and of reaction, etc.

In such cases, the teacher must be prepared to use different methods of educational intervention, meant to improve these pupils' intellectual achievements and effectiveness. He should, however, remain aware of the fact that, whatever he does with them, differs from the aim defined as 'rehabilitation of intellectual potentials'.

Teacher-training must therefore include comparative studies of individual differences, their structural and environmental causes, their intellectual and behavioral expressions. Case-analyses are preferable to systematic courses in psychology of development, of thinking, of learning, of behavior, of personality.

This conclusion is supported by the fact that not only the reversibility of functional damage caused by environmental factors but impairment as well is partial only. We have tried to show that this is due to a variety of causal constellations. While a relatively high congenital level of intelligence may protect the growing child against the destructive influence of negative social or cultural conditions, lack of adequate stimulation through the parents and the school may impair the cognitive development of middle-class children of a no more than average intelligence. In both cases, impairment will be partial only, though for different reasons. It will therefore be much easier here than in 'radical' cases to restore the child's original (high or average) level of functioning. Partiality of impairment finds its expression in a number of facts: The functional area in which it is felt may be compensated by others in which it is less pronounced; the child's motivation for learning may remain more or less intact, without being as radically contradicted by an unrealistic level of aspirations, as in the more typical cases of secondary retardation.

Should we not, then, do everything in our power to concentrate on such cases? Is it not reasonable to presume that cooperation with the parents of children, whose impairment is compensated by a basically normal intelligence or environment, will be easier to secure than with those of severely deprived and retarded children from poverty-stricken or otherwise externalized environments? And should we not gear teacher training to these less radical cases of intellectual impairment, which we can find in every regular school-setting and which may promise easier success?

We do not know much about the relative frequency of the different types of impaired intelligence in any given society. We do not know how to assess the social impact of partial impairment as against that of more radical secondary retardation. We are unable to say how the discrepancies between the achievement levels of so-called normal and of secondarily retarded children are liable to affect the social structure. (And we certainly shall not attempt here to deal with the complex question of research methods and research planning that pose themselves in this connection.) One point, however, should be clear: the functions of the teacher do *not* depend on the degree of his pupils' intellectual impairment but only on the fact that all of them are unable freely to use those cognitive methods that are indispensable for scholastic as well as for social achievement.

It is the need for developing the teacher's awareness of those handicaps (which we have tried to analyse in the preceding chapters) that determines the course of his training, as we shall try to show forthwith. But before going into the details of the implications which this definition of the teacher's basic function has for the structure of training programs, we propose to deal with one more preliminary question: what is the relationship between parents and school, when the aim of teaching is defined as rehabilitation of impaired potentials?

2 PARENTS AND SCHOOL

We have tried to show in another study [26], in which way the externalized parents' attitudes towards the child in his different phases of development determines the latter's level of functioning. Needless to emphasize again that, although relative economic security enables most parents to provide their children with at least a minimum of regularity—either by themselves or through employing auxiliary educators—such external conditions alone are insufficient to guarantee an optimal development of intellectual potentials. Not only the child's inborn qualities act as differential factors of determination; the parents' attitude towards the child's learning activities and towards the school's philosophy, expectations and demands certainly cannot adequately be defined as a function of their social status or their economic conditions.

One of the most pathetic examples of an extreme discrepancy between these two factors (the parents' attitude towards the school and their socio-economic status) can be found in the transition of a family from lower to middle class status: although their children continue to be in need of a rehabilitative teaching program, society may no longer consider them to be so. As a result, they may find themselves in a 'wrong' school. Moreover, their parents may no longer be amenable to interpretations of the school's aims or to advice given by teachers or social workers, because they may believe themselves to be much more sophisticated and much more identified with the educational aims of society at large and of the school, than they really are.

On the other hand, we often witness a most impressive effort on the part of primitive and undifferentiated parents to support their children's learning activities and to cooperate with the school in order to safeguard their progress. Although the parents' expectations and hopes may be unrealistic, they will do everything in their power to accept this essentially alien institution called 'the school' as a condition of change. Their future-orientation may not apply to their own life-span and yet, may produce significant changes in their children's time-consciousness and self perception as learners.

But most parents of socially or culturally retarded children show, as we know, lack of understanding or impatience in the face of the school's endeavours or, at best, are indolent to them. This is, why we speak of 'the school without parents' (see Chapter 5); a school whose methods are based on the presumption that teaching can serve as a means to instil in the child that basic sense of security and trust or of nearness and regularity, which the parents have failed to build-up in him. Does not such a definition of functions imply that the teacher must accept as an unalterable fact the *absence* of the parents as supporting agents? Has he any chance to bring about desirable changes in the parents' attitude towards the school and the child's learning?

We must not forget that, under externalizing conditions of poverty and educational neglect or of cultural disorientation, the parents not only fail to support, but often enough directly or indirectly *counteract* the efforts made by the school. Their value system may be not only different from that of the school but also opposed to it. As a result, the child is liable to take his learning tasks less seriously than the school expects and requires him to do, particularly when these tasks do not seem to have any pragmatic justification. True enough, the externalized child may not identify himself with his parents or introject their images, and yet, may be *conditioned* by their attitudes from the start and may imitate them and their affective modes of evaluation.

This, obviously, has a most important bearing on the training of teachers who want to work with socially or culturally handicapped and retarded children. Whatever they may do to help the child towards better achievements, increased initiative, more security and mobility, will become meaningful for the child's development only when the parents will be convinced that, far from being estranged to them, as a result of his learning, the child will be a *better* child: not only will he be capable of assisting his parents in a variety of social contexts, he will also be able to make them participate in a wider world of concepts and values and thus help them overcome, to some extent at least, the barriers of their own externality of behavior and their illusion of knownness.

It follows that the teachers, in addition to interpreting the school's aims and activities to the parents, must be prepared to help the child overcome his affective tendencies to reject the parents as representatives of an antiquated, negative value-system. Alienation is no solution. On the contrary: it produces tensions in the parents, when they fear they may lose control over their children and, thereby, over the family as a cohesive unit; it produces tensions in the child, when he fears he may be retracted by, and into, the parental value-system. Such tensions are known to account for many failures of rehabilitative teaching. They are often so deeply rooted in the family structure and pathology that a psychologist, a social worker or even a psychotherapist may have to be called in for help. But the teacher too, must be aware of his educational tasks in dealing with these problems of contradictory value system and their emotional and intellectual implications. The parents, not less than the children must learn how to use their imagination; they, too, must learn gradually to replace their illusion of knownness by a feeling of nearness to, and familiarity with, the surrounding reality. Hence, the teacher must learn how to become the parents' teacher as well.

We shall now try to show what implications this definition of the teacher's functions has for the planning of meaningful training courses, for teachers in general, and for teachers of deprived and retarded children, in particular.

3 THE FUNCTIONS OF TEACHER TRAINING

One of the first questions that is usually being asked in this context is the following: What are the causes, and what is the meaning of the universal feminization of the teaching profession particularly in elementary schools? Which is deplored so often as both, result and cause of the teacher's low social status and of the profession's unattractiveness.

It does not seem justified to explain feminization as a *result* of the low status allocated by society to the teaching profession, since male teachers do not, as a rule, enjoy a higher status in those societies that do *not* admit women to the profession. The teacher's status depends on whether or not learning is conceived of as being a continuous process towards the realization of clearly defined spiritual goals. But the function called 'elementary school teaching', as understood today in most countries of the Western world is not differentiated, not independent and not permanent enough to attract highly qualified persons who want to build up a life-career. Perhaps it attracts women—and certainly not always the best qualified ones, intellectually and emotionally—because our society regards it as an 'auxiliary' function only, a supplement to that of the parents and other educational agencies, until the child reaches the age at which 'true learning' becomes possible and meaningful—in the opinion of those responsible for 'higher' learning—that is, when he enters secondary school?

Perhaps elementary school teaching attracts women not only because it requires less continuity, but also, and mainly, because, in the form it has taken today, its character is essentially 'feminine'. Preference of demonstration and concretization over intellectual activity and abstraction, creating a friendly atmosphere of freedom and tolerance rather than a climate of intellectual tension and value-consciousness, seeing the child as being in need of 'maternal' help and protection rather than of 'paternal' guidance—are not all these indications of a feminine approach to the very function of teaching?

Far be it from us to belittle the emotional value of such an approach, particularly for the younger age-groups. But should we not ask whether this is the proper way of preparing a child for the secondary school or for productive adjustment to his future vocational and social tasks? When we exclude the highly intelligent and the highly stimulated children, who will find their place in the secondary school or in other post-elementary training agencies, whatever previous training they may have received, it is safe to state:

a) that the more elements of abstraction the elementary school teacher includes, the better is the child likely to be prepared for the analytic functions of secondary studies;

b) that the more elements of active imagination the elementary school teacher includes, the better is the child likely to be prepared for such functions and tasks of the secondary school as synopsis of relevant facts, synthesis, hypothesis-contruction, objective understanding of texts or of individual motivations, etc;

c) that both types of elements require an attitude towards teaching which differs from that prevailing today in most elementary schools. It is a fallacy to presume that the teacher can provide that basic sense of security which, we have claimed, is the precondition of autonomy in learning and thinking, by ways comparable to those of the mother. Not regularity and reliability of personal relationships —important as it may be—but regularity and reliability of facts and concepts, of imagination and explanation, is the experience which the teacher must make possible.

This is what could be called the 'masculine', the 'spiritual', the 'paternal' type of teaching, which is based on the presumption that learning is not a play, but an ever-repeated challenge, an activity anchored in the ego, and yet ever transcending it. It goes without saying that the child, whatever his personal and social background may be, must have reached a certain age before being able adequately to react to this type of teaching. And yet, even the first-grader *can* and—under conditions of externalization—*must* be made to realize very soon that the casual play atmosphere of the kindergarten basically differs from the school with its objective goals, values and obligations. More important now than spontaneous or adult-directed self-expression is the child's ability to relate himself meaningfully to objective values and goals through the medium of his relationship with 'strangers' (as compared with members of his family), that is, the teacher and the class-group. The teacher must be able and ready to accept this role of a 'stranger' and to represent, in the eyes of the child, the principles of objectivity and universality rather than continue the casual kindergarten atmosphere or make up for early maternal deficiencies. The earlier the child learns to expect and to accept this role of the school and the teacher, the better this will be for his emotional and intellectual development, particularly under conditions of externalization and parental neglect.

Every subject of the training curriculum should be geared simultaneously to imparting essential knowledge and indispensable skills and techniques as well as to developing adequate attitudes.

It is well known that psychology of learning and thinking, on the one hand, and psychology of child-development, on the other, are usually included in teachers' training programs as separate subjects (if the former is included at all). In some professional training courses, particularly in the fields of social work and public health, these and other separate subjects (such as physical growth, cultural patterns, pathology, differential testing etc.) have already been integrated into one course called 'growth and development'. The advantage of such an integrative approach is that in this way theories become easier applicable to the treatment of the individual, provided, we should add, teaching is related in each phase to the reality in which the profession operates.

But it would be a mistake to expect from this approach alone to teaching psychology, or, for that matter, any other subject, a significant change in the future teacher's attitude towards the children under his care. If we define the teacher's function primarily as one of stimulating the child's intellectual initiative, and of developing his responsibility for the tasks of thinking and learning with which he is faced—the total program of teacher-training, including a variety of psychological and sociological subjects, must be geared to teaching: every 'auxiliary' subject must be translated into the language of didactics.

To put it paradoxically: the more the teacher learns how to translate whatever he learns about the emotional and relational characteristics of the child's development into characteristics of his thinking and learning, the better will he be equipped to function not only as a teacher, but also as a psychologist. For, the teacher is *not* a therapist or a mental health councellor, he is primarily an educator. When he operates in a social or a cultural climate of externalization, his educational functions may resemble in certain respects, those of a psychologist or a social case worker; like them, this teacher, too, will try to rehabilitate a socially inadequate individual. But his medium of action is teaching. This definition of functions determines his training needs.

He must learn, as we have already mentioned above, how to

recognize the meaning of the mistakes made by the student, their possible 'roots':

a) in a certain developmental phase, perhaps one preceding his chronological age;
b) or in some kind of emotional conflict which may distort his associations and his thinking, or may otherwise handicap any of his intellectual functions;
c) or in a cultural pattern of thinking which may be incompatible with those implied in a specific learning task;
d) or in a socially conditioned attitude which may contradict objective learning as such.

Hence, the teacher must learn in which way *each developmental phase manifests itself specifically,* not only in behavior, but also in *thinking*; he must, in other words, come to understand, while learning about the child's development, the conceptual equivalents of relational—and behavioral—categories.

He must learn *how to evaluate development,* but not mechanically or quantitatively only, by way of calculating IQ's. Rather, he must learn how to compare the different functional manifestations of a certain phase of development *both vertically,* that is, with those of other phases, and *horizontally,* that is, those of the various functional fields within a certain phase with each other.

He must learn *how to differentiate between truly pathological deviations and those that permit a 'retarded' child with a more or less normal integrational capacity to remain within his group,* provided he is given an opportunity for developing his weakly developed, but trainable, abilities.

He must learn about the ways *emotional disorders*—fears, compulsive self-constriction, aggressiveness—are liable to manifest themselves in the associations, the concepts, the learning, not only of a neurotic, but of every child.

He must learn something about *culturally or socially conditioned value patterns and their specific influence on parental education,* not so much as part of systematic studies in sociology and anthropology, but rather in the way a social worker should become aware of these behavioral factors. Both the social worker and the teacher need basic knowledge of social and cultural patterns of evaluation and education, in order to make their guidance and teaching meaningful. The social worker should use his sociological and anthropological knowledge primarily for the purpose of interpreting the demands of the economic and social environment and the individual's reaction to these demands in the light of his group experiences; the teacher's learning must be geared primarily to discovering the influence such patterns may have on the associations of the individual child during his lessons.

This, however, means that the teacher must learn how to guard against the illegitimate and undesirable interference of prejudices with his own thinking and judging. It means that he must be helped to *become aware of his own unconscious motivations*, as they may manifest themselves in his affective reactions to individual pupils, to certain groups of children, to certain teaching subjects, as well as in the choice and preference of his teaching methods, his exemplifications, his associations, etc. One need not fear the danger of excessive psychologization, because the guidance material will always be taken from, and will always remain related to, the classroom.

It should be clear by now that we advocate a type of teacher training in which the teacher as a person and the application of each detail of his training to actual class-room teaching form the two foci; no teacher, we claim, will be able to fulfil functions of what we have called 'intellectual hygiene', that is, will be able to build up in his pupils a basic sense of security through learning, unless he is himself basically secure. The training course, we claim, must help the teacher gain that security and courage which he needs in order to use his imagination and phantasy (for instance, in suggesting possible interpretations of his pupils' errors in thinking). It will manifest itself in his readiness for experimentation with methods, for improvization, for changing his methods of interpretation, his choice of exemplification, his educational attitude according to the changing needs of his pupils. The training can be said to have been successful if the teacher feels secure enough to use whatever methods or 'techniques' he may have learned as stimuli only for his own phantasy and thinking, if he is free to react to the individual learning needs of his pupils.

Teaching functions so defined will, it is reasonable to hope, be capable of attracting highly qualified men and women in search of a professional career. To the extent that this will happen, it is safe to predict that the status accorded to the profession by society will rise as well, not only because of the higher quality of those teachers, but also in recognition of the more complex nature of their function and of the more thorough and more extended training required.

4 TRAINING PROGRAMS—FRAMEWORK CONTENTS, METHODS

It is being argued that at the age of 18 when in most countries candidates enter the Teachers' Training Schools, only very few will have reached that level of maturity which is a precondition of adequate response to the principles of learning as outlined here. This, however, is not an argument against our conception but, rather, a reason why the age of admission should be raised, say, to 21 (as is already customary in some countries and certainly in other professions, such as social work). In addition, the training should be organized in stages: after a two-year period of basic studies, another one or two-year period, of intensively supervised teaching, may be necessary to make the application of principles and methods learned fruitful and meaningful. Later on, a third period, preferably of in-service training, should follow, devoted to specialization in teaching socially or culturally underprivileged children (possibly also to other specializations, which are, however, beyond the scope of the present analysis).*

No teaching candidate should define himself from the start as a teacher of underprivileged and secondarily retarded children, without having had at least some experience with, and some basic training in teaching, so-called regular classes. True enough, the principles of teaching socially or culturally retarded children, which we have defined in the preceding chapters, are valid for 'normal' children as well; the latter, too, should come to know that rational thinking and imagining contexts of meaning are closely interlinked and not contradictory activities; that differentiation and abstraction, following a number of directions simultaneously, and taking responsibility for the very acts of thinking and learning—are superior to factual learning through self-submission to the authority of data and texts, of teachers and traditions. But only by teaching children for whom the former attitudes towards knowledge and learning are 'natural', will the teacher become sensitized to the needs of those children who require active guidance by the classroom teacher, to *acquire* effective modes of thinking and learning.

* It follows that only a service-oriented agency (and *not* a University department with its obligations towards a usually rather rigid curriculum) is suited for such a training function. For, only a service-oriented agency will be elastic enough to adapt itself to the needs of the students, and will be prepared to see in the training of teachers a sufficient raison d'etre, will regard it as an integral part of its primary function.

We have mentioned that every program of teacher-training must include information on the normal development of perception, of language and thought, of social behavior, through the various age-phases; that it must include information on individual and group-differences due to a variety of structural and environmental causes. Comparisons of essentials, both vertically and horizontally (between phases and between functions) and case-analyses should accompany these basic information courses. The interdependence of cognitive and emotional functions, of thinking and feeling, of learning and behavior, should be shown in the presentation of human growth and development, normal and deviant.

We have asked at the beginning of the present chapter, whether at this general and preliminary stage of training, a distinction must be made between the elementary and the secondary school teacher's needs for understanding the laws and manifestations of growth and development. A more comprehensive study and a wider knowledge of certain subject matters of teaching do not prepare the secondary school teacher better than the elementary school teacher for his educational tasks. On the contrary: the often rather sterile belief in erudition as a value *per se*, which unfortunately characterizes so many of our secondary teachers, is liable to remove them from the adolescent's world of values and conflicts, experiences and expectations much more than the average elementary teacher will ever be removed from his pupil's inner world of phantasies and concepts, fears and hopes. The elementary school teacher usually knows that the subject matter he teaches and the skills he develops in his pupils will be meaningful only to the extent that he helps them build-in knowledge and skills into their future-orientation and into their growing and changing self-perception. Hence, his relatively greater readiness to accept psychological and particularly dynamic interpretations of learning, behavior and development (despite his often less developed intellectual capacities) than that of the secondary school teacher with his often arrogant emphasis on intellectual values and on his own importance.

It follows that the latter certainly needs a solid course of learning about the laws and manifestations of human growth and development, behavior and motivation, differences and deviations, no less, if not more, than the elementary school teacher.

Participation of the two types of teaching candidates in one and the same basic course of phychology seems to be advisable for another reason as well: it is likely to make cross-references of applications and comparison of case material—theoretical as they may be at this stage of learning—much more natural and much more relevant for teacher-training than age-specific courses could ever be.

Psychological, sociological, anthropological and physiological data form natural parts of such an integrated course of growth and development, which should and could be given during the first year of training. Similarly, information should be given to training students on the different school systems and on the demographic structure of the society in which they are expected to work, on prevailing ideologies, typical pathologies and their relative frequency, treatment services available for children and their parents in regular and special educational settings. Here, too, candidates for elementary and for secondary schools could profitably be brought together. We should bear in mind that, the more contact between the two types of teachers is established during their training experience, the better will be the chances for them to become aware of the continuity in education processes.

Teaching methods, on the other hand, belong to the second year of training and should be integrated, in all details, with learning specific subject-matters. The present author contends that general didactics—contrary to the practice, as it can still be found in most teacher training programs—is redundant and almost meaningless: teaching methods should not be taught in the abstract vacuum of so-called didactic theories but only in relation to specific areas of knowledge. It should also be borne in mind that methods of teaching cannot be learned adequately unless they apply to an analysis of thinking processes (since teaching is not *imposition* of knowledge but activation of thinking for the purpose of *acquiring* knowledge).

Teaching methods must therefore be taught in age-specific contexts of learning: Since the elementary and the secondary school teacher must study *different* subject matters, and preferably also in different settings, didactics must be taught in separate groups. It does not mean that methods of teaching are essentially different according to the age-level of the pupils to be taught. But the teaching material *is* different and differently studied (in history or literature, in mathematics or biology, in geography or languages). Hence, its significance as a field of application of methods also differs essentially in the day-to-day work of the elementary and the secondary school teacher.

The same holds good for a discussion of general educational problems, such as value education, participation in social tasks, stimulation of interests, behavioral issues, sex education, parent-child relationships and many extracurricular activities. Differences between the pupils' life experience and phasal achievements require separation of training groups according to the age-levels with which the future teacher intends to work. (In passing only, it may be mentioned that there is no need for loading the basic training program with such discussions and learnings, if only adequate provision is made for later in-service training. Focusing on the here-mentioned general educational problems is much more meaningful and effective if it forms an integral part of an intelligently planned continuation course program.)

All we have said in the present paragraph so far about the components of teacher training applies to so-called normal children, that is, to the training of regular teachers. But it is a well-known fact that the number of children, who, for one reason or another, require specially adapted teaching methods and attitudes is steadily increasing in many countries of the world. An attempt has been made in the preceding chapters to analyze the specific teaching tasks of the teachers of socially or culturally underprivileged children; how they should try to strengthen their pupils' ability to differentiate, to think rationally, to use their phantasy in order to discover the level of meaning behind facts and events; what he should do to help them translate concrete givens into concepts or laws; how the teacher should become sensitized to thinking processes underlying his pupils' faulty answers and solutions; how he should beware of believing in the relevance of 'experience' as such for establishing desirable cognitive patterns (experience, as already said, should be regarded as raw material only for conceptualization and abstraction).

We have mentioned some of the qualities such a teacher needs to fulfil his functions: he must be free of rigid dependence needs, must be prepared to 'follow his students' (to use a Rogerian term), ready to improvise and experiment with methods and explanations, rather than to rely on instruction or systematic guidance; he must be open for the uniqueness and individuality of his students, their backgrounds and motivations, and he must be on guard against the danger of prejudices, fears or irrational expectations.

Now, it may be argued that these qualities are not specifically related to the teacher of underprivileged children only; it is precisely due to them that *every* teacher in the elementary as well as in the secondary school, the teacher of normal as well as of retarded or emotionally disturbed children becomes more adequate in his functions. And yet, so we have said, it is only when working with children, whose impaired intelligence requires rehabilitation through the teacher's adequate interventions, that empathy and readiness to follow the pupils'—presumed and hypothesized—thinking processes, courage and ability to improvise are indispensable. Many teachers in regular classes are known to be rigidly dependent on instructions and 'prescribed' curricula, regrettably deficient in empathy and imagination; and yet, they do *not* cause severe damage to their students, provided the latter are intelligent enough to learn from whatever teacher happens to cross their way, (or provided they are exposed to a comprehensive treatment program such as is often designed for disturbed children).

Where in the training course is the place for developing the qualities we have mentioned here, in the teacher who wants to work with socially or culturally retarded children, and what are the appropriate methods and means?

Two years are certainly not too much for training in subject-matters of teaching, first unrelated, later on related to didactical application. We should remember that in these two years basic information is added on functional growth and development, on individual and group differences, on mental and behavioral deviation, on demographic facts and figures, on social services and on teaching methods in relation to the various subject matters of learning. One or two years of guided teaching practice should then follow. These years should be spent in regular classes of either elementary or secondary schools. Only after such a practice period in regular classes should a course in 'rehabilitative teaching' start, again accompanied by appropriate practice.

We suggest that the two areas of specific functional training (in addition to the learning of subject-matters with which we are not concerned here) should be defined as those of 'the teacher as a person' and 'the teaching methods to be used'. We shall not go into discussing the meaning of these concepts within the first two stages of training. Suffice it here to repeat what we have already said before: that every stage, even the preparatory stage of informative courses in the first year, offers the student some opportunities for relating the contents of his learning to his own personality problems. But the more he is forced into facing his teaching function as a reality, in the class situations to which he is exposed already in the second, but certainly in the third or fourth year (of applications), the less can he avoid self-confrontation with his personality problems.

We have in mind a task much more complex than the one called 'improving the teacher's mental health'.* We have maintained that clarification of reaction-patterns, preferences and resistances are an indispensable precondition of successful teaching everywhere; that *every* teacher must face the consequences of his repressions and of struggling against prejudices, must try to overcome the possible impact of disappointments in his pupils, in the degree of his success, in the conditions of his work. Unconscious or half-conscious reasons for choosing his career may account for later frustrations.† Teaching requires the same qualities as every helping profession: relative freedom from irrational affects, ability to understand motivation, empathy, courage.

But teaching is primarily content-and-value-oriented, aims at enlarging the pupils' mind, at developing his mental skills and functions and not only at clarifying his motivations or attitudes. The case-worker or the psychotherapist can afford to separate from each other the two functional areas, feeling and thinking, and to concentrate on the first only, while hoping and assuming that the second will 'benefit' from setting the first in order. The teacher, on the other hand, depends on the *simultaneous* operation of empathy and analytical thinking, of imagination and rational affect-free interventions. To attain this goal, either within or outside a training course, requires more than mental hygiene, in fact, requires a psychodynamic approach to cognition and a cognitive approach to emotional manifestations.

The proper place for such an approach, as we have already mentioned, is in that phase of training in which 'specialization' takes place, particularly when this specialization is in the area of rehabilitating the lost intellectual potentials of socially or culturally underprivileged children. It is here, in this area of 'special' teaching, that every experience should, and could, be used primarily for an interpretation of the rationale of the different methods employed, that is, for relating methods to the thinking processes that go in the learner. It is certainly *not* a theoretical course in psychology of thinking and learning. It is an attempt to involve the student in

* See e.g. the comprehensive analysis of the subject in F. Redl's and W. Wattenberg's *Mental Hygiene in Teaching.*

† The ways of improving the mental hygiene of the teacher, through group-discussions, individual consultations and other means of increasing self-awareness are well-known (though value-oriented educators who look down affectively upon that kind of 'psychological nonsense' still outnumber almost everywhere their mental-hygiene oriented colleagues).

his teaching tasks, to make him aware of the dialogic character of teaching, of what is going on in each of his pupils, in relation to his acts of teaching, and in him in reaction to the child's reactions.

It is precisely this involvement and this dialogic character of teaching which account for the fact that the specialization period of teacher training is considered the proper period for teaching the psychodynamic approach to thinking and learning. Even analyses of problems of behavior and discipline should serve, in this period of training, as a means to enlarge and deepen the teacher's understanding of his pupils' cognitive problems. Case analysis should *not* be used—as it may be in case-work training or in clinical psychology —to produce a diagnostician, a councellor, a clinician (which the teacher will never be). Case analysis is a means to strengthen the teacher's readiness to search for the remedial function of teaching; important as it may be to reduce symptoms of behavior disorders or other pathologies to their childhood roots and thus to prepare the way to proper therapeutic interventions, the *teacher* must not lose sight of the impact which a child's emotional and behavioral disorders may have on specific thinking and learning processes. He should try to answer the question to which the therapist would be at a loss to give a meaningful reply: what corrective role has learning in behavior disorders? How could teaching material be built into direct or indirect references to the (presumed or hypothesized) meaning of the child's emotional problems? And *vice versa*: how should the behavior problem of the individual child, or for that matter, of his group, be incorporated into the teaching material?

Already before, at the practice stage of training, individual or group discussions of class-'events', comparisons of methods and defining their rationales should be introduced. But it is during the specialization stage that these training methods (and contents) become essential, in addition to other methods, such as role playing, text-analyses and individual contacts of the candidate for specialization with a case worker.

Rehabilitative teaching, we have said, should be accompanied by an ever repeated attempt to *interpret the sequences of a classroom session* and particularly the inadequate answers given by an individual pupil in reaction to a defineable teaching stimulus. Groups of teachers, each of whom may bring with him experiences with a different age group, or with a different subject matter, are a useful medium for the development of those qualities that we have mentioned as indispensable preconditions of successful rehabilitative teaching. It is through group discussions of 'class-events' (that is, of typical or critical learning situations) that the teacher will learn how to relate to his pupils as to thinking individuals; how to be ready to switch from one possible interpretation of thinking—and learning—processes to another one; how to use, accordingly, varying modes of didactic intervention; how to react, how to improvise and how to control his reactions and improvisations.

The same purpose may be served by attending and *observing* lessons given by other teachers and then critically to evaluate what the latter have done. This requires the availability of councellors well versed not only in the s.r. child's cognitive modes of operation and the relevant didactic interventions, not only in the art of observing class situations and processes, interactions between students and teachers, but also in guiding the trainees in the no less complex and complicated methods of affect-free evaluation.*

Another medium, as already mentioned, is *role playing*, through which possible motivations, expectations, reactions and resistances of pupils, parents or teachers (including the trainee himself), can be brought to the level of conscious experience. At the same time, it offers an excellent opportunity to learn all about interview techniques that the teacher of secondarily retarded children must know. Without constant efforts to gain the cooperation of the child in his affective relationships with his parents, or in his often unrealistic relationship to the very learning-process or to his self-perception in present and future roles, the teacher would be unable to function adequately in a class for such children. We need not repeat that the same applies to his contacts with the child's parents. Neither should we underestimate the importance of obtaining the support or, at least, the silent consent of colleagues, to use what might seem to them to be an unorthodox avenue to teaching. For this purpose, too, learning-through-role-playing will be useful.

Theoretical interpretations and elaborations (sometimes even in the form of frontal lectures on motivations, attitudes and attitude-

---

* It is obvious that such an approach requires the setting up of a new profession. Nothing could be more erroneous than to regard the supervisor or, better, the educational guide and councellor whom we have in mind, as identical with the generally known type of supervisor whose administrative responsibilities, more often than not, exclude all opportunities for truly educational interventions. We have in mind a highly qualified practitioner who, after a thorough preparation in didactics, in cognitive analyses, in dynamic psychology of development, of behavior and of thinking, and after meaningful learning about motivation and control of reaction—should work as consultant to teachers.

changes) should accompany the personal experience and insight gained in this way. *Analyzing carefully selected texts* would seem to be the best way of condensing and synthesizing essential thought material, provided these text-analysis sessions are conducted so to stimulate active elaboration of certain basic concepts and ideas in their relationship to practice. The danger of overloading the training program with more or less meaningful (or meaningless) texts and theories should be avoided, since the teacher of these children should not be turned into a theoretician or a man of research.

Nor should he be turned into a therapist or a clinician, as we have already mentioned. And yet, in his many encounters with patterns and symptoms of culture-alien behavior and thinking, with rejecting and rejection-provoking attitudes, with cognition contaminated by feeling and emotions contaminated by externalization—all these encounters make self-confrontation indispensable. This is why the future teacher of secondarily retarded children should be given an opportunity—in the year of training towards his special functions—to clarify some of his personality problems. This may be done profitably through contacts with a case-worker or a psychologist well-versed in the art of working-through such problems in representatives of the various helping professions. (Needless to add that such contacts should *not* be based on the principles of depth-analysis).

What we have said here about the principles of teacher-training, could be summarized as follows:

—if we see in learning an instrument of leading the learner towards relative autonomy and towards internalization of values and concepts;

—if we want to develop in the socially or culturally retarded child the ability to differentiate, to think rationally and, above all, to take responsibility for his acts of thinking and learning; in brief:

—if we want to use teaching as a means for the rehabilitation of socially or culturally impaired intelligence—

we should base teacher-training on comparable qualities: the teacher, too, should learn, how to differentiate, how to react individually to his pupils' manifestation of thinking, how to think rationally, how to become free of stereotypes and of dependence-needs, how to take upon himself full responsibility for his teaching acts and his educational interventions, how to improvise without losing sight of his main trend of teaching, how to handle different methods according to the changing needs of the class or of an individual pupil, how to *be* spontaneous and how to *act* spontaneously.

References

1. ABEL, T. M. and KINDER, E. F., *The Subnormal Adolescent Girl*, New York, Columbia University Press, 1942
2. ALLPORT, G. W., *Personality*, New York, Henry Holt & Co., 1937
3. AINSWORTH, M. D., The Effects of Maternal Deprivation. In: *Deprivation of Maternal Care*, Geneva, World Health Organization, 1962
4. BÜHLER, CH., *Kindheit und Jugend*, Leipzig, Hirzel, 1928
5. BÜHLER, K., *The Mental Development of the Child*, 1933
6. BURT, C., *The Backward Child*, London, University of London Press, 1946
7. CANNON, W. B., *The Wisdom of the Body*, New York, Norton & Co., 1939
8. DAVIS, A. and HAVIGHURST, R. M., Social Class and Color Differences in Child Rearing. In: *Am. Sociol. Review*, 1946
9. DOLL, E. A., The Essentials of an Inclusive Concept of Mental Deficiency. In: *Am. J. Ment. Def.*, 1941, 46, 214
10. EISENSTADT, S. N., *The Absorption of Immigrants*, London, Routledge, Kegan Paul, 1954
11. ERIKSON, E. H., *Childhood and Society*, London, Imago, 1950
12. FEDERN, P., *Ego Psychology and the Psychoses*, New York, Basic Books, 1952
13. FENICHEL, O., *The Psychoanalytic Theory of Neuroses*, London, Routledge, Kegan Paul, 1945
14. FRANKENSTEIN, C., Waywardness in Children, Jerusalem, Szold Foundation, 1947 (In Hebrew Translation)
15. FRANKENSTEIN, C., *The Concept of Cause in the Research of Juvenile Delinquency*, Jerusalem, Szold Foundation, 1954 (In Hebrew Translation)
16. FRANKENSTEIN, C., Structural Factors in the Anxiety of Children. In: *Acta Psychological*, 1956, 12, 321
17. FRANKENSTEIN, C., The Structural Meaning of Aggressiveness. In: *Acta Psychologica*, 1958, 14, 253

18. Frankenstein, C., Low Level of Intellectual Functioning and Dissocial Behaviour. In: *Am. J. Ment. Def.*, 1958, 63, 294

19. Frankenstein, C., Das Unbewusste und die Tiefenzone des Seelischen. In: *Zeitschrift für Diagnostische Psychologie und Persönlichkeitsforschung*, 1958, 6, 158

20. Frankenstein, C., *Die Ausserlichkeit des Lebensstils*, Amsterdam, Meulenhoff, 1959

21. Frankenstein, C., *Psychopathy*, New York, Grune & Stratton, 1959

22. Frankenstein, C., School Without Parents In: *Scripta Hierosolymitana*, Jerusalem, University Press, 1963

23. Frankenstein, C., *Persönlichkeitswandel durch Fürsorge, Erziehung und Therapie,* München, Urban & Schwarzenberg, 1964

24. Frankenstein, C., *The Roots of the Ego,* Baltimore, Williams & Wilkins, 1966

25. Frankenstein, C., Du und Nicht-Ich-Zu Bubers Theorie des Dialogs. In: *Stimmen der Zeit,* 1966, 11, 356

26. Frankenstein, C., *Psychodynamics of Externalization,* Baltimore, Williams & Wilkins, 1968

27. Freud, S., *Drei Abhandlugen zur Sexualtheorie,* Gesammelte Werke, Bd. V., London, Imago, 1948

28. Freud, S., *Der Untergang des Ödipus Komplexes,* Gesammelte Werke, Bd. XIII, London, Imago, 1948

29. Goldstein, K., *Language and Language Disturbances,* New York, Grune & Stratton, 1948

30. Hartman, H., *Ego Psychology and the Problem of Adaptation,* New York, International Universities Press, 1958

30a. Hollingshead, A. and Redlich, F. C., *Social Class and Mental Illness,* New York, Wiley, 1958

31. Jung, C. G., *Psychologische Typen,* Zürich, Rascher & Co., 1930

32. Jung, C. G., *The Archetypes and the Collective Unconscious,* London, Routledge, Kegan Paul, 1959

33. Klages, L., *Grundlagen der Charakter-Kunde,* Leipzig, 1946

34. Klein, M., *Contributions to Psychoanalysis,* London, Hogarth, 1948

35. Kounin, J. S., Experimental Studies in Rigidity In: *Character and Personality,* 1946, 9, 273

36. Lewin, K., A Dynamic Theory of Feeblemindedness In: *Dynamic Theory of Personality,* New York, McGraw Hill, 1935

37. MAUTNER, H., *Mental Retardation*, London, Pergamon Press, 1959
38. MAY, R., *The Meaning of Anxiety*, New York, Ronald Press, 1950
39. MURCHISON, C., *Criminal Intelligence*, Worcester, Clark University Press, 1926
40. OPHUIJSEN, J. H. W. van, Primary Conduct Disturbances In: Lewis, N. D. C. & Pacella, B. L. (eds.): *Modern Trends in Child Psychiatry*, New York, International Universities Press, 1950
41. PARSONS, T. *and* BALES, R., *Family, Socialization and Interaction Process*, Glencoe, Ill., The Free Press, 1955
42. PIAGET, J., *The Moral Judgment of the Child*, Glencoe, Ill., The Free Press, 1948
43. PIAGET, J., *The Language and Thought of the Child*, New York, Meridian Books, 1955
44. RIESMAN, D., *The Lonely Crowd*, New Haven, Yale University Press, 1950
45. ROSENTHAL, R., *Pygmalion in the Classroom*, New York, 1968
46. ROTHSCHILD, F. S., *Das Ich und die Regulationen des Erlebnisvorgangs*, Basel, S. Karger, 1950
47. SARASON, S. B., *Psychological Problems in Mental Deficiency*, New York, Harper, 1959 (third edition)
48. SCHMIDT, B. G., Changes in Personal, Social and Intellectual Behavior in Children Originally Classified as Feebleminded. *Psych. Monogs.*, 1946, 60, 5, 1
49. SLAVSON, S. R., *An Introduction to Group Therapy*, New York, The Commonwealth Fund, 1943
50. SPITZ, R., *La Première Annee de la Vie de l'Enfant*, Paris, Presses Universitaires de France, 1958
51. STODDARD, G. D., *The Meaning of Intelligence*, New York, Macmillan, 1943
52. STRAUSS, A. A. and KEPHART, N. C., *Psychopathology and Education of the Brain Injured*, New York, Grune & Stratton, 1955
53. TERMAN, L. M. and MERRIL, M. A., *The Measuring of Intelligence*, London, Harrap, 1937
54. THORNDIKE, R. L., *Intelligence: Its Nature and Nurture*, Bloomington, Public School Publishing Co., 1940
55. TILLICH, P., *The Courage to Be*, New Haven, Yale University Press, 1960

56. Tredgold, A. F., *Mental Deficiency*, Baltimore, W. Wood & Co., 1922

57. Wechsler, D., *The Measurement of Adult Intelligence*, Baltimore, Williams & Wilkins, 1944

58. Werner, H., Rorschach Method Applied to Two Clinical Groups of Mental Defectives. In: *Am. J. Ment. Defic.*, 1945, 49, 340

Subject Index

* In this index, f.m. stands for 'feebleminded' or 'feeblemindedness' and s.r. stands for 'secondary retardation'.